You

Copyright © 2022 by Visage Books

ISBN 978-1-4958-2209-4 Paperback
ISBN 978-1-4958-2210-0 Hardcover

Printed in the United States of America

CONTENTS

Chapter 4: INFINITE POTENTIAL

Chapter 5: WRAPPINGS AND TRAPPINGS

Chapter 6: BEING GODLY

Chapter 7: PRACTICE

Chapter 8: END GAME

Postscript

Preface

There is a wisdom awaiting you that is not supposed to be a secret. It is ancient, and it is available, but it is widely unknown. It has been hidden for too long, and it is time for it to become revealed. This wisdom will change everything, if we allow it. Where there was conflict, there will be peace. Where there was animosity, there will be empathy. Where there was fear, there will be courage. Where there was shame, there will be self-acceptance and esteem. Where there was scarcity, there will be abundance.

Existence is not meaningless. Humanity is not irredeemable. The future is not bleak. The alienation and despair that lurk just beneath the surface of the modern psyche are not the inevitable human condition. They are the result of misguided ideologies that pervade our global culture and invade our every thought. Each of us - each and every one of us - is so much more than we imagine. We are here for a reason, and we are equipped with all of the capabilities that we require.

The ideas contained in the following pages are not new or progressive. They are as old as the world. The path explored here is a Torah path. Torah is the divine will and wisdom that was transmitted through Moses to a fledgling nation of former slaves so that its light would be disseminated to illuminate a dark world.

The "Bible" that many have been exposed to is radically different from Torah in its authentic essence. Many westerners have turned to alternate sources for wisdom and spirituality because the doctrine that they have been reared on has not offered them the inspiration or solace that they seek. Torah is no more western than eastern or northern or southern. It does not have a geographic bearing or bias. God is not the God of some and not others.

The insights herein are gleaned, in large part, from Chassidic philosophy and the Torah's mystic teachings. They are equally applicable to those who observe Torah's laws strictly, those who follow other spiritual practices, and those who engage in no practice at all. The existence of God is not questioned in these pages, nor is it proven or defined. One need not be a "believer" to explore the Torah's wisdom tradition.

Ultimately, this is a book about you. You may not see yourself in it at first, but by the end you will hopefully recognize yourself more clearly. It is a book about life and its meaning and your place in this big, swirling thing we call existence. There are big ideas and questions addressed, but not with big language or overly sophisticated concepts.

This book might be described as spiritual, or even a bit mystical; but don't worry, it isn't aiming to convert you or convince you or control you. Its goal is simply to present you with questions - and even a few answers - that will eventually acquaint you with someone you deserve to know, someone you will love, and someone to whom you may have sadly never been properly introduced: you.

You may be wondering, justifiably, how the author of this book can pretend to know you if you have likely never met. Part of you may also be bristling at the presumption that this author knows more about you than you know about yourself. Here's the thing: the you that you will find in the following pages is the same you that the author found in the many pages studied before writing this book. What you, and I, and every one of us will come to recognize and appreciate at some point is that we are not the many surface things that distinguish us from everyone else, but rather the single thing that every "you" has in common. In chapter three, we will learn the revolutionary mystic insight of what that "you" truly is. The subsequent chapters will then help us to penetrate and incorporate this life-changing revelation.

This is not a book for any particular type of reader. It will resonate, hopefully, with those who seek, but that is true of all of us. Some seek more intentionally and openly than others. But everyone is seeking something, somewhere, somehow. It is the nature of human life. What is most important as you explore the following pages is curiosity, and perhaps even hope that you will find something (or someone) in these pages that you didn't know before.

Chapter 1: GETTING LOST

The First Question

W here are you?

Right now, as you read this page, where are you?

'In my bedroom,' you might answer. Or 'on the train.' Or 'at the park.' Or 'flying over the Grand Canyon on my way to visit my best friend in Los Angeles.' Or any number of locations you may be at this moment. But none of these will truly answer the question.

Where are you?

Let's begin with a simple exercise. Point to yourself. Where is your finger pointing? Most of us will point to our chest or our face. But is that you? Can you really point to who you are? Perhaps we'll admit that the body is not who I am, because the body changes. We know that most of the cells of our body regenerate within a decade, so most of our body is no longer the same material that it was just ten years past. Our DNA remains the same though, so perhaps we are our DNA. But DNA is not conscious. It replicates, but it does not think or feel. There is something that is lodged within this body, within this flesh and bone that is formed by our DNA. So when we point to our body, we are perhaps indicating that our self is somewhere within this. I can't touch it per se, but this is where it lives.

If so, we have perhaps determined its vicinity, but we have indicated nothing of its nature with the pointing of our finger. We have not identified it or pinpointed it. We have merely located it approximately. But let's not settle for approximates. We were not given the gift of life to treat it haphazardly. We can be lazy with many things, but understanding who, what, and where we are doesn't seem to be one of those things we should cast off with abandon.

Where are you? It is the primary question. Quite literally, it is the very first question that humanity is asked by its Creator:

> And the Lord God called to man and He said to him 'where are you'?[1]
>
> (Genesis 3:9)

The question came on the first day that humanity existed, which was the sixth day of creation. As the story in the book of Genesis details, throughout the first five days, God created the heavens and the earth and all of their components and inhabitants. On day six, He created Adam and Eve and placed them into His garden to work it and perfect it. He provided and allowed them everything, but forbade them only one thing - from the fruit of the tree that grows in the middle of the garden you shall not eat, the tree of the knowledge of good and evil. But Adam and Eve could not resist. Within hours of their creation, they had committed the one act that they had been forbidden. They ate the fruit. They then heard God approaching them, and they hid. God called out to them, "where are you?"

The question was not God's question. God, according to Torah, is omniscient - He knew precisely where they were. The question was for them - do *you* know where you are? Adam and Eve had gotten lost, and all of us since then - their children - have been lost as well.

---

[1] Citations will be quoted in their English translations throughout this book. Transliteration of the Hebrew is included when the original language is relevant. And the Hebrew letters themselves are provided when they are necessary to display additional meaning or implication.

Adam and Eve knew that they were in the garden of Eden. It's not that they had journeyed some great distance from their home and weren't familiar with the way back to where they'd started. Their feet had not carried them far. The issue was not one of geography, and it was not a place that they had lost. It was *themselves*. They were home, but the home was empty. The question was not "what is this place," but rather "are *you* in this place?" The emphasis of the question was not "where" - WHERE are you - but rather "you" - where are YOU? Their surroundings were familiar, but as they wandered through it, they could not identify its inhabitants. Who is this? Who is acting this way?

Prior to eating the fruit, the Midrash[2] tells us, Adam's and Eve's skin was diaphanous. They could see into themselves and each other. Their surface did not conceal their interior. God had created them transparent because there was no separation between their core and their veneer. They were completely unified in body and soul. Their actions matched their intentions. Their essence was manifest in everything they did. They were naked, but they were not ashamed, because there was no split between their most intimate recesses and their outer reality.

But then they ate the fruit. And there was shame. Their skin had become opaque, and they could no longer see where the true 'me' was within them. The translucent skin receded and they were wrapped in the flesh that we, their descendants, are covered in now. We maintain remnants of that primordial skin in our fingernails and toenails. From these we have an idea of what Adam and Eve originally looked like.

After the "sin," Adam and Eve hid, because they were ashamed of what they had done. They suddenly felt their nakedness, because the new flesh was a sign of their failure. Before, they were confident and secure - they knew who and where they were. But now they were unsure. Who am I? Where am I? What have I done? Suddenly they experienced a tremendous gulf between their inner essence and their outward reality. They had ingested the knowledge of good and evil. They had internalized a duality that did not exist in the paradise of the garden. In paradise, there is no conflict, no tension. In this new realm, "east of Eden" where they were exiled, there is perpetual conflict because of the tension

---

[2] Midrash is a collection of Rabbinic teachings that provides additional details and background to the Torah's narratives. See Breishis Rabba 20:12, Pirkei D'Rabbi Eliezer 14:3.

that persists between the interior and the exterior, the soul and the body, the godly essence and its animalistic casing.

In this post-Eden existence, it is therefore difficult to point to precisely who and where we are. We show our face, "PaNiM" in Hebrew, but we rarely show our inner essence, or "PNiMyus." The words for 'face' and 'inwardness' share the same root in Hebrew - "PNM" - because the intention for humanity is that our interior will be the same as our exterior. But we have yet to live up to this ideal. And this is our struggle and the source of our existential angst. *The pain of life is our dissatisfaction with living on the surface. It is the discomfort of wearing a skin that conceals who we truly are. It is the suffocation of our truth under a mantle of facade.*

Where are you?

You can identify your location at this moment - your bedroom, the train, the park, the plane, whatever the case may be - but what is more difficult to identify is the self that is occupying that space. Who are you? What are you? Are you the one who acts this way, thinks this way, feels this way? Is this truly you? Where did this 'you' come from? What made it what it is today? Is it authentic - is it what it has always been? Is it what it was made, or meant, to be? Is it what you would have liked to become?

If I look in the mirror right now, I see a face that I have seen many times before. It has changed over the years, but it is generally the same face I have met in the mirror for decades. I know the name by which that face is called - it's my name. I know that I call it me, but I suddenly realize that it is not me. My name is not who I am, nor is my face or my body. I don't know precisely who I am, but I know what I am not. I am not the skin that dresses my bones, or the bones that support my sinews and flesh. They will eventually be buried in the ground, but I will have already left them lifeless. I am the life behind the face. I am housed here, but I am not visible in the mirror. I am the one looking, but I am not the one seen.

Who am I?! Where am I?! How did I lose myself, and most importantly, how do I find me?!

A Hidden World

It's not your fault that "you" are lost!

This is essential to establish right from the start. You are not lost because you are wicked, or sinful, or deviant. There is no shame in being lost, no guilt to bear or blame to be assessed. It was not Adam and Eve's fault that they lost themselves, and it isn't yours, or mine, or any of us who have gotten lost - and that is to say, all of us. It is no coincidence, no bad luck, and no failure. We were created to be missing. That is the way God designed it.

We can see this in the Hebrew word for "world" - "olam." The etymology of this word is from the root "elem", which also forms the word "helam," meaning "hidden." Tracing the word back to its source enables us to trace God's intention for the universe back to its root. He created the world, "olam," to be a realm of concealment, "helam." Creation is thus a process of getting lost. Our mission and purpose, our raison d'etre, is the process of getting found and finding what has been concealed.

What is it that was to be concealed in this world of hiddenness? The Creator Himself. He would hide Himself behind the veneer of the material world. And along with Himself, He would hide the source and essence of all things, including your essence, or the ultimate you. It would be a realm where surface would prevail over substance. The spiritual would be encased in the corporeal to the extent that it was virtually imperceptible. The inhabitants of this world would be so enmeshed in their physical and material pursuits that they would not only come to mistake themselves for their appetites - in other words to lose themselves in their own skin -   but they would have the ability, and even the propensity, to deny the existence of their Creator.

Why would God possibly create such a world?!

Why would He desire a realm of division and confusion, a place where the truth of things would be buried beneath a veil of distortion? What could be His reason for fabricating beings who could so easily become distracted, misguided, and disoriented? Why would He want His creations to be lost and corrupted? Why would He fashion a universe in which He Himself would be so commonly disregarded or denied?

We could suggest, as many have, that none of this concealment was His intention. It was, rather, a consequence of our failure to fulfill His command. Maybe the world is as dark and confused as it is because of our sin. This is not an uncommon belief, and many are raised with the doctrine of "original sin." According to this perspective, the story of Adam and Eve, which we related above, is pretty straightforward and pretty damning. They were created clear and unified, they transgressed, and as a result, they became lost from themselves and then banished from God's garden. This couldn't have been God's desire or intention, right? Rather, it was obviously a violation of His will. Humanity was punished, this was our great Fall, and since then we have been paying and suffering for our progenitors' primordial sin.

But as popular and pervasive as this rendition is, there's something troubling about it, isn't there? Is God's will so feeble and flimsy that it is defied and derailed within hours of its implementation? Is this what we think of the Creator of the universe?

'Let me generate a world,' we are to believe He said to Himself, 'of harmony and revelation. Let there be light, let there be heavens, let there be water that teems with life, and earth that sprouts forth vegetation and birds of the sky and beasts of the field. And finally, let there be humanity, glorious beings fashioned in My image who will work my garden. Let them walk with Me and know Me. Let them know themselves and be transparent. I will grant them free will, and I will give them everything but the fruit of the tree in the middle of the garden which I will instruct them not to eat." And He did just so. But there was a serpent, and the serpent was silver-tongued and it seduced them. And within hours of their formation, all of God's plans were laid to waste. Afterwards, for eons His creations would suffer and His world would languish.

This is a fairly pathetic version of history. The failure of Adam and Eve pales in comparison to the seeming failure of their Creator who envisioned something idyllic but was forced to accept and endure something far more infernal. Is it possible that God "failed" so miserably?

The Only One

Torah does not support the concept of Original Sin. Nor does Torah believe in "the devil," an evil force that is equal and contrary to God's power. Torah doctrine professes, rather, a concept known as "Hashgacha Protis," which is translated as Individual Divine Providence, and which means that there is nothing that occurs in the universe that is contrary to the will of God. Every incident is an indispensable component of the divine tapestry and plan. A leaf does not blow in the wind if it is not precisely as the Creator intended it to be.[3]

This notion of "hashgacha protis" is predicated on the fundamental tenet of Torah theology and ontology, which is the complete and exclusive unity of God. There can be nothing that occurs outside of God's will because *there is nothing that exists other than God*. This complete unity is stated succinctly in the Torah expression "ain od milvado/there is nothing besides Him."[4] This tenet is so central to our existence that Torah mandates that it should be declared twice daily in the "Shema," a prayer that is known by most Jews, but understood by few. The prayer is derived from a verse in the fifth book of the Torah, Deuteronomy:

> *Shema Yisrael A-donai E-loheinu A-donai echad.*
> Hear O Israel, the Lord our God, the Lord is ONE!
> (Deuteronomy 6:4)

Commonly interpreted as a statement of monotheism, this verse, like all of Torah, operates simultaneously on multiple levels. On the simplest level, the primary contribution of Torah to world history and culture was the notion of one God. The prevalent belief throughout the pagan world prior to the time of Abraham, the first Hebrew, was that the universe was influenced by a vast plurality of deities. Rather than a god

---

[3] Even free will, a subject that is beyond the scope of this work and treated in many volumes that are devoted to this issue alone, is accounted for in the doctrine of hashgacha protis. For more on the subject of hashgacha protis, see Tanya, Shaar HaYichud VehaEmunah, ch. 2, and Iggeres HaKodesh, Epistle 25.

[4] Deuteronomy 4:35

of the sun, a god of rain, a god of wind, and a host of other idols that humanity fashioned and worshipped in pursuit of its needs and desires, Abraham came to understand that there was one God who controlled all of the forces and happenings that swirl around us. It was a revolutionary concept that would ultimately transform civilization and spawn at least three of the world's foremost religious traditions: Judaism, Christianity, and Islam.[5]

Yet monotheism was only a part of Abraham's message. The revolutionary innovation that would be passed down through his descendants was not simply that there is only one God, as opposed to many deities. In its simple reading, the Shema prayer states 'Listen Israel, there is one God." But in its inner essence, it tells us something far more subtle and radical: 'Listen Israel, there is only One: God!'

In declaring "A-donai echad/the Lord is One," the Shema informs us that there is only one existence, and that is God. He is the one and only. There is no being or entity other than Him. Everything that we perceive to be distinct or disparate is in truth only various manifestations of the exclusive infinite Godly reality. The verse begins with the word "shema/hear," commanding us to "hear" this truth - rather than to know it, see it, ponder it, or understand it - because it is too profound and abstruse to be seen or even clearly grasped intellectually. The custom is therefore to close one's eyes for the recitation of this prayer and to cover them with one's hand. We must rely on a more inward and ethereal type of perception for this mystic reality because it is completely beyond the realm of both our sensate and intellectual experience.

Of course, if this is the case, if the Shema is accurate and God is the only true being, then we are forced to wonder what this means about us. If we recite this prayer (twice daily) and thereby negate the existence of anything other than God, are we declaring that we don't exist? We close our eyes and nullify the plurality around us, and then we open them and are forced to function in a structure that we have seemingly just denied. How does this make sense?

---

[5] Torah itself suggests that the religions of the East were also significantly influenced by the Abrahamic tradition, as it explicitly states "And to the sons of Abraham's concubines, Abraham gave gifts, and he sent them … eastward to the land of the East" (Genesis 25:6). The sages indicate that these "gifts" were secret divine names, one of which was the holy name "Ohm," one of the 72 three letter names of God mentioned in Kabbala.

Furthermore, if God is truly One, if there really is nothing other than Him, then what is this illusion of multiplicity, and why does He hide Himself behind it? Why does He allow it to seem as though His project has failed if in fact He is perfectly and completely in control?

———◆———

The Face Of Death

To answer these questions, we must address the issue of human error. When God's creations fail to live up to His standards and expectations, is this an infraction of God's will? As we have discussed, the Torah's principle of "hashgachah protis/individual divine providence" insists that nothing can happen that is contrary to God's intention, because nothing truly exists other than God Himself. If so, then how are we to understand the concept of transgression?

The Torah is replete with stories of human error. A world in which the ultimate truth is concealed is bound to be a place of trial and miscalculation. Of all of the errors that are recorded in scripture, there are two that are considered to be so egregious that they influenced all of history in their wake. The first was the eating of the forbidden fruit, which we have been discussing already. The second was the worship of the golden calf.

As the story of the golden calf goes, Abraham's descendants were enslaved in Egypt. After several generations, God afflicted the Egyptians with ten plagues, forcing the wicked Pharaoh to let His people go. The fledgling nation fled into the desert, where they were then pursued by Pharaoh and his army. God split the sea so that the Israelites could escape, and He then led them to Mount Sinai, where their leader, Moses, ascended to retrieve the Torah. But Moses was on the mountain for 40 days, and the people grew impatient and feared that he would not return. They therefore built themselves a golden idol in the form of a calf, and they worshiped it in spite of all the miracles and wonders that God had performed for them in Egypt, at the Sea, and at the mountain.

Here again, just as in the garden of Eden, God's hopes were seemingly dashed by His rebellious creations. Just as His plan for revelation and unity had been derailed at the outset of creation by the first humans He formed, similarly His "chosen" nation, newly birthed after their redemption from Egypt, shattered His plans for a new age of revelation by building an idol at the foot of His holy mountain. Just as the idyllic existence in the Garden of Eden lasted only briefly, so now the elevation and illumination of the world that was marked by the giving of the Torah would last only briefly. The "sin" of the golden calf immediately sent the creation toppling back again into a state of darkness and disconnection.

Why does this keep happening?!

If God wants us to see Him and experience Him, then why does He once again allow us to cast Him away so quickly and easily? In the immediate aftermath of the golden calf, God provides an answer to this perplexing question. Moses, clearly bewildered by the sequence of events, asks God to explain Himself to him.

> If I have indeed found favor in your eyes, let me know
> Your ways, so that I may know You.
> (Exodus 33:13)

God accedes to Moses' request. He invites Moses to come up once again onto the mountain, and there He will cause His glory to pass before him. But Moses will be granted only a vision of God's back, not His face.

> And He said to him, "You will not be able to see my face,
> for man shall not see Me and live."
> (Exodus 33:20)

Why is it that Moses is not permitted to see God's face? What does this mean that a person can experience God's back, but cannot perceive His face and continue to remain alive?

God's face represents His full and complete revelation, whereas His back represents a more shrouded and limited view and understanding of Him. The inability to see God's face informs us that if we were to experience the full, unimpeded revelation of His infinite reality, which is His complete unity, then we would understand that nothing else, including ourselves, truly exists at all. The verse does not read 'if man sees Me he will perish,' but rather "man shall not see Me and live." In other words, it is not that seeing God's face would cause one to die, but rather that in the presence of His "face" one does not, and never did, truly live. We cannot see His face because in the presence of His face, which is the manifestation of His infinite presence, there is nothing else, and therefore no "we" at all.

With this, we can answer our question of why God hides His unity - because if He didn't, we would cease to be. "Olam," Hebrew for 'world,' is related to the word "helam/hidden" because the act of the creation of the world was an act of concealment. *In order to allow for the existence of any seeming other, God had to allow Himself to be unseen.*

Intentional Error

We can now understand the story of Adam and Eve very differently from the version of God's failed experiment that we presented above. When we view the events with the assumption of "hashgacha protis" - God's complete providence and control - and we begin with the awareness of God's Oneness and His desire to create "others" with whom He could interact, the version of events plays more like this:

'Let me generate a world,' God thought to Himself, 'of concealment and plurality. Where there was originally only Me, let Me now withdraw and obscure Myself so that a creation can emerge. Let there be light and darkness, let there be heavens and earth, let there be life that does not know where it comes from or that it is not truly distinct and diverse. Let there be beings who resemble Me, who sense Me, who are capable of finding Me, but who do not know the full extent of Me. I will place them in My garden to give them a glimpse of their essence and my truth, and then I will allow them to lose themselves, to get lost, to lose sight of their Creator. They will stumble in the darkness, but I will never leave them, because there is no place that they can go where I am not already and always there." So He created the garden and placed Adam and Eve in it; He created the fruit and commanded them not to eat it; He created the snake and its silver tongue; and He set His plan in motion so that He would be unseen and a world could develop in His seeming absence.

Just as the eating of the fruit and the "expulsion" from the garden was therefore not a failure or an accident, we can similarly understand the story of the golden calf not as another frustration of God's plan, but as a necessary condition for it:

From the day of Adam and Eve's creation and exile, there were two millennia of concealment and spiritual darkness. At that point, after twenty generations, God determined that it was time for the gradual process of His revelation to begin. Abraham was born, and he became the first human to innovate and publicize the idea of one God. Abraham's grandson, Jacob, also known as Israel, descended to Egypt, and after the death of his 12 sons, the Bnei Yisrael (children of Israel) were enslaved. Two centuries later, God freed Abraham's descendants from Egypt and guided them, under the leadership of Moses, to Mount Sinai. Here, God performed a national revelation, manifesting Himself to the three million men, women, and children who were gathered at the base of the mountain. At this moment, He provided them a covenant and a scripture that would enable them to begin to light the darkness.

It was then that the children of Israel became the Nation of Israel, and then that they were given their mandate to be "Ohr l'goyim," a light unto the nations. What this means is that they were commissioned to go forth from the revelation that they had experienced, and to share, with all those they would encounter, the message that God is hidden beneath the fabric of creation. The darkness, they would report, is only a thin mask that conceals a breathtaking light beneath. God, they would declare, is One.

But in the radiance of God's oneness, it is difficult to negotiate the mundane imperatives of the material world. How can we leave the warmth and brilliance of the light on the mountain to venture into the darkness and coldness of the surrounding world? In the glory of His presence, all else becomes trivial, and ultimately illusory. How are we to function in a system that is not real? In the awareness of God's Oneness, we become conscious of our own nonexistence. How can we fulfill our mission and task if we believe that we are nothing?

Therefore, immediately after God's revelation, there was once again a reversion to His concealment. The worship of the golden calf precipitated Moses' immediate descent from the mountaintop and his shattering of the tablets that he had received from the hand of God. The channel that had been opened between the heavens and the earth was once again closed, and the clarity of vision which had been momentarily granted to every man, woman, and child was once again clouded and obscured. Here again, as in the garden of Eden, with every experience of intense exposure, there is a subsequent incident of withdrawal. This is imperative because the continued existence of the creation depends on it. If revelation would continue unimpeded, then God's absolute unity would be revealed and would preclude the presence and "survival" of anything other.

Darkness, we suddenly and shockingly realize, is not evil! It is not the province of some demonic force that is working against God's will. Darkness is God's as much as light is. It allows us to be. *Astonishingly, concealment, we have come to understand, is an act of consummate divine love!*

----------◆----------

An Invitation

We can now understand that, as we suggested earlier, being lost is not our fault, but it is rather the nature of the existence into which we have been thrust. Far from the notion of blame and guilt, we can begin to free ourselves from the belief that our confusion and alienation are the result of our failings. We are not lost because we have been cast from God's loving embrace. Rather, it is in order to embrace us that God has created "distance" between us and Him - otherwise, He would merely be embracing Himself.

Guilt is not a productive emotion. It has certainly proven to be a motivating force, and it may in fact account for the majority of what most humans do on a daily basis and throughout our lives. But that does not render guilt productive, nor does it make it positive or desirable. It could, in fact, be suggested that guilt is responsible for most of the destructive thoughts and actions that we visit upon ourselves and those around us. The sense that I am not as I should be, or that I ought to be better than what I have become, often leads us to the subconscious belief that we are deserving of the suffering that we experience. This can subsequently bring us to the self-defeating and self-fulfilling assumption that we are incapable of rectifying our previous missteps. This type of shame and despair embitters us, and when we are bitter, we tend to punish not only ourselves, but everyone else as well.

God did not create us to despair. He did not conceal Himself in order to deceive us or in order to watch us fumble about in the dark. He did not send us from the garden to live lives of anguish and regression. He does not look down upon us from somewhere on high and revel in our struggle. God is not vindictive or vengeful. These are not the traits of God, but of men who have created a god in their own image with which they can intimidate and control others. Shame, fear, and guilt are the weapons of those who are hungry for power. God has no hunger and needs no power. Though His ways are mysterious and our comprehension is limited, we know that just as creation was an act of love, so too all darkness is simply a concealment of His unity which enables us to exist as individuals who will ultimately reunite and recognize our inherent divinity.

None of this is to suggest that light and darkness do not differ within the framework of our reality, or that right and wrong cannot be established and distinguished. None of this absolves us from the responsibility to choose right action over wrong action. And none of this denies the reality that we often choose poorly. We are human, our world is a realm of hiddenness, and we stumble. Yet when we do, we can admit our failings without guilt. We can feel regret without the debilitating hobbles of shame. The regret is the awareness that we did not live up to our potential. We know we can do better, but we also know that it is not we who have created ourselves imperfect. It is not we who have hidden our true essence from ourselves. Our Creator did that. This does not free us from the task of finding the truth, but it relieves us from the disgrace of being lost and imperfect. The task is far less burdensome and far more achievable if we are not plagued with self-doubt and self-loathing.

"Where are you" is not an accusation, but an invitation. Prior to being lost, Adam and Eve were not aware that there was anything within them to be found. They were not looking for themselves - their true selves - because they had no self-consciousness. They were naked, and as they were unaware of their nakedness, they were unashamed. But they were also simply unaware. It was a paradise, a dream with no consciousness, a blissful ignorance. The fruit from the tree of the knowledge of good and evil woke them from their reverie. It shattered the placid glassy veneer of the dream, and revealed to them that there was a whole world of depths down there beneath the surface. "Ayecha," God said to them, "where are you?"

Come, He beckoned them, I did not create you to be unconscious in the garden like the other animals. I have a job for you to do. There is something that I've hidden that I want you to find and reveal. I have chosen you for the task because I love you and I believe in you. It will not be easy, but I will be with you. I am not sending you away - there is no 'away' from Me because I am everywhere. I am not punishing you - you have not failed by eating the fruit, you have simply created the distance that is necessary for your journey to be set.

With a backward glance at the garden, along with a fond remembrance of the ease and bliss that they had known and would not know again, Adam and Eve accepted the mission that their Creator had assigned them. And likewise we, lost and full of uncertainty, but free of guilt and confident in the One Who sends us, are ready to set out east of Eden on the arduous, awesome task of getting found.

Chapter 2: IN THE DARKNESS

Pre-Dawn Departure

W e begin our journey in the dark. The sun may have risen already, but it is dark nonetheless. That is the nature of this world, as we have previously discussed - 'olam/world' is derived from 'helam/hiddenness.' Sunlight does not dispel the darkness, it only simulates illumination. The truth is as obscure at midday as it is at midnight. It is true that God created light on the very first day of the creation. "Let there be light,"[6] He said, and there was light. But the sages teach that this light was immediately hidden away, only to be accessed and utilized by "the righteous in the future."[7] This light that enables genuine vision is referred to as the "Ohr Haganuz/the hidden light," and it is generally inaccessible to most of us now. Physical light is only part of the illusion that enables us to believe that we can see.

---

[6] Genesis 1:3

[7] Rashi (Rabbi Shlomo Yitzchaki, 11th century French sage and foremost commentator on Torah's "simple meaning") on Genesis 1:4.

Admitting that we are lost and in the dark can be frightening. We're uncertain how we got here, or why we're here at all. We don't know what's lurking nearby, and we have no idea which way to go. Fear can stymie us, rooting us in our place, or it can make us want to run, aimless and mindless. But neither of these will help us to get found. This is not a time for panic. It is a time for courage and composure. It is time to assess our situation and gather what we know.

What we know at this point is that hiddenness is intentional, that it is not a result of failure or punishment, but rather it is a prerequisite for our existence. We have also established that *we have been created with a purpose and a mission, and that is to find what has been hidden and lost.* Yet this knowledge leaves us with several questions that we must address in order to help us navigate the journey from our current place of exile to the place of revelation and redemption that we seek.

Our first question is why God requires or desires our existence at all? We can understand that He must hide His infinite presence in order to allow finite creations like us to exist, but we have not yet determined why it is important for Him that we exist in the first place. If we are to suggest that there is a task that He assigned to us, we have to wonder how it is possible for there to be anything that we can do which He could not have done Himself. If we believe that He is omnipotent, and that, according to the notion of "hashgacha protis/individual divine providence," He determines everything that happens at every moment and in every place throughout the universe, then what could our creation possibly provide to Him that He did not already possess?

Our second question is that if this world was truly intended to be a realm of concealment, then why does God provide intermittent moments of revelation at all if they are only to be followed by a return to darkness? Why did we begin in the garden if we were inevitably to be expelled from it? Why did God reveal Himself to us at Mount Sinai and give us His Torah if we would quickly turn from Him and attempt to replace Him with an idol made of gold? Why do we have glimmers of clarity, connection, and inspiration throughout our lives, only to lose them the moment we try to grasp them? Again, according to our premise of "hashgacha protis/individual divine providence" and intentionality, there must be a purpose and necessity for both the light and the darkness. But which is it that God truly desires - an "olam/world" where He is shrouded in "helam/concealment," or a realm of light where the truth of His unity is revealed?

Our two questions are intertwined. The first asks why our existence is so important to God that it justifies His self-concealment and the creation of darkness, which is the root of all confusion and conflict. The second seeks to understand the flashes of stunning revelation that rip across the darkness like occasional lightning bolts throughout the long night. What is this interplay between revelation and obfuscation, how do we reconcile the two, and which is it that God primarily desires? In the dark before the dawn, as we prepare to set out on our journey, we attempt to familiarize ourselves as best we can with God's goals and motivations so that we can most successfully fulfill the mission that He assigns us.

Night And Then Day

Which came first, the chicken or the egg? The question has confounded multitudes, but in the creation story at the beginning of the Torah, the answer is clear. God created the animals fully formed, and then He commanded them to reproduce - so the chicken came first, and then came the egg. From the same creation story, in the very first verses of the Torah, we can address another profound order of precedence: which came first, the darkness or the light? The question may not be as catchy as the one about the chicken, but it is certainly significant and informative.

> In the beginning of God's creation of the heavens and
> the earth. Now the earth was astonishingly empty, and
> darkness was on the face of the deep and the spirit of
> God hovered over the face of the water. And God said,
> "Let there be light," and there was light.
> (Genesis 1:1-3)

From these opening verses of Torah, we see clearly that darkness preceded light. First there was darkness "on the face of the deep," and then God said "let there be light." It is for this reason that on the Hebrew calendar, the date begins not with morning, but with nightfall. Describing the creation of each of the days of the first week, the verse states "Vayehi erev, vayehi boker - it was evening, and (then) it was morning."[8]

Like every detail of Torah, the sequence is consequential. God created darkness and only thereafter light because that is the progression that He designed and intended for this world. First there was to be darkness, because darkness serves an important function - it allows a world to exist, as we discussed in the previous chapter. But darkness is not the goal or the ultimate objective. After the darkness, there was to be light; and not just any light, but a light that could only be achieved after dwelling in the dark.

When a light is switched on in the darkness, we are momentarily blinded. It may be a dim light, a light that we could tolerate easily and comfortably at any other time, but in contrast to the darkness, it is glaring, and we are forced to blink or shield our eyes. Such is the reality that was expressed by the wisest man in history, King Solomon, when he wrote that wisdom is better than folly, just as light is better than darkness. The mystics wonder at this statement. Did it require the deep insight of King Solomon to understand that wisdom is superior to folly? Or, for that matter, that light is preferable to darkness? Yet a careful reading of the Hebrew original indicates that Solomon was alluding to a far more subtle and profound truth.

> V'ra'isi ani she'yesh yisron la'chochmah **min** hasichlus k'yisron ha'or **min** hachoshech.
> I saw that there is an advantage to wisdom **FROM** folly like the advantage of light **FROM** darkness.
> (Ecclesiastes 2:13)

The mystics point out that the word "min" which appears before both the words "hasichlus/folly" and "hachoshech/darkness" is commonly translated as "than," but it literally means "from." The verse therefore expresses not merely that wisdom is greater *than* folly, or that light is greater *than* darkness, but that the advantage of wisdom comes *from*, or *subsequent to*, folly, and the advantage of light comes *from*, or *sub-*

---

[8] Genesis 1:5

sequent to, darkness. What King Solomon offers here, therefore, is not a simple statement of the obvious, but rather a profound insight into a) the nature of what wisdom and light are and how to attain them, and b) why the world we inhabit is filled with folly and darkness.

True wisdom, he informs us, comes from, and after, folly, just as the most blinding light is that light which follows darkness. One cannot be truly wise until s/he has made errors to learn from. One cannot come ultimately close to something until s/he has experienced distance, alienation, and longing which then drive her/him passionately toward that which s/he has lacked. One has never experienced true and blinding light until s/he has first dwelled in, and adjusted to, the darkness.

<hr />

Step By Step

Every voyage begins with a single step. We have taken our first step.

The first step is the understanding that there are steps. There are phases and stages to the world and God's plan for it. We cannot merely establish a polarity of light and darkness and ascribe to God a desire for one or the other. Such a simplistic conception does not recognize the inclusion of all aspects of creation within the divine unity. Any attempt to delimit God to one thing or another is inherently a failure to recognize His presence in, and therefore His intention for, everything that He has created. If something exists, then there is a reason it exists and a purpose for its existence. This is not to say that everything is "holy," desirable, or permissible, but rather that everything can and must be traced back to its origin, which is the ultimate truth that has been hidden within it. Darkness, as we have seen, is not evil. It is a veil with which God conceals Himself so that we are not obliterated in His infinite presence. While concealment is therefore a gift and an act of love, it is not an objective in itself. It is our point of embarkation. It is the beginning of a journey that will lead us to an unprecedented revelation of unimaginable light.

The recognition of steps is not only a prerequisite and jumping off point, it also assures that we are setting off on the right foot, so to speak. The journey will be long and arduous, but it need not be painful or unpleasant. The awareness of steps is the antidote to frustration, depression, and despair. It is the cure before the wound. Life, for many, is full of pain, but it needn't be. What is certain, in a world of darkness and concealment, is that there will be trial and struggle. However, these are not synonymous with pain. Pain is the result not of challenge, but of the assumption that there is no benefit in the challenge, and no purpose in its endurance. When, on the contrary, we are conscious of the underlying reason and productive function of a trying situation, we are able to endure it, and even pursue it, no matter how uncomfortable or troublesome it may be. As Freidrich Nietzche wrote, and as Viktor Frankl explained in his work *Man's Search for Meaning*, "He who has a why to live for can bear with almost any how." The recognition of steps enables us to set out in the darkness, to be unafraid and undeterred because we are aware that not only is there a purpose and reason for this concealment, but it is temporary and it is merely a dim passageway that will usher us to someplace luminous.

With such consciousness, we face the journey ahead not with trepidation and resignation, but rather we embrace the darkness because we know that it is not only a necessity, but a benefit. We venture into the darkness headlong because we know that our goal awaits us on the other side. This enables us to answer our second question, which is that if God created this "world/olam" as a place of "concealment/helam," then why does He keep introducing these glimmers of light and revelation that gleam momentarily and then quickly fail. Why place Adam and Eve in the Garden of Eden if He knew that they were to eat the fruit and be exiled within hours of their creation? Why bestow the Torah on Mount Sinai if He knew His people would fashion a golden calf soon thereafter? Why do we experience brief moments of clarity throughout our lives but dwell primarily in tumult and uncertainty? Is it concealment that You desire, God, or is it revelation?

The answer, we now understand, is both. More specifically, as discussed above, the answer is one and then the other. He desires darkness and then light, and ultimately light that comes from darkness. The reason for the glimmers of unenduring light is to provide us glimpses of the truth so that we remain aware of the end-game and can thereby continue to withstand the challenges of this interim darkness and persevere. The goal is therefore light, but there is something that the darkness provides that the light does not and cannot. The darkness provides the distance that makes the subsequent light appreciable.

With this answer to our second question, we must now address our first. What is it that the darkness and concealment provide to God? If, as we have established previously, He concealed Himself so that we could exist, what is it that our existence does for Him that He could not have done Himself? What is it that a vast multiplicity of flawed and finite beings can accomplish that an omnipotent and infinite unity cannot?

***

All One, Alone

"In the beginning, God created the heavens and the earth."

This is the common translation of the first sentence of the Torah. We begin with the beginning, which seems to be a reasonable place to start. But this is not truly the beginning, because something existed beforehand. We know this not only because God Himself obviously predated the creation if He created it, but also because the grammar of the verse makes it clear that this is not a reference to the very first moment of existence.[9] The word "Breishis," the very first word of the Torah which is translated as "in the beginning," always modifies the word that comes after it, and therefore more literally means "in the beginning OF." As such, the verse does not mean "In the beginning, God created the heavens and the earth" as it is generally rendered, but rather "In the beginning OF God's creation of the heavens and the earth...."

The difference is subtle, but substantive. If the verse were truly intending to discuss the very beginning of all creation, then the proper Hebrew word would have been either "Barishona" or "B'tchila," both of which means "at first." "Breishis," on the contrary, indicates that we are not talking here about the absolute beginning of all things, but rather the beginning of a particular stage in the larger context of existence. The process that is initiated at the opening of the book of Genesis is the creation of the world that we inhabit, but this is not the only world, nor is it the first. If this were truly the beginning, then we would not seek to un-

---

9 Rashi on Genesis 1:1

derstand what preceded it. But if, as the verse literally indicates, this describes only the dawn of our existence and the realm in which we exist, i.e. the heavens and the earth, then we will want to know what there was before we were. What preceded the creation of our world, which is what is recorded in the beginning of the Torah.

On the face of it, the Hebrew Bible[10] is focused on our world and our function within the context of this particular creation. Therefore, it does not explicitly concern itself with pre-history or the spiritual realms and alternate realities that coexist with ours. This Bible, beginning with Genesis and ending with Deuteronomy, is what most people understand to be the Torah. However, Torah more generally refers to far more than the five books of Moses. It comprises all of the divine wisdom that has been communicated to and by the sages, including the Talmud, or oral Torah, as well as the vast literature and tradition of Kabbala. Kabbala is the esoteric and hidden tradition which has been passed down through the ages. Among other things, it explores other worlds and the interplay between our reality and those which are beyond our immediate perception. The esoteric wisdom provides a glimpse of the ultimate beginning, prior to the creation of any world or any being, when there was only God.

At that point, God was One. God was All. God was All One, or Alone.

'Alone' generally connotes a state of isolation and separation. In God's case, of course, these terms do not, and cannot, apply. He is not isolated because He is everywhere at once. He is not separated, because there is nothing other than Him from which He can be distinct. 'Alone' in God's primordial sense means that there is no one, and no thing else. Oneness is a difficult concept to imagine, and though we meditate on it multiple times daily with the recital of the Shema prayer (as we discussed above), it continues to elude our mortal comprehension. We cover our eyes when we say Shema because vision is irrevocably tethered to the facade of plurality - the moment we look, we see so many things that seem to be separate from ourselves and from each other. But close your eyes and imagine for a moment an empty space that stretches infinitely in every direction. There are no walls that bound the space, no floor or ground below, or ceiling or sky above. The space just goes on forever.

---

[10] Otherwise known as the "Chumash" or the Five Books of Moses

Now remove yourself from the space as well so that there is not even a distinct being observing the space, there is only space. Yet the space is not truly empty. Something fills and pervades it. It is the space itself. It is all there is, and it is everywhere. It is not dark, or light, and it has no hue, or sound, or weight, or scent. It is everything and nothing at once. It is all, it is one. It is alone.

'Alone' is often correlated with 'lonely,' but of course they are not the same. Loneness is not synonymous with lonesomeness. We often tend to associate negative feelings with being alone, but it carries no inherent emotional state. For some, the idea of being isolated may be frightful or sad, but for others, the privacy and tranquility of seclusion are desirable and pursued. For God, we cannot say that His singularity presented a lack, or any feeling of incompleteness, because these very terms cannot apply to something that is everything. Yet in some way, which is beyond the reach of our intellectual comprehension, there was a desire within God for something else, something other.

How could One who is all, and who has all, want or need? Infinite, omnipotent, and omniscient, God could have, or be, or know anything He desired. But there was one thing He could not do: He couldn't give. He couldn't give because there was nothing other to give to. One cannot truly give to Oneself; and even if One could, One cannot be given to when One already possesses and includes everything that is.

Good Nature

Why did God create the universe? What was His reason? What did He want? Further, as we have asked earlier, what could our creation give Him that He didn't already have? What was He seeking that was worth concealing Himself and initiating a world of darkness in order to have it?

Volumes have been written on the question of the divine why. One very concise, and simultaneously very profound, reason for the creation of our universe that has been provided by the mystics is:

Teva hatov l'heitiv.
It is the nature of one who is good to do good.
(Emek HaMelech, Shaar Aleph)

God, according to this explanation, created the world because He desired to give. Or to put it slightly differently: God did not simply desire to create the world, but rather His giving nature necessitated the creation of the world, so to speak, because there had to be an outlet for His inherent and essential nature to manifest His beneficence. It is the nature of one who is good to do good, and therefore in order to express His natural goodness, God required a recipient to whom He could convey His generosity.

But how could God find a recipient if He was the sole existence? He would have to create an "other." But where could this other be created if there was no place that God did not already inhabit Himself? He would have to withdraw Himself, so to speak, from some portion of infinite space in order to make room for this new realm of otherness. But can One who is infinite create a space that is empty of Him? Theoretically, God is omnipotent, and therefore, there is nothing that He cannot do. However, by suggesting that He can create a space that is devoid of His presence, we are bounding His infinity; yet, if we affirm his ubiquity and suggest that there can be no place where He is not, then we are challenging His omnipotence.

The mystics resolve this paradox with the concept of "tzimtzum," or contraction. God contracted Himself to create a void where His presence was not revealed. It's not that this space was truly empty of God's presence, but rather that His presence here was concealed. By creating the world - "olam," again related to "helam" meaning hiddenness - God is not truly withdrawing Himself, but He is rather concealing His omnipresence. He does so in order to manufacture the appearance of otherness so that He can express His irrepressible benevolence.

If there were a brief introductory paragraph before the first verse of chapter one of the book of Genesis, it might read something like this:

In the beginning, the true beginning, before the beginning of the Creation of heaven of earth, God was All One, and He desired to give. In order to do so, He first needed to create an other, or many others, to be the recipients of his giving. Yet there was no place for any other, because

He filled all space and place. Therefore, in order to fashion a creation, first He needed to conceal Himself. Thus, the very first thing that God created, before He initiated the Creation as we know it, was darkness, which was not truly a creation, but rather a shrouding of His presence. Darkness is not truly void of God, because He remains One, everywhere and everything. Darkness is rather a concealment of the essential reality of His Oneness.

From this preface, we can better understand the first verses of Genesis:

> In the beginning of God's creation of the heaven and the earth, the earth was astonishingly empty, and darkness was on the face of the deep, and the spirit of God was hovering over the face of the water. And God said 'Let there be light,' and there was light.
>
> (Genesis 1:1-3)

We can now understand why there was already darkness and emptiness prior to the establishment of our world - because these were prerequisites for this realm of hiddenness. We can now comprehend "why the spirit of God was *hovering over*" the space rather than pervading it - because He "withdrew" Himself, so to speak, through the process of "tzimtzum" in order to make room for otherness. We can also appreciate why His first creative utterance was "Let there be light" - because darkness was only a preparatory contingency, and since light was the ultimate end-game, He announced and introduced its creation first. Darkness is concealment, withdrawal, and restraint, while light is revelation, effusion, and lovingkindness. The sole purpose of the former in God's scheme of creation was to enable the latter.

This reality has been explained with a simple but powerful analogy: There was a King with inexplicable capability, power, and wealth, but he had no one to share his gifts with because no one could tolerate the incredible force, immensity, and bliss of his presence. He possessed everything anyone could ever desire, but he wanted nothing more than to share his abundance with others. One day, as he sat alone at his tremendous table in the royal dining room, he had an idea. He took portions of himself, fashioned them into human form and outfitted them with various costumes and masks, and placed them in the chairs around the table. Each of them soon forgot that they were wearing masks and eventually came to believe themselves to be individuals rather than portions of the king himself. Delighted with his "guests," the king provided them every type of delicacy and "everyone" rejoiced in the royal feast.[11]

This dynamic is alluded to early in the creation narrative with the verse, shortly after the creation of Adam:

> Lo tov heyos ha'adam levado.
> It is not good for man to be alone.
> (Genesis 2:18)

On the simple level, this statement refers to the first man's solitary predicament. Because God saw that it was not good for Adam to be alone, He therefore created Eve to be his partner, as the verse continues "I shall make him a helpmate opposite him." But the Chassidic masters teach that, like all verses in the Torah, there is a mystic secret contained in these words, and that "haAdam/man" in this verse simultaneously refers to God Himself. Adam is the name that was given to the first human, but it also refers to "Adam Kadmon," a kabbalistic term that is best translated as "primordial Man" and which denotes the Godly "image" or "structure" that existed before the creation and to which the human image corresponds. Translated in this way, the verse is informing us of the very reason for the creation: 'It is not good for God to be alone, I shall make a helper corresponding to Him.'

When was God "alone?" Before He fashioned the creation. Why was it not "good" for Him to be alone? Because "good," by its very definition, is the bestowal of kindness from one to another. If there is no one to be, or to do, good to, then there is no good at all. Therefore, it was not "good" for God to be alone, and thus in order for good to exist, God needed to create an other to whom good could be given. Therefore, "I shall make a helpmate corresponding to him" - God fashioned a being that was in His image, an Adam/man that was corresponding to "Adam

---

[11] This analogy has been offered by Gutman Locks, author of "There is One", "Coming Back to Earth" and other enlightening books.

Kadmon/His primordial image," in order to "help" Him by enabling Him to express His goodness.[12]

With this, we have now answered both of our questions. We had previously established that our world was a realm of intentional concealment, and that the reason for the creation of darkness was to cloak God's unity so that something other - ie. we and all of the creation - could exist. But we wondered why our existence was necessary, and what it is that we can provide to God that He could not have provided Himself. And we now understand that we are here in order to provide God a recipient for His love and kindness.

But still we are lost. Still, we are in the dark. While these answers shed some glimmer of comprehension on the origin and nature of our being, and provide some ray of comfort in the awareness of our blamelessness for the darkness that surrounds us, they still tell us nothing of our objective or of the direction that we should pursue. As we set out on our journey, we need to know where we are going, why we are going, and indeed whether we should be going at all. If we are created simply to be recipients of divine charity, then can we not merely sit in our place and collect what God desires to give? Does this not fulfill our purpose? Or is there something that we were put here to do?

Adam and Eve were sent out of the garden. Moses and the fledgling nation were set free from Egypt, and then sent away from Mount Sinai. History has been a series of exiles and excursions through foreign and often oppressive lands. We are scattered throughout the globe and always yearning for a messianic eventuality that will deliver us from the darkness and usher us back to our home. Yet we are not simply waiting. We are not merely floating on the tides of history and allowing ourselves to be buffeted by the stormy seas. We have a role to play and a job to do. We are lost and in the dark by Godly design, but we are not sitting idly by and awaiting rescue. We are sent out to find our way, to find ourselves, to find the Creator Who has hidden Himself in order for us to exist.

If darkness is concealment of God's oneness, then light is its revelation. The first divine proclamation, "Let there be light," is more than an act of creation, it is an indication of our mission and purpose. While

---

[12] See Torah Ohr, Parshas Breishis, maamar Lo Tov Hayos HaAdam Levado, where the Alter Rebbe discusses this idea.

we were created to be the recipients of God's love and kindness, our task is not simply to be passive receptacles. True love does not merely bestow, because passive receipt is not what is best for the beloved. True love provides one's lover the opportunity to be active and to give in return, because the dignity that one earns by giving is far more valuable than all the riches and gifts that one can passively receive. God therefore gives us the ability to be good and Godly ourselves by providing us a task that we can do for Him. What is that task? To illuminate the darkness, to shed light on what is hidden, to reveal Him in a realm in which He has concealed Himself.

What then does our creation provide to God? Not only the ability for Him to give, but also the revelation and publication of His presence in a world that is capable of denying His existence.

———◆———

The Mission

As we head out on our journey, though there is darkness all around us, we can find clarity for our mission from a variety of sources. One is hidden in plain sight in the very first words of the Torah:

> Breishis bara E-lohim es hashamayim v'es haaretz.
> In the beginning of God's creation of the heavens and the earth.
> (Genesis 1:1)

The chassidic masters have suggested that these words contain our ultimate mission statement and a concise expression of the very meaning of life. While we have previously translated this verse as "In the beginning of God's creation of the heavens and the earth," the richness and elasticity of the Hebrew language enabled the rabbis to intuit a profound message in these words. "Breishis," commonly rendered as 'in the beginning of," can also be read as "the first thing" or "the primary thing." "Bara" means "creation," and can also be rendered as "revelation," because creation is essentially an act of revelation in that whatever is being created did not previously exist, and thus it has now come into a state of being and awareness. Translating the words this way, and adding the rest of the verse, we find in the very opening of the entire Torah, a clear and simple instruction:

> **Breishis**/the primary thing is **bara**/the revelation of **E-lohim**/God **es hashamayim v'es haaretz**/in the heavens and the earth.

"The primary thing is the revelation of God in the heavens and the earth." It is a simple statement, but its implications are deeply profound. When God gave us the Torah, a compendium of His will and wisdom, He provided an answer to our most fundamental question - what is the purpose of our lives - right in the opening words. *We are here to make the Creator known throughout His creation.*[13]

What does this mean? How exactly are we to reveal God in the heavens and the earth? Is it simply a matter of declaring "there is a God"? While such a statement and awareness is significant, and while there have always been those throughout history who have denied this reality, it hardly seems to be the sum total of our life's work and our very raison d'etre. Billions of people around the globe believe in God in some form or another and declare and demonstrate their allegiance daily. Can we say that each of us is fulfilling our personal mission and expressing the meaning of life simply by acknowledging God's existence or presence? Is believing in God the same as "revealing" Him? For that matter, is one "revealing" God simply by virtue of serving Him? In other words, is it possible that one can have faith in God, and beyond that s/he is even dutifully devoted to fulfilling God's will to the best of her/his abilities, but s/he is still not "revealing" God and therefore not yet fulfilling the mission statement that is etched into the Torah's opening verse?

"The primary thing is the revelation of God in the heavens and the earth!"

How do we do that? What is He asking of us, and what can we do to fulfill it? How many of us are actually able to accomplish this "primary thing" for even a moment throughout the entirety of our lives? Most of us are not even aware that this is our purpose and directive. And now that we do know, what are we supposed to do to actualize it?

---

13 See Kesser Shem Tov, Hosafos daled and hei

Seeing In The Dark

In order to "reveal" God, first we have to perceive Him. We must see God ourselves so that we can then disseminate the knowledge of Him around us. As we have been discussing, seeing God is no easy task, because He has, by design, not made it easy. The world we inhabit is a realm of darkness and concealment because otherwise we would be unable to exist. Yet He wants us to see through the darkness. He wants us to find Him where He is hiding. He wants us to divulge His presence under the shroud of His concealment, to unmask the blinding light that crouches silently and disguises itself in the shadows. In addition to embedding this mission statement in the opening verse of the Torah, God has also implanted this intention in the name of the nation to which He would give the Torah, Israel.

The name Israel, or "Yisrael" in Hebrew, has many explanations. The most common and explicit is the way it is expounded by the angel who changes Jacob's name to Israel after the two have wrestled and Jacob has been victorious. As the story goes, Jacob is on his way back to the home of his parents after he has spent two decades abroad in order to distance himself from his murderous twin brother Esau. The night before he is to encounter Esau after all these years, he is visited by an angel who wrestles with him until dawn. Some say it is Esau's guardian angel, and others suggest it is Jacob's own angel who has come to test and strengthen him. As the sun begins to rise, the angel tries to return to the heavens, but Jacob refuses to release him until he will grant him a blessing. The blessing that the angel gives him is a new and holy name:

> And (the angel) said, "It shall no longer be said that your name is Jacob, but rather Yisrael, for you have nobly contended with God and men and you have prevailed."
> (Genesis 32:29)

The name "יִשְׂרָאֵל/Yisrael" can be broken down into two words, "שַׂר/sar," which connotes nobility and victory, and "א-ל/E-l," which is one of the names of God. Because Jacob struggled against the angel of God and was victorious, his name was changed to Yisrael, meaning "one who has wrestled victoriously with God." The "Children of Israel," Jacob's descendants, would wrestle with the divine throughout history, struggling to reconcile the physical and the spiritual, to understand the darkness and the light, to decipher God's intentions and overcome His tests and challenges. For this reason, "one who wrestles with God" is an appropriate name not only for Jacob, but for his progeny as well.

The Kli Yakar[14] provides an additional interpretation of the name Yisrael which applies more directly to our theme of finding and revealing God. Similar to the first explanation above, the Kli Yakar breaks the word down into its two component parts. But in this case, rather than "sar" and "E-l" as above, he renders it "**shar**" and "E-l." Because there are no grammatical markings in the Torah scroll, the second letter of the word can be read as a both a "שׁ/shin" (with the vowelized dot on the right side of the letter), which is pronounced "sh," and a "שׂ/sin," (with the vowelized dot on the left side of the letter), which is pronounced "s". While the angel translated the first segment of the word as "sar/wrestle" as discussed above, the Kli Yakar translates it as "shar," which means "to see." As such, the name Israel, according to the Kli Yakar, thus means "One who sees God."

Interestingly, the Kli Yakar further teaches that according to some opinions, the name of the angel that fought with Jacob was "Samael," which, according to Jewish mysticism, is the name of an angel otherwise known as "the satan." Though as explained in the first chapter, Torah does not believe in a devil that works against God's will, the concept of "satan" is derived from Torah sources and is a force created by God to provide an alternative option so that we can *choose* to do the divine will rather than being forced to accede to it by compulsion. As such, the satan is as much a part of God as everything else, and its ultimate will is that we should be strengthened by the challenges that it presents us. How does the satan challenge us? We see this through understanding its name. "Samael" is a compound of the Hebrew word "suma," which

[14] Torah commentary by the 16th century scholar and mystic Rabbi Sholomo Ephraim of Luntschitz

means "blind," and "E-l", which, as we saw earlier, means God. As opposed to Yisrael, which means "one who sees God," Samael means "one who is blind to God." Satan/Samael is the force that tries to blind us to God's existence and presence.

The classical commentator Rashi points out that in the fight between Jacob and the angel Samael, the word for their struggle is "ye'abek," which shares the same root as "avak" which means "dust." The Kli Yakar teaches that when Samael/satan struggles with us, he kicks dust up in our face in order to blind us and maintain our inability to see God's presence through the darkness. Furthermore, as the story continues, though he is unable to defeat Jacob, the angel reaches out and injures his thigh. Why is it Jacob's thigh specifically that the angel injures? Because, the Kli Yakar explains, the thigh represents concealment, the part of our body that we cover, as it says in the Talmud, "just as your thigh is hidden, so are the words of Torah hidden."[15]

From all of these details, we reinforce our new awareness that our mission is to see and reveal God. Simultaneously, we find that there are potent and persistent forces in the universe that will constantly battle us in order to keep us from fulfilling this mission. Yet with all this, we must remain cognizant of the fact that it is God Himself who created the darkness and our blindness. It is God who creates the environment in which it is difficult for us to see Him. It is He who sends His servant Samael to kick dust in our eyes, to injure our thigh, and to maintain our myopia. And yet He creates the nation of Israel as a force of vision and light in the darkness. He provides Israel the Torah, and instructs them to teach its wisdom to the other nations. In so doing, He provides us all the potential to be victorious over Samael, and to see what was heretofore invisible.

Double Darkness

We are now equipped with a distinct statement of our purpose - "the primary thing is to reveal God" - as well as some new insights into

---

15 Sukkah 49

our nature and the nature of our reality. But in spite of the various clues that God provides us, the vast majority of us don't even realize that He has hidden Himself or that we are supposed to be seeking Him. This is because He is not only hidden, but furthermore, He has hidden His hiddenness. In other words, not only is God concealed, but He has concealed the fact that He has concealed Himself, and therefore many, if not most, of His creations are not even conscious of the fact that there is something that is missing.

This dynamic is alluded to near the end of the Torah in one of the final chapters of the book of Deuteronomy. God speaks to Moses before his death and informs him that he will soon pass from this world, and following his death the people will stray from the path he presented them and will worship the idols of their neighbors in the land. As we have seen before, it is known by God that the people will lose themselves in the confusion and distraction of the world. Even in the desert, where the divine presence was apparent daily in the provision of manna from heaven as well as other overt miracles, the people repeatedly erred and went astray. How much more so would they falter after Moses' passing and the cessation of the direct flow of divine transmission that Moses conveyed. As a result of the people's turning away from Him, God informs Moses, He will hide Himself from them.

> And I will hide My face on that day.
> (Deuteronomy 31:18)

This is curious. Hasn't God just begun to reveal Himself to the people? After two millennia of complete concealment, He has identified Himself to Abraham, Isaac and Jacob, and then He has rescued their children from slavery and given them the Torah so that they can find Him and reveal Him throughout the creation. Furthermore, isn't their transgression (and all transgression) attributable to the fact that He has already hidden Himself too much? If He wanted their compliance and devotion, wouldn't it make sense to make Himself more apparent rather than less? Can He really blame them - and us - for turning to "other gods" when He has made it so difficult for us to detect Him in the darkness of this concealed realm? Why would He now decide to conceal Himself further?

What is also puzzling is the specific language of the Hebrew verse: "V'Anochi **haster astir** panai bayom hahu." It is simply translated as "I will hide my face," but the word for "hide," "astir," is repeated twice - "haster astir" - so the literal reading is "I will *hide hide* my face." The common explanation for such repetition in Torah is that the word is doubled for emphasis, so the verse would read "I will certainly hide my face." But the mystics interpret the words more literally as, "I will *hide the hiding* of my face." With this reading, they identify a reference here to the primary existential quandary of this reality: not only is this world, "olam," founded on concealment, "helam," but this situation of concealment is itself concealed so that we are not even aware that the we are in the dark. We are so discombobulated that we have come to confuse the darkness for light, so blind that we don't even realize that we cannot see.

We might describe such a reality as a game of hide and seek where one player hides, but the others don't even know that they are playing, and therefore they don't look for him. Why would God create such a "game" in which the players are unaware that they are playing? We have already established why God hid himself, in order that we, and anything other, could exist. But why did He then choose to hide the very fact that He was hidden? Why make the darkness so dark that we don't even see our inability to see? Because, as we have established previously,[16] the darker the darkness, the greater will be the ensuing light. Therefore, with every glimmer of revelation, there is an increase of concealment that immediately follows. Yet within each of those glimmers resides the power and potential to overcome the darkness, as we find in the subsequent verses of this same conversation between God and Moses. Immediately after informing Moses that He is going to hide His face, God continues:

> And now, write for yourselves this song, and teach it to the Children of Israel. Place it into their mouths, in order that this song will be for Me as a witness for the children of Israel.
> (Deuteronomy 31:19)

---

[16] in the section "Night and Then Day"

Now, God tells Moses, in order to combat the darkness that is ahead, teach the children of Israel to sing these words of my Torah. There will be darkness, God informs us, and this darkness will be so thick and so disorienting that we will be unable to recognize that we are in the dark at all. But there will always be a light, a remembrance, a song that is heard by our ears even when our eyes fail us and prove completely unreliable. Many will forget the song - either they will tune it out intentionally or lose it beneath the clamor of their appetites and distractions. But as God continues to assure Moses:

> It will be, when they will encounter many evils and
> troubles, this song will bear witness before them, for it
> will not be forgotten from the mouth of their offspring.
> (Deuteronomy 31:21)

There will always be those, God promises us, few and scattered among the nations, who hum in the shadows and remind us that it is not too dark to see that we are in the dark. In other words, God has not hidden Himself completely. He has given us a lantern to penetrate the doubled and redoubled darkness. He has given us a song to guide us audibly and spiritually when our more external senses fail. He has given us a job to do, to find what has been lost, to remind those who have forgotten, to forge headlong through the gloom.

The first step then is to know that we are supposed to be looking for something. Before we can reveal what has been hidden, first we must reveal that there is something to reveal. Once we do that, then we can begin to search. And once we begin to search, only then can we find what we are looking for. If we are not looking, we will certainly never find it. Not only don't we know where to look, we don't know what we're looking for, and we don't know that we are lacking, and therefore looking, at all.

Most of us have some sense that we are missing something, some nagging sensation of emptiness deep within us. There is a void, a yearning, a thirst, but we don't know how to fill or slake it. So we try to ignore it. We distract ourselves with every manner of entertainment and diversion. Or we attempt to numb or drown our emptiness with substances, chemicals, or other addictions that may temporarily mitigate our angst, but which can never fully eradicate it. This is the darkness that conceals the darkness. The only solution is to admit and confront the presence of absence within us. There is something missing. I am deficient of something. That is not a defect or a shortcoming, it is the nature of the human condition. I need not panic in response to my lack. I needn't try desperately to deny and disown it. I am not abnormal or defective. On the contrary, it is how I and all of us were created. There is no one whole, but there is, rather, a hole within each of us. Our lifelong task is to fill it, but first we must acknowledge it is there.

The Joy Of The Search

Once we have established that we are intentionally lost and that God is intentionally hidden, once we have recognized that our task is to reveal Him and simultaneously find ourselves, once we have begun to understand the purpose of the darkness and our ability to see through it and eventually transform it, now we are just about ready to set out to fulfill our mission. But there is one thing more that we will need before we go. That is "simcha/joy," as we are instructed "serve God with sim-cha/joy."[17] Without joy, we will surely fail. This is because joy is not sim-ply a tool that will assist us along the path, nor is it the prize that awaits us at the end of the path, but rather joy is the path itself. Those who be-lieve that they will only find happiness when they have traversed and transcended the darkness will forever find themselves in the dark. It is the ability to sense and experience joy *within* the darkness that will lead one where s/he needs to go.

True and lasting happiness is not an emotion, it is a practice. It is not something that happens to you, but something that you must sow and cultivate constantly. Moments of joy may be happened upon, but if so they are fleeting and unreliable. In order to maintain happiness, one must exercise joy and develop the proper "muscles" to grasp and hold onto it. Torah provides a detailed regimen for such a practice with 613 "mitzvos" or commandments. One of the most essential and powerful

---

[17] Psalms 100:2

components of this regimen is daily prayer. Torah practice includes three prayer services a day in order invite one to step away from the facade of the physical world and to reconnect to the reality that is hidden beneath. At the beginning of the morning prayer service, one recites a prayer called "Hodu." The third verse of this prayer reads:

> Happy of heart is the one who seeks God.
> (Psalms 105:3)

This statement is puzzling. Why is one happy if s/he is looking for something? If s/he is seeking it, then this means that s/he has not found it, so why would s/he be happy? Seemingly, it would make more sense if it read 'happy is the one who *finds* God.' But the one who is looking, who looks daily and constantly but does not find what s/he seeks, wouldn't s/he be more inclined to be frustrated or anxious rather than happy? We might say that such a person is passionate, or driven, or hopeful even, but why happy? Are we happy when we lack what we seek, or is it when we achieve our goal that we are truly joyous?

The message here is powerful, and it is placed at the beginning of the daily service because it is essential for one to remind her/himself of it as s/he sets out anew each morning: Joy is not merely in the achievement, but in the pursuit. It is not only in the reward, but in the attempt. It is the knowledge that that which one seeks is there to be found! One is happy when s/he believes wholeheartedly that s/he can find what s/he is searching for, and that s/he is on the right path. S/he sings in the dark because though s/he may be lost, though s/he has not yet discovered what s/he is after, s/he knows that it is close and that there is nothing that can ultimately keep her/him from it. S/he is happy because s/he knows that s/he was made to search, that this is precisely what s/he was placed in this realm of darkness to do.

Unhappiness is not the result of our goal being as yet unfulfilled. Unhappiness is the abandonment of the search, the resignation and despair that come when we convince ourselves that we will never find what we are after and we decide to try no more. God does not exist, we determine, or perhaps He is out there somewhere but I do not have the strength, wisdom, or wherewithal to find Him. The moment we give up, any joy we knew is gone. Further, this surrender will lead to a sense of failure and a deeper melancholy that stems from the sense that I am not good, I am not doing what I should be doing, I am not being what I should be. Unhappiness is guilt and shame, self-judgment and self-loathing.

Happiness, on the contrary, is the sense that the world, with all its imperfection, is just as it was created to be, and I, with all my imperfections, am just as I was created to be. I was created imperfect. I was placed into an "olam/world" of "helam/concealment." That is nothing to be ashamed of, and nothing to be afraid of. The darkness is not frightening, it is God hiding Himself because He wants me to exist so that He can give to me. He wants me to seek Him and find Him and reveal Him, and He created me with the ability to do so. He will not make it easy, because ease is not love. Ease will keep one small and feeble, while challenge will give one strength and confidence and dignity. Challenge provides the fortitude to withstand the darkness and find what we are looking for.

On an even deeper level, the one who seeks God in the darkness is joyous because s/he knows a secret that those who believe that God is only to be found in the light do not know. S/he knows from the Shema prayer that, as we discussed earlier,[18] God is One, the one and only. Therefore, s/he recognizes that the darkness is God as much as the light is, and so no matter how dark it gets, God is always present and there is nothing to fear. This is what King David expressed in Psalms:

> If I say, surely the darkness shall cover me, the light shall
> be night about me. Even the darkness is not dark for
> you; but the night shines like the day; darkness is as
> light with you.
> (Psalms 139:11-12)

If we believe in the darkness, if we fear it and fail to recognize that it has no true existence other than its function in God's will to conceal the truth of His oneness so that we are able to exist, then even the light itself will be like night. In other words, if we don't recognize God's oneness and His presence in every single aspect of creation, then we will feel constantly anxious and alone because life itself will be devoid of

---

[18] in section "The Only One"

sense and meaning and purpose. When, however, we recognize that the darkness is not truly dark, but rather it is only a place where Godliness is temporarily concealed, then the night itself will shine like day. With such consciousness, there is only joy. And with such joy, we are ready to set out, confident that, with divine intention and assistance, we will find what we have lost. We will rediscover ourselves and our Creator, and we will make them manifest and evident for all.

Chapter 3: GETTING FOUND

Exile

W e are on our way. But which way are we supposed to go?
We have established that our task is to find and reveal what has been hidden, but now we must determine where we are supposed to look. If we are here to reveal God, we need to know where He hid Himself. Furthermore, we realized at the very outset that we, ourselves, are lost. How can we find anything else, if we do not even know how to locate ourselves? As it turns out, this is not a problem. The first step in getting found is recognizing that you are lost, even if, and especially if, you feel that you are at home.

The Torah begins with exile and ends on the doorstep of a homeland with the promise of exile's end. On the first day of our creation, we were expelled from the garden, and throughout our history, we have wandered and waited for the day when we will be able to return home. The very first communication that the Torah records between God and Abraham, the first Hebrew, is a commandment to leave his home.

Vayomer A-donai el Avram **lech lecha** *me'artzecha u'mi'mo-ladetecha u'mi'beis avicha el ha'aretz asher* **areka.**
And the Lord said to Abram, 'Go forth from your land and from your birthplace and from your father's house, to the land that I will show you.

(Genesis 12:1)

Like his first forebears, Adam and Eve, Abraham's journey begins by being sent away. The primary condition of a relationship with God seems to be displacement. Why?

Abraham would settle in the land of Canaan and raise his son Isaac there. Isaac would live his entire life in his birthplace, but his son Jacob would be forced to flee from Canaan to escape the murderous wrath of his brother Esau. He would return decades later, but his son, Joseph, would be sold by his brothers into slavery in Egypt. Later the entire clan would be forced by famine to relocate to Egypt, and this would mark the beginning of the exile that would stretch throughout the vast majority of the Torah. Subsequent to the events recorded in the five books of Moses, the young Israelite nation would enter the land of Israel, where they would live for roughly a millennium before the brief Babylonian exile, and then another half millennium before the Roman exile which has left them wandering throughout the ensuing two thousand years.

The fact that exile is such a central theme and trope in Torah is no coincidence. Exile is the natural state of this "olam/world" of "helam/hiddenness" that we inhabit. We have been exiled from paradise, alienated from the truth of who and what we are. We are never "home" in this world because this is not where we are from, it is not our origin or our destination. Wherever we may find ourselves, we are simply passing through, dwelling temporarily. We are looking for something, and as long as we do not find it, we are not settled or at ease. We cannot rest as long as we remain lost, and we are always lost because that is the very nature of this world that we inhabit.

The exiled individual is to be aware constantly that s/he is *in* the world, but not *of* the world. This is not our true home. This exile appears to be a curse, but in fact it is a blessing. It keeps us from being comfortable here, from mistaking this for our proper habitat or environment. It reminds us that we have something to do, that we need to expose the truth behind the ruse. Those who are comfortable and "well-adjusted" in this false reality are not healthier or better off - they have actually bought into the lie. They have accepted, and adapted to, life in prison. The hiddenness is hidden from them, as we discussed earlier. This is far worse than if one feels the discomfort of being lost and therefore strives always to be found.

In examining that first instruction which God communicated to the first Jew - "Go forth from your land and from your birthplace and from your father's house, to the land that I will show you" - the Chassidic masters[19] identify the blessing that is hidden within this expulsion. "Go forth" is a translation of the Hebrew words "lech lecha," which literally mean "go to you." If God wanted simply to direct Abraham to go from his home, He could have more succinctly stated "lech me'artzecha /go from your land." The additional word, "lech _lecha_ me'artzecha," can be translated the same way, but the sages teach that there is nothing superfluous in the Torah. Even the inclusion or exclusion of mere letters signify hints or allusions to profound additional insights. Therefore, an additional word is no accident or coincidence. "Go _to you_ from your land" is God's intimation to Abraham, and to all of us after him, that exile is the first step in the quest that He has assigned us. You will not find yourself without leaving where you are comfortable, He tells us. Get up and begin the journey. You have to find yourself, and you have a long way to travel to do so.

Just as the verse begins with hidden guidance, so does it conclude. Where is it that we are going when we leave where we began? At first glance, the verse seems to leave that answer vague and unidentified - "to the land that I will show you." But once again, the Chassidic masters note that the Hebrew contains an allusion that provides us a deeper answer and a greater certainty. The final word, "areka," means "I will show you." In the simple translation, this modifies the previous word, so that we understand it to indicate that what God will show us is the land. However, the word can also be read by itself, as "I will show _you_" - not that I/God will show something else (the land) _to_ you, but that the thing that I/God will show _is_ you. The verse thus informs us that when we

---

[19] See Likkutei Sichos, parshas Lech Lecha by Rabbi Menachem M. Schneerson, the Lubavitcher Rebbe

leave our place of origin and comfort, when we undertake the journey that God assigns us and we follow the way He designates, He will ultimately lead us to find precisely what we have been seeking all along - ourselves.

"Where are you," God had asked Adam at the very beginning of creation. For two thousand years, Adam's children remained lost and misguided. And then one of his descendants discovered the One and only God in an environment where all of his peers were worshiping any idol they could get their hands on. To this man, Abraham, God provided the beginning of the answer to the question that He had posed to his first ancestor. 'This world is a realm of concealment,' He told Abraham. 'From the very first days, humankind has been lost. But rise up and follow me, and I will take you from your exile to the place where you will be found.'

Where is this "land" where we will be found? Where is it that God is leading us? We have been wandering for millennia, and we still haven't found it. It is not on any atlas or map. It is nowhere that we can visit by plane, or boat, or any other means of transportation. It is not above us or below us, nor is it someplace foreign or exotic. It is not in the heavens and not across any sea. There is only one direction that will take us to God's land and to the ultimate 'you' that is hidden there.

That direction is *within*!

Inward Bound

It is no secret that if we want to find ourselves, we must look within. We have heard this from any number of teachers, spiritual guides, therapists, and healers from a diversity of backgrounds and ideologies. Over 3,300 years old, Torah has been directing us inward throughout the millennia. The Hebrew nation's exile, enslavement, wandering, and longing to return home is one sweeping allegory for the existential dilemma of losing our connection to our essence, and our history-spanning effort to reconnect. As mentioned earlier, our first progenitors, Adam and Eve, were originally in perfect communion with their interior - so much so that their skin was translucent and there was nothing that separated their inner essence from their outer reality. With their eating of the apple, however, they grew opaque, they were subsequently exiled from the garden, and we have been looking for our true selves ever since.

The central Torah concept and practice of "teshuvah" reflects this constant movement back and inward. Commonly translated as "repentance," "teshuvah" literally means "return." Throughout our lives, we are working perpetually on this process of getting back in sync, or returning to our original state of purity and integrity. We have lost our bearing and our center. Our goal is not to find new uncharted ground, but to go back to the place and state from where we came. Our actualization comes not from becoming something different and better, but rather from simply getting back to, and manifesting, what we were created and intended to be.

"Shabbat/the sabbath," which is the pinnacle of the week and a focal point of Torah time in general, is closely aligned with this concept of "teshuvah/return." The Hebrew words "teSHuVah" and "SHaBbat" share the same root, "SH-V," which means "return."[20] The sabbath is the day when one is to cease all worldly labor and activity in order to relinquish her/his focus on the external reality and redirect consciousness on her/his inner essence. This allows one to reconnect to her/his truer self, and then venture out into the workweek once again when the sabbath ends.

Furthermore, the entire system of 613 "mitzvos," which create the backbone of Torah life and practice, is similarly predicated on this idea of return and reunification. Commonly translated as "commandment," the word "mitzvah," according to the mystics, is derived not only from the Hebrew "tzivui," meaning "command," but also from the Aramaic word "tzavsa," which means "bond." Every one of the daily actions and prohibitions included in the 613 mitzvos that comprise Torah law - from the most global like "Thou shalt not kill" to the most picayune like washing hands before eating bread - is intended to reorient one to the awareness of, and attachment to, the soul which resides within her/him.

Torah practice is thus an attempt to reconnect, re-bond, and re-unify one's experience so s/he is not divided from her/his inner essence and cut off from who and what s/he truly is. Yet in spite of this ancient wisdom that counsels us to turn within, and in spite of a variety of more

---

[20] In Hebrew, the letter ב is sometimes 'b' and sometimes 'v' depending on its attending vowel.

modern and popular wisdoms that echo this biblical call, this has not discouraged many of us from seeking satisfaction and relief everywhere except inside of us. We look to entertainment, to money and material gain, to fame and other markers of societal recognition, to gluttony and various forms of intoxication. This is perhaps because, as we discussed earlier, what we sense inside of us is a void, an emptiness, and we believe that the only way to fill it is to bring something in from outside of us. To compound our confusion, we have been taught to pursue material pleasure and distraction by a society that profits from personal dissatisfaction and external gratification. Furthermore, the interior search is demanding, requiring discipline, commitment and hard work, while indulgence and inebriation, on the contrary, are easy and quick.

Yet "deep down inside" we know that none of these diversions will work. Sooner or later, we will conclude that all of these schemes and strategies to quell our inner longing with something external will only increase the void. And then we will begin to look inside. When we do, what will we find there? With hard work, and a good guide, we will find what we have been looking for - ourself. But that's not all. Torah teaches that we will find far more. We will find, in the deepest recesses of our being, that the self that we were missing is very different from, and infinitely greater than, what we thought it was. A tremendous surprise is awaiting us!

The Face Within You

So what's in there?

What is it that we will find in that most inward place? We can call it our self, our essence, our core, our inner spark - but none of those terms help us to understand what it is. Religiously, we can refer to it as our soul, but what is a soul? In Hebrew, there are numerous words for soul: "nefesh," "ruach," "neshama," "chaya," and "yechida." We might wonder why there is such a variety of different expressions for the same thing. The anthropologist Franz Boas studied the Inuit people of Alaska in the late nineteenth century and discovered that the eskimos have dozens of names for snow. This is because they identified many different types of snow - dry powdery snow, wet slushy snow, hard icy snow, just to name a few - and when something is such an integral part of your existence, you learn to differentiate between its various forms. In Torah, the soul is like snow to the eskimo - it is not something that one encounters only occasionally, but rather one lives with it and interacts with it every moment. It is not simply a detail of our existence, it is rather the very crux of it. We are not merely beings with souls, but it is our souls that make us beings. There is no existence without the soul, and there is nothing that exists that does not have a soul of some form or other. Even inert matter, like stone or mineral, has a soul according to Torah. The soul is the spark of vitality that enables the creation to be.

The various names for the soul refer to its different aspects, functions, and manifestations. For example, the "nefesh" level of the soul manages physical action, while "ruach" guides one's emotional makeup, and "neshama" regulates intellect. Yet while this informs us, to some extent at least, what the soul *does*, it still does not tell us what it *is*. The soul governs us, and even more than that, it vitalizes us, gives us existence, and underlies everything that is. But where does it come from, what comprises it, and, perhaps most pertinent to our line of inquiry, how are we to identify it and reunite with it, particularly if we have no clear idea what it is that we are seeking?

To complicate matters further, we seem to be ignoring an apparent contradiction that makes our search all the more confounding. On the one hand, we are instructed "Lech lecha / go to yourself," which seems to indicate that the object of our investigation is our self, which we have otherwise identified as our soul. On the other hand, we have established earlier that our fundamental mission is "bara E-lohim," to reveal God. So which is it? Is our search directed at finding ourselves, or at finding God? If we are looking within, we would seem more likely to find ourselves. But is this search not distracting us from the larger objective that we are responsible for, which is finding and revealing God?

A verse from Psalms will help us to resolve this confusion and identify the ultimate target of our search:

On Your behalf, my heart says, "seek my face." Your face,
O Lord, I will seek.
(Psalms 27:8)

This verse, like all of the verses of Psalms, is poetic, somewhat cryptic, and open to a variety of interpretations. Written by King David, and expressed by each of us who recites it, the verse addresses God and informs Him that our heart speaks to us on His behalf. There is a voice from deep within us, in other words, that speaks for God and instructs us to "seek My face." What is unclear, however, is whose face we are to seek - does "my face" refer to God's face or to our own? If the voice is ours, emanating from our heart, and it urges us to seek "my" face, then it seems to be our own face that is to be sought. If, however, the voice is speaking on God's behalf, as the beginning of the verse indicates, then "my" face may in fact be referring to the face of God. However, the voice may also be speaking on God's behalf and expressing His desire that we should seek our own face. Some clarity is provided by the second half of the verse, which indicates "Your face, O Lord, I will seek." Yet we are left with a question of which and whose face the first part of the verse refers to.

Before we can answer this question, we must understand what is meant by the word "face." What is this "face" that we are seeking, whether it is God's or our own? Can it be said that God has a face? And if it is referring to our own face, then why does it need to be sought when it is plainly visible? All we need to do is look in a mirror. However, as we explained earlier in the first section of chapter one, the Hebrew word "**PaNiM**/face" is closely related to the word "**PNiM**yus/inwardness," and refers not only to one's physical visage, but also to one's innermost essence. While there would seem to be a great distance and difference between one's face (her/his outermost and most superficial attribute) and one's soul (her/his innermost core), we have explained earlier that they are ultimately supposed to be perfectly attuned and aligned. It is only on account of the "hiddenness/helam" of this "world/olam," that they are alienated from one another. And this is what the voice of our heart is telling us in this verse on God's behalf - that our task in the darkness of this world is to find the "Panim/face" that we have lost. That face is obviously not the one that stares back at us in the mirror, but rather our true face, our deepest inwardness, the "face" of our soul.

The first part of the verse thus declares "On Your behalf, God, my heart tells me to seek **my own** face," my own self and soul, from which I have become disconnected and lost. But if so, then why does the second half of the verse say that it is "**Your** face," God's face, that we are to pursue? The verse thus presents us with the seeming contradiction that we have noted above. We are instructed to seek our self, as God's instruction to Abraham, "lech lecha/go to yourself," denotes. But we are informed in the very first line of the entire Torah, "breishis bara E-lohim/the primary thing is to reveal God," that our fundamental mission statement is to seek and reveal God. Which is it, and how are we to focus on one when we are distracted by the other?

In his work *Tanya*, the Chassidic master Schneur Zalman of Liadi,[21] also known as the Alter Rebbe, reveals the profound esoteric secret hidden in this verse of Psalms. Within our innermost interior, we will find not only our own soul, but we will discover what constitutes that soul:

> *Nitzot Elokus she'bchol nefesh Yisroel.*
> A spark of God that is in every soul of Israel.
> (Tanya, Igeres Hakodesh, Igeres 4)

The foundation of our soul, the Alter Rebbe informs us, is a portion of God that He has concealed within us. *We, and every component of our physical universe, are sparks of God that have been hidden within a material exterior in order to create a realm of multiplicity.* As we discussed in chapter two, God desires such multiplicity, and therefore He masks these fragments of Himself a) so that He can express His infinite nature to give, and b) because the light that is revealed subsequent to darkness is far more brilliant than the original light itself.

With this remarkable insight from the Alter Rebbe - that the soul is a veritable spark of God - we have answered several of our questions at once. We have asked, what is the soul that we are seeking? We have simultaneously wrestled with the seeming conflict of goals and instructions: is it our own soul that we are to be looking for, or are we to focus our search on the discovery of God? Whose "face" is it that the voice of our soul directs us to seek, and how can we find either if our intention is unclear? Finally, we understand that the direction of our search is certain, and the goal of our search is not ambiguous or multiple. To find what we

---

[21] Founder of Chabad-Lubavitch Chassidic dynasty 1745-1812

are after, we must move inward. And when we penetrate, with endless persistence and devotion, to our innermost interior, we will find our soul. And when we plumb the deepest depths of our soul, we will find not only our own face, but ultimately, the very face of God!

The first portion of King David's verse, "Bakshu panai/seek *my* face," and the second portion of the verse, "es panecha A-donai avakeish/*Your* face God I will seek," are not conflicting or confounding, because they are phases of the same search and aspects of the same reality. "Lech lecha/go to yourself," and "Breishis bara Elokim/the primary thing is to reveal God," are not contradictory instructions because our essential self and God are not distinct or separate, they are One!

The face of God is within you! It is your own inwardness and your deepest self!

In Me?!

Where are you? It was the first question with which we opened this book, and the first question that God asks Adam and Eve, and through them all of their descendants. It is the invitation with which He beckons us to seek and find what has been lost or hidden. We know now what we are looking for, and we know now where to begin our search. What we have lost is the awareness of what we are. What we are is pure Godliness that has been concealed and disguised. What we must do is uncover that reality. Where we must go is deep within ourselves to find the face of God so that we can allow it to be revealed.

Knowing that God's face is within us does far more than provide us a direction for our search. It also informs us of our fundamental nature and our inherent worth. It compels us to confront the reality that we are intrinsically Godly. It inspires us to express our infinite potential. It fortifies us with the ability to overcome all challenges. It reminds us that we are good even when we feel or act bad, and thus allows us to be better versions of ourselves than what we become when we forget our intrinsic greatness.

This is an extraordinary and intensely uplifting notion with tremendous ramifications which we will explore throughout the remainder of this book. But before doing so, it is important to admit that it is also an audacious claim that some may find uncomfortable or even objectionable. Reluctance to accepting such an idea may be predicated on a variety of considerations. The first may be the perceived burden that it confers - if I am Godly, then must I be perfect? What kind of limitations and restrictions does this inherent divinity impose on me, and what if I don't want the responsibility of such a lofty potential?

Resistance to the notion of inner Godliness may alternatively be based on deep religious conviction and an image of the self that is far too base and lowly to contain, or even to compare to, the divine. Religious conditioning, particularly in western culture, has drawn a sharp contrast between the human and the Godly. The human is viewed as animalistic and sinful, and the Godly is seen as an external force that can rescue or redeem us from our inherent wickedness. Suggesting that God can be found within us would thus be demeaning to God, if not downright blasphemous. Many of us have been reared by religious leaders and teachers who have convinced us that we are weak and selfish and unworthy. Our "self," we have been told, is our ego, and our ego is what we must deny and transcend. God, in such a worldview, is surely not within us. We would certainly not identify God with ourselves, but rather we are exhorted to crush and eradicate our self in order to achieve a relationship with Him.

But what if my ego is not my true self? *What if my ego is not what I ultimately am, but rather it is a disguise that has been wrapped over me in order to conceal my essential divine reality and unity?*

Of course, there are valid reasons to make a distinction between the self and the divine, and there are real risks involved with identifying God with the self. To be sure, there have arisen within the past half century numerous modern "religions" and pseudo-spiritualities that have veered toward self-worship on account of various misunderstandings of the notion of a universal and internal Godliness. Mystical truths, in the wrong hands, have been twisted and perverted - sometimes deliberately, and sometimes inadvertently - to result in outcomes that are completely contrary to their intentions or origins.

For all of these reasons, and in light of all of these reasonable objections, it would be legitimate for one who is skeptical, or for whom the concept of the face of God within is new and uncertain, to say "prove it." At least give me some additional supports for this idea.

For those, on the other hand, who find the idea attractive and inspiring, it is also worthwhile to explore evidence and support for such a revolutionary and potentially life-altering claim. It is one thing to invoke pseudo-spiritual and pop-psychological platitudes to suggest that we are Godly beings. It is quite another thing to provide textual citations from ancient and authoritative sources which can reveal the existence of the very face of God within us. Furthermore, when the sources will be shown to exist within the framework of an age-old codified system, they will be understood in the context of a rich and established tradition of thought, and their implications and ramifications will not be left subject to haphazard interpretation or personal whimsy.

All of this is to say that we need to further explore the biblical sources for the claim that the face of God is within us. Is this truly supported by scripture and consistent with the tradition that has been transmitted throughout the generations from Mount Sinai until today? Where can we find authentic evidence for such a notion, and if it is so, then why does it seem so radical, questionable, and unfamiliar?

What we will find by digging even a little bit beneath the surface of the Torah text is that this reality is hidden in plain sight, and that the idea that the face of God is embedded within us is not what is shocking. Rather, with all of the indicators pointing to it, what is truly remarkable is that we have any doubt that it is there! What we will discover through the sources is not merely the existence and nature of our Godly essence, but we will furthermore come to know what we have been created to do, where we have to go to do it, and how we are to get it done.

Face In Face

Moses, in describing the events on Mount Sinai when God gave the Torah to the Jewish nation, states that God spoke to the people "face to face."

Panim b'panim dibber A-donai imachem bahar.
Face to face God spoke to you at the mountain.
(Deuteronomy 5:4)

It's difficult to understand what this could mean. Does it imply that the people saw the actual face of God as they stood at the foot of the mountain? This is problematic on a number of different levels. First, we know that God does not have physical attributes. How then could one suggest that His face was visible? Secondly, as we discussed earlier in chapter one, God informed Moses that "you will not be able to see my face, for man shall not see Me (God) and live."[22] If so, how could it be that He spoke to the entire nation "face to face" and they survived? Once again, the English translation is baffling, and we must look to the Hebrew original in order to clarify our confusion.

The wording used by Moses in the verse, "Panim b'panim," does not literally mean "face to face" as it is commonly translated. That would be the literal translation of "panim **el** panim." The Hebrew word "el" means 'to', while the Hebrew prefix "b'" which Moses uses in the verse, means "in." The expression "Panim **B**'panim" therefore literally means "face IN face," and the full verse would thus be translated "face IN face God spoke to you at the mountain." This is very odd, particularly because there are other verses in the Torah where the expression "face *to* face" is used, and in those cases the proper expression "panim *el* panim" is employed.[23] Why in Moses' description of the interaction at Mount Sinai does it use the unusual expression "panim *B*'panim," and what could it mean that God spoke to us "face *IN* face?"

To reinforce our question further, in the chapter previous to the one from which this verse is taken, Moses warns the nation against the worship of idolatry by stating:

But you shall greatly beware for your souls, for you did not see any likeness on the day Hashem spoke to you at Horeb (Sinai).
(Deuteronomy 4:15)

---

[22] Exodus 33:20

[23] For example, see Genesis 32:31 and Exodus 33:11

If it was not clear before from Moses' unusual wording, then from his admonition here it becomes obvious that we did not speak to God "face to face" as the English translation implies. Rather, the expression "panim B'panim/face IN face" denotes an experience of something at the giving of the Torah which has nothing to do with any physical or visual phenomenon.

As we have discussed on multiple occasions already, the Hebrew word for "face," **PaNiM** is closely related to the word **PNiMyus,** "inner essence," and can therefore refer to an experience of one's deepest interior as opposed to one's most surface features. As such, what Moses describes by utilizing the phrase "face IN face" rather than "face to face" is a mingling of "faces," an infusion of one inner essence into another. The giving of the Torah, we come to understand, was not simply the transmission of a book of laws and narratives. While the ten commandments and the Biblical text that Moses brought down from Mount Sinai contained a Divine wisdom that would revolutionize the world, there was something even more profound that was conveyed at that moment. Many have missed the nuance of the language of the verse that we have been discussing, but a careful reading of the Hebrew text renders the secret that Moses is alluding to completely apparent:

"Panim b'panim dibber Hashem imachem bahar" - **at the mountain, God infused His face, His quintessence, into our face, our innermost core.**[24]

This provides an entirely new and earth-shattering context to the events at Mount Sinai and the understanding of what the Torah is. Far more than a rule book and a chronicle of historic events, Torah is a mechanism through which we can access the infinite potential that is embedded within us. Beyond Moses' intimation of this reality through his unusual language, we can also see this from the very first word of the ten

---

[24] See Likkutei Torah, Parshas Reeh where the Alter Rebbe discusses this subject: "And behold it is written 'face to face Hashem spoke with you' because at the time of the receiving of the Torah there was drawn down into every single individual of Israel the aspect of Havaya into the aspect of their 'face' in every spark of their neshama, and this is the concept of receiving the statement 'I am the Lord your God,' the explanation of which is that the aspect of the name Havaya should shine and be revealed within you."

commandments, which are the encapsulation of the entire Torah and the very words that Moses and the nation heard on Mount Sinai.

> **Anochi** A-donai E-lohecha asher hotzeisicha me'eretz Mitz-
> rayim mi'beis avadim.
> I am the Lord your God who took you out of the land of
> Egypt, out of the house of bondage.
> (Exodus 20:2)

"Anochi" means 'I', and it is the first word of the first commandment. But the common Hebrew word for 'I' is "ani," and the sages ask why this far less common usage is employed here. One answer they provide is that the word "A-No-CH-I" is an acronym for the phrase "**A**na **N**afshi **C**hatavis **Y**ahavis," which means "I wrote and gave Myself."[25] From this, we further understand that what God delivered to us through the giving of the Torah was not just His wisdom or His will, but it was His very self.

But where is this "self" that He gave us? Is it on the tablets that were engraved on the mountain and brought down to us by Moses? Is it on the parchment of the Torah scroll? Is it in the breath of the words that were passed down verbally through the oral Torah? The answer to this is found in Moses' statement "panim b'panim." The "Self" that God delivered to us is His "panim / face," and the place where He deposited it is in our "panim / inner core."

In Your Face

We may be inclined, from this discussion of the events at Mount Sinai, to mistakenly assume that the face of God was not within us prior to the giving of the Torah. Clearly the events at Mount Sinai marked a revolutionary moment in history and something new and profound was introduced into the universe, and into us, at that time. But what about the previous 2,448 years from the time of Creation until then?

---

25 Talmud Bavli, Shabbat 105a

If, as we've noted earlier, the soul is the life force of all beings, and, as we quoted from the Alter Rebbe, that it is "a spark of God" that exists in each of us, then certainly God was within us from the moment of our creation. What then does it mean to say that the giving of the Torah marked the moment when God placed his "face/panim" into our "pnimyus/inner essence," as we discussed in regards to the phrase "panim B'panim/face IN face" above?

We will gain some further insight by exploring another verse that also expresses these themes. In the book of Deuteronomy, God proclaims:

> *Reeh **Anochi** nosein **lifneichem** hayom bracha u'klala.*
> See, I give before you today a blessing and a curse.
> (Deuteronomy 11:26)

Simply translated, this verse means that God is providing the nation on that day a choice between a blessing and a curse. The subsequent verses then go on to explain that the blessing will come if God's will is obeyed, and the curse will result from the opposite. Afterwards, the blessings and curses are laid out in detail. Like all of Torah, the verse operates on this basic level, but also reveals deeper truths beneath its surface. Its more hidden meaning is once again gleaned from examining the precision of the Hebrew text.

Two of the words in the verse bear particular relevance to the analysis that we have been pursuing. First, there is once again the word "Anochi," which we have already identified as an unusual usage and a less common translation for the pronoun "I." Secondly, we find the word "pnei/face," which we have been discussing at length, within the word "lifneichem."[26] Neither of these word choices are haphazard or insignificant. The Alter Rebbe asks why "lifneichem," which is translated as "before you," was used here rather than the more simple and straightforward "lachem/to you." If God merely wanted to express that "I am giving *to you* today a blessing and a curse," then He could have more simply stated "Ani nosein *lachem* hayom.../I give to you today...". Substi-

---

26 "פְּנֵי/pnei" is another form of the word "פָּנִים/panim," both meaning "face." The Hebrew letter 'פ' can be pronounced either 'p' or 'f' depending on its vowelization. Therefore "face" can be vocalized as either "pnei" or "fnei."

tuting "lifneichem" for "lachem" provides a far more profound implication, as does inserting "Anochi" instead of the more common word for I, "Ani." "Lifneichem" can mean "before you," or it can be translated as "within you." Both meanings are a function of its root "pnei/face." "Before you" is an expression of something being 'in front of your face.' "Within you" is an expression of another connotation of "panim" which we have mentioned several times now, "pnimyus" or inwardness. In this sense, "lifneichem" would more literally mean "in your face" or inside your inner-ness.

Based on the use of these terms, the Alter Rebbe's translation of the verse reveals its mystic secret:

> "See, I place 'Anochi' within you today, a blessing and a curse."

On this deeper level, the verse is not simply stating that God is placing a blessing and curse before us, but that He is placing His level of "Anochi," His deepest self, within us, and this can manifest as either a blessing or a curse. The "blessing" is when we are aware of this divine reality and we publicize it. The "curse" is when we remain ignorant of what we truly are, and we therefore neglect our duty to make it known to others and thereby transform the entire creation. Once again, we are presented with a shockingly blatant and succinct statement of God's insertion of His essence within us. Our task is laid out in the first word of the verse, "Reeh/See": we are instructed to perceive this hidden truth, and to then make it revealed so that others can see it as well.

Yet what remains to be understood in the verse is the word "hayom/today." When is this "today" on which God implanted His level of "Anochi" into our "pnimyus/innermost core?" The verse is stated some time in the fortieth year that the nation is journeying in the desert after their exodus from Egypt, soon before they enter the land of Canaan. However, it was not at this moment that God infused Himself in us. There is a principal in Torah analysis that is known as "gezeira shava" which means "identical terms." When identical words or phrases are utilized in different places in Torah, one is able to interpret them in one context based on how they are similarly used in other contexts. The word "hayom/today" aligns the verse with another verse in Deuteronomy

"Atem nitzavim *hayom*/you are standing *today.*"[27] The Zohar comments that the word "hayom/today" in that verse is a reference to the first day of Adam and Eve's creation. This is because the same word is found in the phrase from the talmud, "zeh **hayom** techilas maasecha zichron l'yom rishon/this day is the beginning of your works, a remembrance of the first day."[28] If we read "hayom/today" in our verse ("See, I place Anochi within you *today* ...") as a reference to the day of humanity's original creation, then we find that the time when God instilled His inner essence into our innermost core was the very moment of our inception. Humanity was conceived and created with God's level of "Anochi" as our crux and foundation. It is what we are in essence and in fact.

If this is the case, then what was the innovation at the giving of the Torah? How is it, as we discussed in the previous section, that we and the world were dramatically transformed when we stood at Mount Sinai after we went out of Egypt two and half millennia after our creation? If the soul, which is God's "face," was in our "face" all along, then what did we gain with the receiving of the Torah? What is the significance of the fact that God spoke to us "panim **B**'panim/face IN face" at this point if He had already embedded His face within us thousands of years earlier?

While we might be tempted to suggest that He gave us "more" of His face at Mount Sinai than He had given us at our creation, this is untenable because there cannot be more or less of the infinite. However, there can be a greater revelation of something that already existed in a more hidden way. And this is precisely the additional dimension that became manifest when the Torah was given. At that point, with the giving of the Torah, humanity was provided a far greater ability to locate the face that God had already hidden within us at our creation. The Torah was, and is, a way for us to relate to and reveal the infinite that was previously too blinding for us to detect. The "Anochi" that He gave with the giving of the Torah was a mechanism for us to see the "Anochi" that was already in there but was previously impossible to grasp and maintain. In this sense, Torah can be seen as an eyepiece that allows us to perceive,

---

[27] Deuteronomy 29:9

[28] Tractate Rosh Hashana 27a; Ramaz, Zohar Chadash beis 32,2

and even stare without being blinded, into the blazing infinite light that shines from within our hidden nucleus.

In *The Ethics of the Fathers*, it is taught: "Precious is man for he was created in the image of God. Even more precious is that it was made known to him that he is formed in the image of God."[29] The face/image of God was always within us, but we weren't aware of that and truly able to know what that meant until we received the Torah. The Torah's inner dimensions enable us to plumb our depths to understand and express our true nature and potential.

———————

Not So Fast

We have answered a number of our questions at this point, but another question, which is perhaps even more troubling, now confronts us.

Our initial question, and, as we have pointed out, God's initial query in the Bible, was "ayecha", **Where are you?** The question itself led us to the awareness, which we often try to ignore, that we are lost. And this prompted us to ask our second question: **Why are we lost?** To this, we responded that we are lost because this is precisely how God intended it. This prompted the obvious follow up: **Why would God create us to be lost?** And here, we explained that this "olam/world" was to be a realm of "helam/concealment" so that we, and anything "other" than God, could exist (or at least perceive itself to be existing). This existence was necessary in order for God to express His infinite giving nature - "teva hatov l'heitiv/it is the nature of the good to do good."

We then asked: **What is our task in this darkness?** And we concluded that we are here to find what has been lost and concealed, and then to reveal it in order to manifest a light that would shine extraordinarily bright in comparison to the darkness that preceded it. Ready to set out in order to undertake this search, we next pondered: **Where are we to look?** We recognized our propensity to seek satisfaction and fulfill-

---

[29] Pirkei Avos 3:14

ment in a wide variety of places where we know it will never be found, and concluded that the proper direction can only be within.

At this point, turning inward, and anxious to be on our way, we paused to clarify some confusion about the ultimate object of our search: **Were we to be looking for ourselves** - "lech lecha/go to you" - **or for God** - "Breishis bara Elokim/the primary thing is to reveal God"? The startling and exhilarating response was that we are seeking both simultaneously, and that the one is hidden within the other: "panim B'panim dibber Elokim" - God instilled His essence into our core. Inspired by the new awareness of our personal divinity, we inquired: **How can we find the face of God within our own inner face deep within us?** And we were encouraged as we learned that there is a map which we have been given that will lead us there. That map is the Torah.

With all of these questions and their respective answers, we have penetrated a good way into the darkness already. However, we are now presented with a quandary as we rest to catch our breath. As we realize that our goal and destination is still not at all apparent to us, the obvious and unsettling question creeps up on us: **if we have the Torah which is to serve as our guide, and if we have had it for nearly three and a half millennia already, why are we still lost, and why does God remain concealed?**

The answer is that it is no fault or error which has resulted in the continued darkness. As we touched on in chapter one, this is precisely what God intended when He created this "olam/world" to be a place of "helam/concealment." As we elaborated in chapter two, He created darkness prior to light - "it was evening and then morning" - because there is a benefit in the progression from the one to the other. That is that light which comes after darkness is more brilliant than light by itself. Therefore, every moment that there is continued darkness and concealment, we are building toward an ever greater eventual revelation. It was never God's intention that we should quickly move from exile to redemption. If He had desired that to be the case, then, as we have discussed regarding the principal of "hashgacha protis/Divine providence" and God's complete control of everything that happens, it would have been so. The fact that we have languished in exile for the majority of our history, and the fact that human existence has been marked by consistent conflict, confusion, and frustration, is not an accident or an indication of either Divine or human failing. Rather, it is the precise process through which God's ultimate goal of the meticulous transformation of darkness to light will be accomplished. And though it may seem to be moving too painfully slow from our perspective, we must remind ourselves that everything must and will move at God's pace, which is precisely the right pace.

The advent of the Torah was not meant to immediately usher in an age of total revelation. It was not intended to overturn the creation or eradicate the laws and systems that God had previously put in place and set in motion. The complete disclosure of God's essence and reality would cause the world to revert to nothingness in the face of His absolute oneness. This would be utterly contrary to His initial intent in the creation of a multiverse where His unity would be concealed and otherness could exist. Therefore, He provided a tool with which bits of light would be gradually revealed within the darkness. Every commandment prescribed in the Torah would create an individual act of illumination, a breaking of a small shell which contained and concealed a morsel of divine light. Through the aggregate performance of innumerable such acts throughout history, the darkness would slowly be transformed and an age of unprecedented radiance would evolve.

The end of this process is known as "yemot hamashiach/the days of the Messiah," the messianic era when "the earth will be filled with the knowledge of God like the oceans fill the sea-bed."[30] At that point, all of the world and its creations will recognize the face of God within them. Until then, we remain in the dark with the lantern of Torah which lights the path in front of our feet and urges us forward step by step.[31]

--- * ---

[30] Habbakuk 2:14. More on this subject will be discussed in Chapter 8.

[31] There have been many predictions and forecasts throughout history as to when the messiah will come, but none of this is relevant to our daily purpose and labor. A person's job is to work toward it constantly.

From 'Knowing' To 'Showing'

The fact that the world we inhabit was created to be a realm of concealment does not absolve us from our task of working toward illumination and revelation. The fact that the possession of the Torah does not enable us to instantly actualize all of its insights does not diminish its truth or our responsibility to pursue and manifest it. The fact that we are unable to clearly see and reveal the face of God within us does not render us less Godly or free us from the opportunity and duty to exercise our inherent Godliness.

Another way to state all this is to acknowledge that **knowing that the face of God is within us does not mean that we have found it**. Rather, it simply gives us an indication of where to look. Having a map with an 'x' on it to mark where the treasure is hidden is obviously different from finding and possessing the treasure that the 'x' represents. Yet there is tremendous value to the map, for without it, we may spend all of our days hunting for the treasure in all of the wrong places, or worse yet, not knowing that the treasure exists at all. Torah provides us the map. It informs us that there is a priceless and infinite fortune awaiting us, and it offers us instruction on how and where to find it. But it gives us no guarantee when we will reach our destination. That is dependent, in part at least, on the effort that we are willing to exert. It is also, and primarily, dependent on when God chooses to bring the final redemption and take the world out of this last period of exile. The Sages teach that His decision to do so is contingent on our deeds. We never know which act of illumination will be the one that finally puts us over the top and completes the requisite amount of light that will overcome the prevailing darkness. Until then, we are working constantly to move from knowledge to revelation, from intellectual and spiritual awareness of the existence of God's presence within us, to the clear and universal perception and experience of this reality.

We can witness this dynamic in the words of the daily prayers that were established by the Torah sages during the time of the second Temple in the fourth century BCE. Each day begins with a declaration of acknowledgment of God's presence, and then proceeds with prayers requesting the ability to expose this truth and render it perceptible. The first of these two stages is expressed in the very first words which one is to recite immediately upon awakening every morning:

> *Modeh Ani lefanecha melech chai v'kayam, shehechezarta bi nishmasi b'chemla.*
> I offer thanks to You, living and eternal King, for You have mercifully restored my soul within me.
> (Siddur Tehillat Hashem, p.5)

Simply understood, this prayer is an expression of gratitude to God for restoring one's life this new morning and allowing one to live another day. Sleep, according to the sages, is one sixtieth of death,[32] in that the soul partially abandons the body and ascends to the heavens when one sleeps. When one awakens, the soul is restored, and therefore one gives thanks to God for its return and for entrusting her/him with such a precious endowment yet again. Gratitude and appreciation for the gift of life are certainly valuable principles with which to begin every day, but there is an even deeper message hidden within this initial declaration that is uttered within the first moments of consciousness.

The third word in the prayer, "lifanecha," should look familiar to us by now. It is similar to the word "lifneichem" which we recently discussed from the verse "Reeh Anochi nosein *lifneichem* hayom/See I place before you today." While the simple meaning of the word "lifanecha" is "to you," its root is "pnei/face" and its literal meaning is thus "to your face" or "in your face." Just as we saw above,[33] if the intent of the phrase were simply "to you" (expressing our gratitude to you, God), the word "lecha/to you" could have been employed. The use of "lifanecha" tells us that we are simultaneously referring to something more, which is once again some allusion to God's "panim/face."

We can understand what we are saying here about God's face by exploring the deeper implication of the first word of the prayer, "modeh", which is translated plainly to mean "give thanks." The word's root, in addition to thanks, also means to confess, to admit, to submit, to acknowledge, and to bow. Understanding "modeh" in this sense, and

---

[32] Talmud, Berachot 57b

[33] In section "In Your Face"

reading "lifanecha" in its more literal translation, the prayer takes on a very different implication. Rather than "I give thanks to you," we can now read the beginning of the phrase as "I acknowledge your face" or "I admit/submit/bow to your face." Translating the entire prayer in this context, we can render it as follows:

"I acknowledge your face, living and eternal King, which You have returned within me, my soul."

Understood this way, the first utterance as one begins every new day is an acknowledgement and admission of the face of God which He has placed within us. One reminds her/himself that this is what the soul is - we live and are sustained only by virtue of the fact that God infuses His innermost essence into us. We recognize the tremendous extent of His mercy and His faith in us that leads Him to entrust us with such a precious part of Himself.

Imagine awakening daily with this affirmation and this resolve. The recognition of our core divinity and the proclamation of what we ultimately are will certainly transform our consciousness and positively influence the day ahead. Yet with all of this profound awareness and acknowledgement, one must 'admit' and 'submit' to this truth rather than perceive it. This is the implication of the word "modeh," according to the Alter Rebbe.[34] It is an admission and submission to something that one cannot see clearly, but which he recognizes to be true nonetheless. "Modeh ani lefanecha/I acknowledge your face" is thus our daily admission, the moment we awaken, that God's face is within us though we don't yet see it clearly. We are furthermore submitting to the reality of our divine essence, even if we are not feeling particularly Godly. And we are committing to doing our best to make that Godliness visible through our actions throughout the day ahead.

Yet our goal is not to stay at this level of "modeh/admission" where the truth is hidden but acknowledged. While we are charged with the task of expressing Godliness through our actions within this time of exile and concealment, our ultimate goal is not to remain in the dark, but to eradicate and transform the darkness. This means that while our day begins with an admission of an unperceived truth, this is only a first step

[34] Likkutei Torah, Devarim p.1, Tzion B'mishpat Tipadeh

- albeit an extremely profound first step - and we do not stop here. From here, we will offer, throughout the day ahead, a series of impassioned requests for this truth to emerge from its obscurity and to become overt. Where do we find this request expressed? In the seemingly simple, but generally misunderstood, wording of the most common daily prayers.

Blessed Are You

"Baruch attah A-donai/Blessed are You God" is the well-known formula that begins many Hebrew prayers. Prior to performing many rituals acts, or even simple deeds like eating, one will recite a blessing that begins with these words and then concludes with a summary of the action that is about to be performed. This is commonly understood as a statement of gratitude for what is about to be partaken of, or a sanctification of the forthcoming deed by expressly stating one's consciousness of God's involvement with everything we do. In addition to utilizing this phrase frequently throughout the day in connection with one's particular actions, the three daily prayer services include dozens of mentions of this phrase.

But what does it really mean to say "Baruch attah A-donai/ Blessed are You God"? Who is blessing God, and what is the implication of God's being blessed? Are we suggesting with this expression that we are blessing Him? Isn't it rather, we who are blessed *by* God? Does God need our blessing, and is He not already blessed whether we bless Him or not?

In general, to bless something means to confer on it some sacredness, or alternatively to bestow upon it a prayer for some desired benefit or divine assistance. God, who is already sacred, and who can have whatever He desires, does not require our blessing in any of these senses. To bless can also mean to proclaim that something is holy, and in this sense, though God is holy whether or not we proclaim Him to be, there is some value in our proclamation. However, the Hebrew word "baruch" has a much deeper implication, the understanding of which can literally transform one's entire practice and consciousness.

The root of "baruch," ב-ר-ך in Hebrew, is found in the Talmud in the word "מַבְרִיך/mavrich," which means "to draw down," as in the phrase "*hamavrich es hagefen*/to draw down a vine"[35] and plant it in the ground so that it grows a new plant. It is also found in the word "בְּרֵיכָה/breichah," which means "pool." Both of these derivatives provide us a more thorough understanding of what it means to "bless." Just as "mavrich" means to draw down, and just as a pool is a place where rain has gathered after falling from above, a blessing is an attempt to draw down, consolidate, and manifest something in this lower realm which originates in a loftier source above.[36]

Understood in this sense of "drawing down," the phrase "baruch atta A-donai" becomes both a request and a mechanism for God to be revealed in this world of concealment. Rather than "blessed are You, God," it is now rendered, "may You be drawn down and revealed, God." This forms the introduction to manifold prayers and blessings in Torah practice because this is the ultimate intention of the variety of actions and meditations which one performs throughout the day. "May You be revealed" through my eating of this food; "May You be revealed" through my lighting of these candles; "May You be revealed" through the washing of my hands. Each of these acts becomes a way for one to manifest the Godliness that is concealed within her/him, or within the item that s/he is about to consume or utilize. And each prayer one recites beginning with these words is an entreaty to God to assist her/him in the task that God assigned each of us with the first words of His Torah, "breishis bara Elokim/the first thing is to reveal God." We recognize that this is no easy job, and we, therefore, ask Him frequently for His help to fulfill it.

We thus see that, as stated above, we begin each day with a statement of the acknowledgment of God's presence within us - "modeh ani lefanecha/I acknowledge your face" - even though it is not clear or

---

[35] Sotah 43a

[36] Above and below, higher and lower, up and down and other such terms do not refer here to physical space or location. Rather, they are borrowed terms that allude to a thing's closeness to, or distance from, the revelation of its Godly source. While God is everywhere and therefore equally close to all things, the "higher" something is in the hierarchy of realms, the more its divine reality is revealed, and the "lower" something is, the more this reality is concealed.

visible to us. And we then work throughout the day, and indeed throughout our entire lives, to make that reality not only known with intellect or belief, but also shown to our physical eyes and palpable consciousness - "baruch atta A-donai/may You be drawn down and revealed, God." Our first task, then, is to assure that the presence of God's face within us is recognized and acknowledged. But this is only a beginning. From here, we devote our daily and lifelong energies to taking this truth from the realm of knowing to the state of showing. That is, by repeatedly "blessing" God so to speak, one works to draw Him down and reveal Him in all the places that He is not yet seen.

Halleluy-ah

We have now explored several of the biblical sources for the indwelling of God's essential presence within us, as well as citations from the daily prayers which are intended to focus us on this divine reality and our task of exposing it. Before we move on, it is worthwhile to identify one other component of the liturgy which serves a similar purpose. Though there are many more prayers or terms that could be added to this list, the following phrase, similar to "baruch atta A-donai," is very commonly known and is recited repeatedly throughout the prayer service. It is, therefore, familiar to many, but its inner meaning is not commonly understood. Beneath its surface, it also conveys this idea of drawing down and revealing one's inner Godliness. It is the term "Halleluy-ah."

Hebrew speakers and non-Hebrew speakers alike are familiar with the word "halleluy-ah." It has even crept into the English language as an exclamation of gratitude or an interjection that is commonly understood to mean "Praise the Lord!" The Hebrew word "halleluy-ah" is actually a compound of two words: "hallelu," which means "praise," and "Y-ah," which is another name of God. Together, the word does literally translate as "praise God." But what does it mean to praise God? Just as we asked earlier what it means to "bless" God, now we must explore what "praising" Him connotes. What exactly is one declaring when s/he says "halleluy-ah/praise God" either dozens of times throughout the established prayer service, or at any other time s/he chooses?

To praise something generally means to express approval of it. When we praise a person, we mention his or her positive qualities, indicating our feeling of admiration or appreciation. To praise God is likewise a statement of recognition and gratitude. We acknowledge His greatness and His generosity. But why do we do so? God does not need our praise. He does not have an ego or a longing for congratulation or validation. Our intention in mentioning His sublimity may be to remind ourselves of the source of our blessings, to publicize His sovereignty to those who are not aware of it, and to express our gratitude and allegiance to Him with the hope that He will continue to favor us with His guidance and kindness. While all of this provides plenty of good reason to extol God, the word "halleluy-ah" carries an additional nuance which can elevate our "praise" to a far more profound level.

The chassidic masters point out that the word "hallel/praise" derives from the root "H-L" which means to light or ignite. This is evidenced in the following verse from the book of Job:

> BeHiLo nero alai roshi l'oro yeilech choshech.
> When **He lit** His candle over my head; by His light I'd
> go through darkness.
> (Job 29:3)

In this sense, "halleluy-ah" means to ignite the "Y-ah" or to make it shine. What is this "Y-ah" that we desire to kindle and irradiate? "Y-ah" is one of the names of God, and more specifically, it is the first two letters of the divine name "Y-H-V-H" (which is articulated as "A-donai" in order not to pronounce the holy name). This first half of the name, "Y-H," alludes to the concealed aspect of God, and the second half of the name, "V-H," alludes to the aspect of God that is more revealed in the world. The expression "halleluy-ah" is thus a supplication for the "Y-H" to be illuminated and emblazoned throughout the darkness. It is yet another affirmation of our goal, which is to make our hidden Godliness shine. The true "praise" of God is the revelation of His oneness. Nothing we can say or do can possibly express His greatness more than the simple manifestation of His essential hidden truth.

Where is this essence concealed? As we have illustrated, it is within our essence. It is buried beneath our flesh and all of the layers of this "olam/world" of "helam/hiddenness" that were created to conceal it. The "panim/face" of God is buried in our "pnimyus/core." We want it to shine so that we can see it and find our way back to it. It is a beacon that we strive to light so that we know how to get back home. Each "halleluy-ah" is the striking of the flint, so to speak, the blowing on the spark to help it glow, the stoking of the flames so that they grow into a blaze that can no longer be concealed, ignored, or denied. In this sense, we can understand the teaching that Moses' face shone with beams of light when he descended from Mount Sinai:

> And it came to pass when Moses descended from Mount Sinai, and the two tablets of the testimony were in Moses' hand when he descended from the mountain and Moses did not know that **the skin of his face had become radiant** while He had spoken with him.
>
> (Exodus 34:29)

As a result of his intimate contact with God throughout his forty days and nights on the mountain, the light within Moses glowed so brightly that it could no longer be restrained. The "face" of God which was implanted within him burst forth and radiated from his own face. So bright was this radiance that Moses wore a veil in order that those around him would not become blinded. This expression of one's inner Godliness is what we aspire to ourselves, and this is precisely what we are praying for with each utterance of "halleluy-ah."

On the surface, one is offering thanks and devotion to a God that is somewhere beyond us, in an effort to bring Him close, or to convince Him to continue to care for us. But on a deeper level, the intention of terms like "halleluy-ah" and "Baruch atta A-donai" is not to praise something outside of us, but to remind ourselves to express what is within us. Prayer, and religious service in general, is commonly understood as means of requesting favor and benevolent treatment from a distant, superior being who looks down upon us with judgment and frequent displeasure. Yet as we have seen from these examples, the goal of Torah prayer is to arouse the Godly face that is within us, to awaken the ultimate us, and to enable it be expressed.

We could even go so far as to suggest that *all of Torah practice - the entire system of study, worship, and ritual observance - is a series of meditations and practical actions intended to constantly redirect one's consciousness and awareness to what s/he truly is - pure Godliness - and to help one to remove the darkness and crust that conceals this holy truth.* The prayer that underlies every prayer is that wherever I go and whatever I do, may I be conscious of my divine reality, may I express it, and may I live according to it. As we conduct our lifelong search and mission, as we move through the darkness, may we be aware that the light that we seek is within us. May we conduct ourselves and our search in the way of dignity and integrity that befits a divine being. And may our light burst forth to illuminate our way and the way of those around us.

This revolutionary consciousness will change our life and significantly assist us in our search and on our journey. We have come a far distance already, although our odyssey has barely begun. We now know where we need to go, and we have lit the inner torch to guide us through the darkness. This is not to suggest that the path ahead will be easy however. Even as we catch glimmers of how holy we ultimately are and how infinite our potential, we remain in a thick shadow that obscures our vision and clarity. We frequently wonder, "if I am Godly, then why don't I feel Godly; and on the contrary, why do I feel so ungodly so often?" The darkness does not give way readily because it serves the divine purpose of maintaining the illusion of multiplicity which allows for our individual existence. Therefore, we must live in the dark and carry the light.

The constant remembrance of the infinite Godliness within us will enable us to continue on our way even as our surroundings threaten to overwhelm us with fatigue and despair. In the following chapter, we will move further along our pathway as we begin to explore how the consciousness of the inner face of God will transform our every moment from one of uncertainty and human frailty, to one of determination, dignity, and fully exploited potential.

Chapter 4: INFINITE POTENTIAL

The Next Question

We began this book with one question, and now we are ready to introduce another. The initial question was "ayecha/ where are you?" It is, as we discussed, God's first and eternal question. It is our invitation to undertake the search that will involve us every moment of our lives. It is our safeguard against complacency, and our reminder to never allow ourselves to be lulled into the trance of this world's deceptive facade. It is our mission statement, to constantly seek that deepest aspect of ourselves which is not apparent and not fully actualized.

Throughout the previous chapters, we have addressed this first question and have begun to provide an answer, or at least a path that will lead us to the answer. Where are you? You are within. "You," the true and ultimate you, is the face of God that is embedded within your innermost core. That is what we are seeking, and that is what we are challenged to reveal. This answer is a tremendous step, but it is only the beginning of the journey. The proposition of "ayecha" is not merely to know where "You" can be found, but to eventually render this "You" unhidden so that the question need no longer be asked. Our goal, as we explained, is to move from "modeh/knowing" to "baruch/showing," from the stage of acknowledgement in which we admit to our truth though it is concealed, to the stage of revelation in which this truth is seen and no longer merely a matter of faith or belief. This is our daily and lifelong labor.

In the process of addressing the question "where are you," we have also touched on several other questions: 'what are you,' 'who are you,' and even 'why are you.' You are pure Godliness that has been placed in a world of concealment and covered in flesh so that God can express His infinite love to an "other," and so that there can be a light which proceeds from darkness which is more brilliant than the original light itself (to summarize in one long sentence what we developed at length in the first three chapters). Now that we've devoted some time to 'where,' 'what,' 'who,' and 'why are you,' we're ready to ask the next question:

How are you?

The question here is not 'how' as in 'how did you come to be,' or 'how is it possible for you to exist as an individual being when God is a complete and singular unity.' We addressed both of those questions briefly in our previous discussions, and a more thorough exploration of these issues are beyond the scope of this book. The mechanics of creation and the devolution of distinct physical matter from a nonmaterial celestial unity are treated at length in Kabbala and some of the more esoteric works of Chassidus. It is a fascinating and complicated subject, but it is not what we are concerned with here. The 'how are you' that we are asking at this point is 'how are you doing,' or 'how are you feeling?' It is an inquiry of your well-being, and an expression of interest and concern.

One might wonder if this question is as pressing as the others. After all, God does not ask it as clearly and directly as He asked the first. While "where are you/ayecha" is explicitly mentioned in the Torah text, 'how are you' is not. Therefore, one might be left with the false impression that God does not care how we feel, and that our feelings are irrelevant to our pursuit of the mission He assigns us. This could not be further from the truth, nor is such an attitude at all conducive to assuring our mission's success. God loves His creations infinitely, and He wants nothing more for us than to experience His love and care. This, as we have discussed,[37] is one of the fundamental reasons that He created us and all of the framework in which we exist, in order to have someone(s) to whom He could express His love - "teva hatov l'heitiv/it is the nature of the good to do good." This idea is similarly expressed in a phrase from Psalms:

> Olam chesed yibaneh.
> The world is built on lovingkindness.
> (Psalms 89:3)

We see here that "chesed/lovingkindness," is not just one of the building blocks of creation, it is its very foundation. Yet there will be many who question or doubt God's love and concern for them. If God loved me, they will contest, then my life would not be so difficult. If He loves me, they will ask, then why does He not make this love obvious? What kind of love is it that is unseen and disputable? If He truly loves me, then why can I even question the existence of His love?

To these questions, the first response is empathy. This empathy comes with the awareness and the admission that life is not easy and its challenges are many. The questions are not only valid, they are not only normal, but they are healthy and even holy. The tears that all of us have shed in our moments of loneliness and uncertainty are sacred tears. They are not signs of our weakness, but of our humanity. Being human means being lost, as we have discussed at length. Being in this world of concealment means being uncertain, as we seem to be separated from our source and our truth. The greater our feeling of distance from God, the greater is our yearning for Him, and the greater will be our efforts to find and reunite with Him. So the questions and doubts are not only understandable, but they are productive.

This said, we have addressed the subject of God's seeming absence at length already. The only way that God can love us is to conceal Himself from us. If He were to be revealed, if the full nature and glory of His being were to be manifest without the contraction, limitation, and obscuration that He has imposed on Himself, then nothing other would continue to exist. Ultimately, this awareness is the most compelling con-

---

[37] See chapter 2, section "Good Nature."

firmation of His love for us. He concealed Himself in order to create us and give to us. Therefore, He certainly cares how we are feeling and doing. Though He may not ask us "how are you" as explicitly as He asks us "where are you," His concern for us is implicit in His love for us. Though we have suffered as individuals and as a species throughout our history, this must not be seen as a sign of God's disinterest or His absence, but as a part of His plan and His concealed presence. As we discussed in chapter one, the doctrine of "hashgacha protis/divine providence" indicates that there is nothing that occurs anywhere or at any time in God's creation that is beyond His purview and His concern. He cares for every one of His creations and is involved with our every step and our every movement.

So how are you?

Be honest. Do not be afraid to ask yourself this question, and do not think that you are not supposed to focus on your feelings or your well-being. God wants to know. Or rather, He knows, of course, but He wants you to pay attention to your inner state. This is not self-indulgence, it is self-awareness. It is not for the sake of self-service, but for the sake of self-improvement, self-transcendence, and ultimately self-actualization. How do you feel - not just at this moment, but in your life more generally? If you were to stop at multiple random moments throughout the day and spot check your emotional state, what would you find? There would undoubtedly be a range of emotions at various times and in various circumstances, but if we were to aggregate these moments in order to create an average, what would your baseline be? By and large, do you feel fulfilled and positive? Do you feel clear and confident? Do you feel pleased with who you are and what you have done with the time you have been allotted? Or do you feel uncertain? Do you feel adrift and alone? Do you feel anxious, or ashamed, or inferior, or blemished, or unworthy?

We will find that our answer to the question "how are you" will be inextricably linked to our first question, "where are you," and to its subsidiaries "what," who," and "why" are you, which we have been addressing. With the proper approach to those initial questions, the answer to the question of our feelings will be tremendously positive. Asked "how are you," we can consistently respond 'I'm great!' Such a response is possible when it is not merely a statement of how one feels, but a recognition of how one IS. I AM great, and therefore, I feel great. I know where the ultimate me is to be found; I am aware of the true nature of my essence; I see the "Pnei Hashem/face of God" within my "pnimyus/inner core," and I subsequently appreciate my enormous value and capabilities. This awareness will foster not only profound joy and confidence, but it will enable us to act in accordance with our inherent greatness.

Feeling Great, Being Great

Earlier, in chapter two, we identified our goal and purpose in life as it is disclosed in the very first verse of the Torah: "Breishis bara Elokim es hashamayim v'es haaretz/the primary thing is to reveal God in the heavens and the earth." In chapter three, we then discussed God's first command to Abraham, "lech lecha/go to yourself," and we learned that our lifelong task is to discover our true self which is hidden deep within us. We wrestled with this seeming contradiction, asking whether our ultimate task is the revelation of God, or the discovery of our self. We reconciled the two directives with the insight that God is hidden in our core, and therefore, finding the one will allow us to find and reveal the other. But what does not seem to be included in either of these statements of our life's work is the imperative to be happy or to feel good. Therefore, it would be reasonable to wonder what role, if any, happiness plays in the pursuit of our mission and goal. Perhaps it would be possible to suggest that as long as we are working to "lech lecha," i.e. find ourself, and "bara Elokim," i.e. reveal God, it is not relevant whether we are joyous, miserable, or somewhere in between.

To forestall any such conclusion, the Torah commands "ivdu es Hashem b'simcha/serve God with joy."[38] The point of life is not to suffer in servitude, or even to merely obey stoically and mechanically, but to serve with pleasure and delight. It could be said that if we are not serving God with joy, then we are not serving Him properly at all. This is because proper service will necessarily bring us joy. It is not that being

---

[38] Psalms 100:2

happy is the goal, but rather that joy is the inevitable bi-product of pursuing our goal of finding our true self and revealing God.

We saw this earlier[39] in the verse from the morning prayers, "happy of heart is the one who seeks God." What is it about this search that makes one joyous? It is the knowledge that the face of God is within us even if we cannot see it clearly, and even if we have yet to make it revealed. It is the awareness of our inherent and essential greatness that makes us feel great. And it is this sense of our tremendous potential, and the feelings of incredible optimism and elation that arise from it, which will ultimately enable us to manifest the greatness that is hidden within us. From all this, we begin to understand that the awareness of the Godly face within us is both the source of our joy and its outcome: knowing our Godly essence and core creates immense positivity, and then that positivity enables us to fulfill the arduous task of withstanding and overcoming the darkness so that we can finally bring God's face to a state of revelation.

It is no secret that one's attitude is a major determinant of her/his reality. One's self-image will significantly shape the figure that s/he projects. It is not surprising, then, that a society which downplays the inherent goodness and interconnectedness of its members will produce a culture that is, at best, individualistic and libertarian, and at worst, decadent, narcissistic, and cruel. To understand why modern culture has veered into stark divisiveness and increasingly frequent violence, we need only recognize the angst and despondency of several generations that were reared on notions of existentialism, atheism, nihilism, and naturalism. These and a host of other 'isms' have encouraged them, either subtly or more blatantly, to question their intrinsic worth and their fundamental goodness.

Even in homes and communities that clung to "traditional" and "religious" values, the prevailing concepts are not much more encouraging or optimistic. Adherents have been inculcated, again either subtly or more vehemently, with the belief that they are sinners by nature. They are convinced that they have been conceived and born in lust and immorality, and that they must constantly do their penance and strive against their backsliding inclination. It is hard to blame those who turned to the 'isms' and turned away from these dogmas that constantly

---

[39] Chapter two, section "The Joy of the Search"

pressed them down and tried to convince them that they were base and degenerate beings who could only be redeemed if they complied with various strictures and requirements.

But whether one is a "believer" or a skeptic, the conceptions of self that have characterized modern humanity - be it a weak and wayward brute, a mannered animal, or a fleeting figment of nothingness - have often left us less than inspired or empowered. This would be sad but inevitable if the truth were as bleak as these ideologies portrayed them. But as we are, in fact, divine, and as the face of God does indeed reside within us, therefore, these misconceptions of our being and misrepresentations of our nature have been responsible for so much avoidable suffering, heartache, and squandered potential.

Human Nature

To appreciate the profound difference between the Torah's conception of a person and other non-Torah views, it is helpful to compare and contrast the terms that are used to describe humankind. The word with which the Torah designates humanity is "Adam." Though the term is also the proper name of the first man, it is employed more generally to refer to the species of beings of whom Adam was the first. Eve, too, was included in the name Adam, as we can see in the verse that introduces them:

> And God created man (ha-adam) in His image; in the
> image of God He created him; male and female He cre-
> ated them.
> (Genesis 1:27)

"Adam" here is used to refer both to "him" and to "them." In English, we see a similar duality in the word "man." While the term more specifically refers to a male person, in a more general sense it can be employed as a reference to "mankind." In such a usage, it is a shortened form of the term "human," which categorizes the entire species. The derivation of "human," and of the Latinate "homo," which classifies an even wider range of primate species, is from the Proto-Indo-European term "(dh)gomon," which means "earthling" and is itself a derivative of the root "dhghem," which means "earth." A human being, according to the etymology of the term, is an "earthling," one who inhabits the earth and who derives from the earth.

The Hebrew "adam" shares this connotation of earthliness. The word "adama" means "earth" or "ground." On the simple level, it is because the human being was formed from the dust of the ground that s/he is called "adam."

> And the Lord God formed **man (ha'adam)** of the dust
> from the **ground (ha'adama)**, and He breathed into his
> nostrils the soul of life, and man became a living soul.
> (Genesis 2:7)

However, the sages teach that there is another reason why humanity is referred to as 'adam.' While the term links the human to her/his earthy origins, it has an additional connotation as well. 'Adam' is also derived from the word "adameh," which means 'like' or 'similar.' The rabbis[40] teach that humanity was given the name "adam" because we are "adameh l'Elyon/similar to the Most High."[41] In this sense of the word, our name indicates our loftiness and our resemblance to our Creator.

This comparison to God is also emphasized in the verse from the first chapter of Genesis quoted above which states that we were created "in His image." What does it mean to be created in the image of God? As we know, God has no form or image per se. The expression conveys that there is something about the human creation that carries God's likeness within it. However, as God is one and all, then would this not be true of every one of His creations? Yet it is stated explicitly and exclusively in regard to mankind. This is because the human being is the entity in which God infused Himself most distinctly. The human has the ability to know that God is within him/her, to comprehend that s/he is created in God's image, and to make that image manifest.

---

[40] Including the Shelah Hakadosh in his introduction to "Toldos Adam." The Shelah, Rabbi Isaiah Horowitz, lived in Israel from 1555-1630 and was a renowned mystic known by the acronym of his work "Shnei Luchot Habris".

[41] Isaiah 14:14

The human being, according to Torah, is thus "adam," a fusion of opposites, as we see from both of these connotations of her/his name. S/he is comprised of both the "earth/adama," and of Godliness, "adameh l'Elyon/similar to the Most High." The English/European 'human,' on the contrary, is strictly a creature of the earth. Nothing in her/his name suggests any relationship to the celestial. What has been lost in translation is the duality - the presence of holiness within the profane.

We can further see this limited view of mankind in the usage of the term "human" to express deficiency and weakness. We say that one is "only human," to explain his/her frailty and to excuse her/his fallibility. We invoke "human nature" to describe our selfish tendencies and baser inclinations. When "human" is utilized in such a pejorative fashion, it is not only a justification and rationalization for our misbehavior, but it is a self-fulfilling prophecy. We cannot help ourselves, we assume, because it is simply the way we are. But when we are "adam," on the contrary, when we are both "adama/earth" and "adameh l'elyon/similar to the Most High," then we cannot say that we are "only human." Unlike "human," "adam" is a term of great esteem. It would make no sense to say one is "only Godly" as an excuse for reprobate behavior. When one realizes that s/he is "adam,' and not merely human, then s/he will not continue to be satisfied with being only earthly and failing to express the Godliness within her/him.

When we explore the nature and essence of what we truly are, we will carve through the misconceptions and deceptions, and we will ultimately reveal our true grandeur and holiness. We will find that we are tremendous and full of infinite potential. We have a purpose and every ability to fulfill it. This awareness imbues incredible self-esteem and dispels all of the insecurity and angst that has characterized so much of human existence until now. It removes the sackcloth of self-recrimination and self-flagellation and enables us to change into the robes that are fit for our royalty. We will expect more of ourselves when we understand our true selves, and when we see ourselves as nobles rather than brutes. We will live our best lives when we realize that our lives are precious and divine.

Being And Becoming

There is an idea that we are not 'human beings,' but rather 'human becomings.' The notion is that we are ever evolving, and that we must never limit ourselves to the state in which we find ourselves at the moment. Rather, we must always allow ourselves, and push ourselves, to grow and progress further. In Torah, this idea is expressed frequently. As we discussed in chapter three, God's first direction to Abraham was "lech lecha/go to yourself." The process of self-discovery is one of constant going. We must travel "from your land," in other words from the place where we began, and we must wander through the desert, through a variety of exiles, throughout the millennia, in order to approach our eventual destination. From the first day of human creation, we were exiled from the garden, and we have been trekking and "becoming" ever since.

But while this notion of "human becoming" expresses the imperative for perpetual progress and improvement, there is a truth to the concept of "human being" that is also profound and frequently overlooked. Because we are "adam," and thus "adameh l'elyon/similar to the Most High," we are already, by our very nature, that which we aspire to being. The idea of 'becoming' implies that we are not yet what or where we are supposed, or destined, to be. We must do something, change something, or create something that doesn't already exist. However, Torah teaches that we need not become something different, other, or new in order to fulfill our mission and purpose. Rather we must simply return to what we inherently are. This, as we mentioned in chapter three,[42] is the concept of "teshuvah." Although the word is commonly translated as "repentance," the Torah's notion of self-improvement and self-actualization is not that one must punish her/himself for who s/he is, or turn away from where s/he has come. This punitive approach to the self is the implication of the word "repent," the root '-pent' deriving from the Latin 'poenitire' meaning 'make sorry.' 'Teshuvah,' on the contrary, literally means "return," and our work is not to suppress or eradicate some wayward nature, but rather to constantly peel away the things

---

[42] See section "Inward Bound"

that have covered and concealed our essence so that we can express and expose the purity and brilliance that has always existed within.

The difference here is not merely semantic. One's basic conception of humanity, and of the universe more generally, is fundamentally different when we are aware of the goodness and Godliness that is lodged in our own center and in the center of every component of existence. Rather than a dark, difficult, and malevolent world that needs to be battled, conquered, and redesigned, we find ourselves in a realm of obscured luminescence which merely needs to be stripped of its screens and shrouds. Rather than laboring arduously and endlessly to construct something that does not yet exist, our task is simply to uncover the brilliant and intricate edifice that has been built into us and around us and which is waiting to be unveiled. What's more, the veil itself is not wicked or destructive - its purpose, as we have seen, is to protect us from a light so bright that we cannot withstand its infinite gleam.

None of this is to suggest that our task is easy or that there are not real and profound challenges that we face daily. Yet our ability to meet and overcome these challenges will be significantly augmented when we are cognizant of both the Godliness that is within them - i.e. the divine wisdom and benevolence that is, as yet, beyond our line of vision - and the Godliness that is within us - i.e. our immeasurable strength and potential. We can see this in an expression that is commonly used to encourage those who are facing a daunting endeavor: "you have it in you," we tell them, assuring them of their ability to succeed. What we are reminding them with this reassurance is that the capability and fortitude that they require is not something that they need to obtain or manufacture, but rather it is something that they already possess and embody. The implication, of course, is that it is easier for us to access something that we own than it is to acquire something that we lack. And while it is not always simple for us to tap the deep stores of power and aptitude that are contained within us, we are far more likely to draw upon them and harness them when we know that they are there.

In short, while some would suggest that our goal in life is to express our human potential, what we are proposing here is that our task is to reveal that we are not actually "human," but we are rather "adam," and thus we are inherently divine. We are not created to 'become,' but to shed those things that conceal what we already are. We need not create or generate light, we need simply to stop suppressing and impeding the infinite light that crouches within us. Our work is not creation or even transformation; it is release, expression, and revelation. We must let go of the mask and let it fall away, and we will eventually understand that wearing it, or holding it in place, is more exhausting than allowing it to drop.

The Lubavitcher Rebbe[43] used to greet people outside of his Brooklyn headquarters on various special occasions. Long lines would form, and people would wait for hours to see the Rebbe in person and to receive from him a word or two of blessing. It is said that the Rebbe had the most penetrating eyes, and standing in his presence one would have the sensation of being seen through and through. People from various walks of life would queue up in front of his headquarters at 770 Eastern Parkway. Some of them were the Rebbe's devoted chassidim, some were Jews from other denominations who had heard of the Rebbe's salutary blessings, and some of them were secular and unaffiliated individuals who weren't quite sure what had drawn them there. On one of these occasions, one of those in line was a young man who had been struggling for years with various internal challenges. He had recently begun to pull his life together and to turn away from the self-destructive behaviors that had dogged him until now. He came to the Rebbe with one of his relatives who, when they reached the front of the line, gestured to the young man and said to the Rebbe, "he's becoming a good boy." The Rebbe looked at the young man and smiled. He then turned to the relative and corrected him: "he's always been good, he just didn't know it."

Not In Heaven

Knowing what we are will render us far more capable of expressing our true potential. It is true that we are still in the darkness. We still have a long way to travel and much to accomplish. As long as we are in this "olam/world," we are still immersed in a place of "helam/hid-

---

[43] Rabbi Menachem Mendel Schneerson, the seventh Rebbe of the Chabad chassidic dynasty, 1902-1994.

denness," and we have yet to complete the task of revealing the light that is concealed within us and within everything. However, the awareness that the "Pnei Hashem/face of God" is embedded in our "pnimyus/inner core" is crucial for our lifelong task of taking it from a state of being known (modeh) to a state of being shown (baruch). This awareness is not merely the first step of the process, it is the lantern that lights the way for every step that follows. The question and challenge of "ayecha/where are you" is still on the table. However, with the question of "how are you," we have begun to feel a bit lighter and more buoyant, and this lightness makes the darkness a bit less oppressive and foreboding.

It is interesting that the term 'light' in one sense describes the quality of weight or weightlessness, and in another sense, it describes the quality of illumination and visibility. The two are related of course. The less heavy one feels emotionally, the more bright her/his surroundings seem to be. The more despondent and immobile one feels, the less her/his inner light glows, and the less luster s/he is able to share with her/his environment. Therefore, the awareness of our inner Godliness, even as it remains concealed in our deepest depths, has made us both more agile and more radiant, and the path ahead as we continue is thus less treacherous and intimidating.

We can now move along the path with purpose, direction, and even urgency, but without pressure, guilt, or anxiety. The darkness is not our fault, but it is our responsibility. It is our concern, but not our worry. We are good, we are Godly, and furthermore we recognize that the Godliness within us is the same Godliness that enwraps us. The darkness is not evil, for there is no true evil. There is only the One God (A-donai echad) and the various mechanisms through which He allows Himself to be either hidden or revealed. Seeing the world as such, we are able to pursue our mission not as a burden or a trial, but as an opportunity and a purpose. Seeing oneself as such, we replace self-recrimination with self-esteem. We lose our ego as we find our infinite essence. We harness the strength of something so much larger than ourselves, and we are thus humbled in the enormity of our task, but we are simultaneously confident in the One who has sent us and who dwells within us.

As our optimism continues to swell with the recognition of our tremendous potential and our inherent worth, concurrently we are bolstered by the realization that our goal is far closer than we had once imagined. It is so close, in fact, that it is within us:

> For this commandment which I command you this day, is not concealed from you, nor is it far away. It is not in heaven, that you should say, 'Who will go up to heaven for us and get it for us, to tell it to us, so that we can fulfill it?' Neither is it beyond the sea, that you should say, 'Who will cross to the other side of the sea for us, and get it for us so that we may hear it and fulfill it?' No, **the thing is very near to you; it is in your mouth and in your heart so that you can fulfill it.**
> (Deuteronomy 30:11-14)

Here, God assures us that what He asks of us is not as distant or difficult as we believed it to be. It is, in fact, right here inside of us!

This closeness - the fact that what we seek is "not in heaven" and "neither is it beyond the sea" - provides us tremendous hope and inspiration. We are "inspired" in the true sense of the word - we are uplifted and invigorated by the "spirit" that is "in" us. While it is true that God has hidden Himself from us in this "olam / world" of "helam / concealment," and it is therefore the case that we may spend the entire span of our life here seeking Him, the primary question that will determine the nature of our search and the quality of our time is whether we are searching around us or within us. If our search for Him is always leading us to far flung places or ideas that are perpetually somewhere other than the mundane reality in which we find ourselves, then we will forever be reaching for something just beyond our grasp. But when we recognize that He is within us, that He is with us wherever we go and no matter how debased our surroundings, then our quest to find Him is no longer so daunting and difficult.

We need not climb tremendous mountains or perform monumental feats. We need not journey to a remote monastery or decipher some cryptic and forgotten language. He is right here. We need not acquire Him because we already have Him, and He already has us. We are in His loving arms, and He is in our core. We simply need to be aware of God's presence and permanence within us and then to allow Him to manifest and express Himself through our being. This is true "teshuvah/ return." It does not mean that we must return to some place that we have strayed from and left behind. We must only stop looking and moving outside of ourselves for the thing that is always right there within. We must be still and delve inward, returning to where we begin and where we have always been. There we will find that everything we have ever needed and desired has been awaiting us in the One place that we have never truly left. This process of opening and releasing will not be without effort and travail. But it will be far less grueling than the fleeing, fighting, crushing and reconstructing that we believe to be necessary when we conceive of ourselves as inherently flawed, empty, or forsaken, or when we locate God somewhere outside of us.

Chapter 5: WRAPPINGS AND TRAPPINGS

Skin And Light

The journey, as we have discussed, is not to some distant, remote land or some elusive, exotic locale. The journey is not outward at all, it is within. The "you" that we are directed to seek is buried in our core, where it is fused with the "Pnei Hashem," the essence of Godliness that we were created to reveal. In the previous chapter, we clarified that while this inward voyage will be lifelong and will present frequent challenges, it need not be dismal or painful. With the proper understanding of our essential nature and potential, it can (and therefore must) be joyous. At this point, in order to travel to the destination at our innermost depths, we must open a path, and we must shed the layers of plaque and crust that we have built up around our core. To do so, it will be worthwhile to further explore the nature of, and reasons for, these coverings, and to understand why the process of removing them has spanned the entire course of history.

In chapter one, we explained that our first forebears, Adam and Eve, were created diaphanous. Their skin was translucent because there was no barrier between their interior and their exterior. In that Edenic realm, there was a complete harmony in the creation, and there was no split dividing the Godly essence of things from the casing that contained and expressed it. With the eating of the fruit of the tree of knowledge of good and evil, however, Adam and Eve internalized a duality - good AND evil - and they were now forced to inhabit a world of division and opposition. Immediately after consuming the fruit, they hid. This reaction was a result of their sudden fear and shame, neither of which exist in a state of unity and holism. Self-consciousness and guilt only materialize when we conceive of ourselves as distinct and, therefore, incomplete or defective. "Where are you?" God called to them, and Adam answered:

> I heard Your voice in the garden, and I was afraid because I am naked; so I hid.
> (Genesis 3:10)

God knew that they had eaten the fruit. He knew that they would. It was a necessary part of the process that began with His complete oneness and culminated in a complex system of otherness and multiplicity. This world was not meant to be translucent and to constantly manifest the Godly essence that resided in its core. It was time to clothe Adam and Eve and conceal their naked truth.

> *Vayaas Hashem Elokim l'adam u'l'ishto **kasnos ohr** vayalbisheim.*
> And the Lord God made for Adam and for his wife **coats of skin**, and He dressed them.
> (Genesis 3:21)

In the simple sense, this verse indicates that God fashioned "kasnos ohr/coats of skin," which we understand to be garments of leather. But the sages explain that on a deeper level, the skin with which God covered them was not animal hide, but rather their own flesh. Prior to eating the fruit, Adam and Eve were clothed not in skin, but in garments of light. This is taught in the Midrash[44] which states that in the Torah scroll of Rabbi Meir, one of the words from the above-quoted verse is written with a slight but significant difference. In the phrase "kasnos ohr," which means "coats of skin," the word "ohr" is spelled with a letter "א/aleph" rather than the letter "ע/ayin," as it is spelled in the Torah today. The Hebrew word "ohr" can be written either "אוֹר" (beginning with the letter "א/aleph") or "עוֹר" (beginning with the letter "ע/ayin"). The two spellings are pronounced the same, but with an "א/aleph" - "אוֹר" - the word means "light," and with an "ע/ayin" - "עוֹר" - it means "skin."

The discrepancy of spelling in Rabbi Meir's Torah scroll teaches us that before the eating of the fruit, the human body was composed of glowing light which projected the luminescence that radiated from its Godly core. After the eating of the fruit, the "א/aleph" was replaced by an "ע/ayin," and the "light/אוֹר" was replaced by an opaque fleshy "skin/עוֹר." The interior was cut off from the exterior, and the source was hidden away. Subsequently, Adam and Eve were sent from the garden of Eden, and we have been lost ever since. As we explained in chapter one, it is not simply that we have lost our way geographically, but rather the perpetual wandering and seeking throughout our history is a reflection of our inner exile. We have lost our way because we have lost our self. With the installation of a skin that partitions our interior from our exterior, we have been divided from our essence, and we are therefore unaware of who and what we are.

While this state of concealment and exile can be challenging, it is, as we have pointed out repeatedly, precisely God's will and intention. He created a world in which His unity would be concealed so that otherness could seemingly exist, and love and kindness could thereby be expressed.[45] The first garment that enclothed and obscured our core was therefore crafted and placed upon us by God. It was holy and purposeful. Though it cloaked our inner light and thereby resulted in darkness, it was not undesirable or antithetical to the divine plan. There is sometimes need for withdrawal, limitation, and restraint.

---

44 Breishis Rabba 20:12

45 As explained in chapter two, section "Good Nature"

However, God's intention with the concealment of His infinite light was not that it should remain trapped and forgotten inside of us in perpetuity. On the contrary, this state of estrangement was only to be temporary. With the exodus from Egypt and the liberation of the nascent nation of Israel, a new period would begin in which the barriers would be broken and the truth of our existence would begin to be revealed. The Torah's narratives provide a metaphor of the spiritual drama that plays itself out within each of us. We had been enslaved - in other words, our spiritual substance had been restrained and repressed by the confines of our physical bodies and our animal instincts - and now it was time for that inner truth to be liberated. Weeks after the exodus from Egypt, the nation arrived at Mount Sinai where the Torah was given as a tool with which one could penetrate and dismantle the screen that separated the outer and inner worlds. Throughout the ensuing millennia, we have been engaged in that process.

But why has it taken us so long? Is the skin that God wrapped us in so thick that it requires thousands of years to be infiltrated and removed? Is the Torah so ineffectual that it cannot instruct us how to fulfill its intent? Is God Himself so passive and detached that He cannot remove the covering that He had applied now that it is no longer serving His ultimate purpose and intention?

Of course, the answer is that the flesh is not impenetrable, the Torah is not ineffective, and God is not disinterested or uncaring. If the goal were to separate the soul from the body, that could, and can, be done instantaneously - it is called death. However, the process of revelation was never intended to be contrary to life or to negate the world of limitation and concealment in which life exists. The divine aim has always been to bring about revelation *within* the creation itself. In other words, the goal is not to divorce the body and soul, but to fuse them so that the physical will not oppose or obscure Godliness, but it will rather express it. This is why the Midrash discusses the consonance of the words "אוֹר/ohr," meaning light, and "עוֹר/ohr," meaning skin. Ultimately, as we discussed in the previous chapter, the human being, "Adam," is supposed to be both "adama/earthy" and "adameh l'Elyon/Godly." S/he is supposed to be garbed in flesh, "עוֹר/ohr," that comes from the earth, and that flesh itself is meant to beam with the light, "אוֹר/ohr," of the Godly core that it contains and conveys.

According to the doctrine of "hashgacha protis/divine providence"[46] and the complete and constant dominion that it presupposes, it is clear that if He so desired, God could remove the covering with which He enveloped us at any moment. However, His will is not for us to be disembodied spirits hovering in some ethereal realm. Nor is it His will that He should once again be 'alone/all one' as He was before the creation. Nor is it His intention to contravene the process that He has established for His creations. The objective is that we ourselves should become cognizant of the spark that burns within us, and we should then fan the flame of our Godly core so that it glows so brightly that it will permeate our fleshy skin and burst forth to flood our surroundings with its gleam. Therefore, God leaves the task to us, and He also supplies us with the Torah that lays out our mission and informs us how we can fulfill it.

If so, then why does it remain so difficult for us, and why do we continue to languish in the dark? The unfortunate answer is that rather than uncovering our core and opening a pathway so that it can be accessed and revealed, we tend to spend our lives doing precisely the opposite. We add layers to the husk that encases us, and we close off the passageways to our inner depths so that they will not be breached.

Why do we do that?

———————◆———————

Shame

While the original layer of flesh with which we were enwrapped was installed by God, the countless layers that have been added over it were imposed by ourselves either consciously or unintentionally. The original casing was fashioned by God in order to serve the piece of Himself that He invested inside of it. It would do so by distinguishing the Godly spark from all of the other similar sparks, by housing it, and by carrying it. The additional coverings that we have added have served either to hide and protect our core from external threat, or to repress what is within us in order protect the outside world from the (supposed)

---

46 Discussed in chapter one, section "The Only One"

darkness that seethes beneath our surface. From the time of Adam and Eve's "fall," we are subject to constant fear and shame, afraid of either what is around us, or what is within us, and often both.

It is therefore the basic misconception of our essence and being which has led us, throughout the majority of our history, in the opposite direction from our goal. Rather than probing inward and working to remove the strata that we have built up over and around our center, we have moved ever outward to seek gratification externally. We have simultaneously wrapped ourselves in an ever-increasing mantle of garments in order to bury and conceal our core. The misconception is predicated on one of two errors: we have mistakenly believed that our essence is dark and malevolent and it must be repressed, or we have mistakenly believed that it is weak and vulnerable and needs to be protected. Neither of these conceptions of our inner foundation is even remotely accurate. Our "pnimyus/inner core" is the "Pnei Hashem/Face of God!" It is pure Godliness, and as such it is both infinitely good and impregnable.

How and why did our image and appraisal of ourself come to be so far from the truth?

This, of course, was no accident. It was, as is everything according to our doctrine of "hashgacha protis/divine providence," part of the divine plan. It was necessary for humankind to view itself as "ungodly" in order to create the type of otherness that God required in order to express His desire to give.[47] Were we to know that we are simply portions of Godliness concealed, then the guise of multiplicity would be dispelled, and His complete unity and infinity would be perceived. This was the reason for the "sin" in the garden of Eden and our subsequent expulsion. We had to believe that we were ungodly in order to forget that we are nothing but Godliness enclothed. Through the commission of "sin," we would view ourselves as lowly, and thus something other than divine.

Yet if God truly wanted us to believe that we are separate beings that exist distinctly from Him (and therefore we are "others" who He can love and give to), then could He not have simply created us without any consciousness of our Godliness? Why did He create us in Eden and then expel us, rather than simply creating us outside of the garden in the first place? Why did He endow us first with translucent skin that revealed

---

[47] As we discussed in chapter two, section "Good Nature"

our inner light, and then cover us with animal flesh that would hide the light beneath it? This is because by beginning in Eden, we have a record of our true origin. We have evidence that we do not exist with "original sin," but rather with original purity and Godliness. Our origin story is that we were at first completely Godly. Subsequently we "sinned" and our Godliness became concealed. But that sin is not what or who we originally and essentially are. It is merely a cloak that obscures what is beneath it.

The first two and half millennia of our history - from the time of the exile from Eden until the giving of the Torah - was a period of increasing concealment and forgetfulness. So hidden did our true essence become that we were completely convinced of our separateness and otherness from God. Throughout these many generations, the darkness solidified, and we lost all memory of that time and place where we began. And then it was time to remind us. With the giving of the Torah, God provided this recollection. The intention of the Torah's reminder of our origins is not to admonish us that 'you have been bad,' but to inform us that 'you have been hidden.' God assures us that this concealment and forgetfulness are not our doing, but rather His. I created you as a pure reflection of Myself, He tells us. I sent you forth from the garden to populate a world in which you and I are hidden. Now I am calling on you to remake that world, to transform it from a place of darkness to a realm of revelation. In the thousands of years since the giving of the Torah, there have been those who have been working on that project. However, the darkness has been difficult to penetrate. There are a variety of reasons for this difficulty, but primary amongst them is the resistance that so many of us have developed to the recognition and admission of our inherent Godliness.

When we are in denial of our divinity, whether we are truly ignorant of it or we are unwilling to admit it, we are susceptible to the hazards to which shame and self-doubt expose us. These include destructive habits and patterns of self-sabotage. When we believe we are worthy of punishment, we hold on to pain and suffering. We create illness and failure subconsciously, as mechanisms to punish ourselves for our wrongdoing and purge us of our guilt. In addition to these internal abuses, we subject ourselves to external manipulation and mistreatment. When we recognize our tremendous worth, on the other hand, we are strong and invulnerable to exploitation. When we feel guilt and self-recrimination, we are weak and lost and desperate. We become vulnerable to those who offer us salvation and security and all of the things that will fill the void within us and enable us to control our "evil" nature. Therefore, throughout history, "leaders" who would subjugate us and dominate us have labored to convince us that we are debased and needy. For it is far easier to maintain power when one's subjects are disenfranchised and burdened with shame.

Beyond those who crave superiority and control, there have been countless other leaders who are less self-serving and malevolent, but who simply want to maintain order and security. They have witnessed greed and perversion around them and within them, and they have therefore become convinced of their inherent wretchedness and sinfulness. True believers, they truly believe that the path to redemption is through self-flagellation and the embracing of an external savior who will harness their innate barbarity and rid them of their sins. Whether it is therefore with malicious intent or sincere devotion and desire for a connection to the divine, these figures and institutions in our lives have convinced us to suppress and cover over precisely what we need to pursue and release.

God's response to all of these forces that generate shame and steer us outward rather than inward is consistent throughout His Torah: "Panim b'panim dibber Hashem imachem bahar / face IN face God spoke to you at the mountain" - He infused His face, His quintessence, into our face, our innermost core.[48] "Reeh Anochi nosein lifneichem / See, I give Anochi within you" - He has placed His hidden depths within our innermost nucleus.[49] I am within you, and you are Godly, He informs us repeatedly. It is time for us to discard the erroneous ideas of original sin and human inadequacy, and to accept what we truly are and thereby begin to reveal it.

———————————

[48] See chapter four, section "Face to Face"

[49] See chapter four, section "In Your Face"

Sin

None of what we have discussed so far negates the fact that we are imperfect.

Recognizing our Godly essence does not preclude the awareness of those aspects of ourselves that defy and conceal our higher instincts and deeper nature. Just as God created light, He also created darkness, and as we discussed in chapter two,[50] darkness was created first, and it currently predominates in this world of hiddenness. It is vital for us to be cognizant of the fact that darkness is no less Godly than light. To assume otherwise would be to propose a duality which is completely contrary to the fundamental thesis that "A-donai echad/God is One" and there is nothing other than Him. The darkness serves God's desire to conceal Himself and create otherness, as we have discussed at length. This, however, does not absolve us of the responsibility to choose light over darkness. While God created darkness, He charged us with the task of dispelling it through the revelation of the light that He hid within us and within every aspect of the creation. However, He simultaneously garbed us within a casing that enables us, and even inclines us, to choose wrong at times. It is no surprise or secret to God that we are fallible. He created us that way. His love for us is not contingent upon our perfection. If it were, He would not have formed us with the ability and proclivity to violate His will.

We therefore need to understand the nature of sin and why God allows it to exist. We have addressed the latter question in part in our discussion of the first sin, Adam and Eve's eating of the forbidden fruit. Sin, we explained, allows God to maintain the illusion of something distinct and contrary to His unity. If there were no sin, no free will, no ability for us to choose anything other than God's way, then it would be difficult, if not impossible, to attest to our differentiation and independence. If we were simply automatons that were programmed to perform a strictly delineated set of actions, then we would not serve the purpose of being others to whom God could give and show love. One can have affection for a doll or a toy, but if it is unable to feel and choose, then it cannot experience love no matter how much we may try to express it.

---

50 Section "Night And Then Day"

The goal of God's darkness is to allow for the existence of beings that are "in His image" - with a full complement of desires, will, and capabilities - but who are able to perceive of themselves as being distinct from their source.

"Sin," then, as counterintuitive as this may sound, is part of the divine plan. This is certainly not to say that God wants us to sin, but He created us with the capacity to do so, and He is not shocked or caught off guard when we do. To take it a step further, contrary to popular belief, *God is not injured, insulted, or even angry when we sin!* How can we make such a claim? Is it not in opposition to explicit verses from the Torah like, "They have angered Me with their vanities,"[51] and, "And G-d's anger will flare?"[52] Will such a claim, furthermore, not encourage one to flaunt God's will and therefore bring more darkness to the world than light?

Indeed, we are treading on precarious ground here, and there is a genuine risk that the presentation of these concepts, taken out of context and divorced from the explanations that will follow, can result in the very opposite of their intention. For this reason, we must proceed here with great caution. There is good reason why such discussions of the Torah's inner depths have been restricted and sequestered. Throughout the majority of our history, the study of Kabbala and the Torah's esoteric secrets was limited exclusively to those who were tested and deemed thoroughly versed in the revealed dimensions of Torah. Furthermore, one was required to reach the age of forty before he would even be considered for such initiation. This is because insights such as the ones we are discussing here could be confusing and even harmful to those who did not already have a strong foundation in Torah study and practice, as well as the life-experience and maturity to understand the wiles of the ego and one's baser inclinations. The analogy has been given to one who, while walking in a field, falls into a pit because her/his eyes were directed at the stars rather than what is in front of her/his feet. First, we must be very familiar with the ground around and before us, and then we can begin to gaze up to study the heavens above us.

In spite of these valid concerns, the latter mystics, beginning with the Baal Shem Tov in the 18th century, determined that the time had

---

[51] Deuteronomy 32:21

[52] Deuteronomy 11:17

come to begin revealing the Torah's secrets to the masses. This was, in part, in order to combat the coming "Enlightenment" and the age of rationalism that would tear so many away from their faith and their connection to God. Only through a deep and thorough understanding of God's unity and our place in His creation can we withstand the temptations and attractions of the modern age and recognize that they will not lead us to joy, peace, and freedom, but rather to insatiability and anguish.

In this light, we can appreciate a parable that was told by the Alter Rebbe. It had come to his attention that there was a heavenly charge against his teacher, the Maggid of Mezeritch,[53] for the crime of spreading the precious secrets of Torah to the masses, where they were squandered and frequently misunderstood. In response to the charge, the Alter Rebbe told the parable of a great king whose son, the prince, was deathly ill. All of the kingdom's doctors were summoned, but nothing would remedy the lethal illness. One wise man came and informed the king that the only possible cure was an elixir that could be made from the dust of an exceedingly rare gem, the only one of which was embedded in the king's crown. The jewel was priceless, but the king did not hesitate to have it removed from his headpiece. As it was about to be ground to dust, some of the king's advisors tried to dissuade him. We don't know if the elixir will work, they told him, and even if it does have the proper healing properties, the prince is unconscious and it is possible that none of it will make it down his throat. Even if only one drop penetrates, the king replied, and even if there is only a minute possibility of saving my beloved son's life, it is worth far more than the most priceless gem. He ground the stone and made the elixir. A mere drop was ingested by the prince, but it was enough to save his life. So too, the Alter Rebbe taught, his teacher's efforts to save God's lost and ailing children with the secrets of the Torah were justified in spite of the priceless gems that were squandered in the process.

With this preface, we can return, with great care and discretion, to the subject of sin, and the audacious - and potentially dangerous - assertion that God is not ultimately "angered" by our transgression of His will. So far, we have approached this notion from the perspective of the utility and benefit of sin in God's ultimate plan. Though sin itself may be

---

[53] circa 1700-1772. Disciple of the Baal Shem Tov and teacher of the Alter Rebbe.

undesirable, as part of the process of the larger divine end-game, it serves a purpose that is ultimately positive, in spite of its seeming and temporary negativity. That is, it enables God's creations to be fully fleshed-out beings, as opposed to mere robots who are programmed to do only what our Creator demands. Just as we saw in chapter two that darkness was created in service of the more brilliant light that would eventually follow it,[54] so too sin, understood in this way, is a stepping stone that can ultimately be evaluated properly only in the context of the broader time-line of history.

We can even take this idea a step further and demonstrate that not only is God not angered by our misdeeds, but in the deepest sense (as opposed to the surface reality of this earthly plane), He is not affected by our actions at all. The sages have found support for this divine impassivity in the following verse:

> I am God, I have not changed.
> (Malachi 3:6)

The implication of this statement is that the temporal and finite world has, and can have, no impact on the eternal and infinite God. Just as He was One before He created the world, so is He One after the creation. This is difficult to comprehend from our human perspective, but we must remember that God is not subject to time or space or any of the other "natural laws" which He created and in which we function. From our viewpoint, pre-creation and post-creation represent an enormous change - it is the difference between existence and non-existence. But from God's perspective, the entire span of history and the entire expanse of space is not even as proportionate to His ultimate reality as one drop of water in comparison to the sea. For while one drop is an infinitesimal amount in relation to all of the 26.64 septillion drops that mathematicians have determined to be contained in the earth's oceans,[55] it is still one part of that number. In relation to infinity, however, even numbers in the septillions like the one above do not account or amount to even a minute

---

[54] Section "Night And Then Day"

[55] 26,640,000,000,000,000,000,000,000 - with an estimated 1.332 billion cubic kilometers of sea on Earth and 0.05 ml of water in a drop

fraction of a fraction. It is in this regard that we can come to the conclusion of the insignificance of our deeds. Scripture verbalizes this reality as follows:

> If you sinned, what effect do you have on Him, and if your transgressions are many, what do you do to Him? If you are righteous, what do you give Him, or what does He take from your hand?
> (Job 35:6-7)

What can our trivial actions amount to, Scripture asks. Can our sins truly have any effect on God in the grand scheme of His infinite Oneness? For that matter, does our righteousness actually impact Him in any way?

It is a sobering line of reasoning, and one that does not necessarily bring us comfort. While we can find some solace in the notion that our errors and misdeeds do not anger God and do not provoke in Him a desire for punishment or vengeance, the suggestion that our deeds are meaningless and irrelevant certainly is not inspiring and, on the contrary, it can feel extremely defeating. If this is the case, then what meaning is there in our existence, and what difference does it make what we do or how we conduct ourselves? Furthermore, how do we reconcile either of these ideas with the verses from the Torah which, as we quoted earlier, explicitly refer to God's anger and vengeance?

Layers

To address the previous questions, we must begin with the awareness that everything in life is comprised of various levels and layers. The Torah is said to have many "faces":

> Torah has 70 faces.
> (Midrash Bamidbar Rabba, 13:16)

This means that a single Torah concept can be understood on seventy different levels, all of which are valid and true even as some may be conflicting or contradictory. Rabbi Yitzchak Luria, the holy Arizal,[56] taught that there are actually 600,000 various interpretations for every Torah idea. In general, Torah study is referred to as walking in an orchard, the Hebrew word for which is "Pardes." In addition to meaning orchard, "PaRDeS" is also an acronym for four words:

"**P**shat," which means "simple meaning."
"**R**emez," which means "allusion."
"**D**rush," which means "homily."
"**S**od," which means "secrets."

Torah is called a "pardes/orchard" because it can be experienced on all four of these general levels of interpretation.

Very generally speaking, we can break this down to two primary categories: there is the revealed surface of things, and then there are the hidden depths beneath and within. We have been speaking primarily in this book about these two levels of "pshat," the simple and surface level of understanding, and "sod," the secret depths that are concealed beneath the surface. Throughout our discussion, we have made frequent reference to the "panim/pnimyus," which is the "sod" or secret inner dimension, and the 'olam/world' (derived from the world 'helam /hiddenness') which is the "pshat" or the simple visible reality in which we operate and beneath which the secrets are concealed. While the secrets are more "true" in the ultimate sense, the surface also represents a truth and reality that we must recognize and negotiate. While these levels are starkly different, and they can even contradict one another, nevertheless they can, and do, exist simultaneously. It is taught that one of the highest levels of wisdom is the tolerance of paradox. The sages state it this way:

Eilu v'eilu divrei Elokim chayim.
These and these are the words of the living God.
(Talmud, Eruvin 13b)

---

[56] 1534-1572, one of the foremost Kabbalists in history, who created the system of Lurianic Kabbala.

The implication is that though concepts or perspectives may diverge dramatically, they can both be true depending on the perspective and level of reality that they reflect. We have seen this repeatedly already in our discussion of God's complete unity, and our simultaneous existence and independence. On the one hand, there is nothing but God; but at the same time, He created us as others, and we therefore exist. On the deepest level, there is only One, but on the level of this world, there is vast multiplicity. We have seen this also in our exploration of the story of Adam and Eve in the garden. On the revealed and simple level, they sinned by eating the fruit, and they were therefore punished and expelled. On the deeper level, their act was precisely what was necessary in order to further God's design, and their journey from the garden was not a downfall, but rather an opportunity to bring the light that God had implanted within them out into the surrounding darkness.

On the level of "pshat," the revealed surface of our existence, sin does indeed "anger" God. While it is ultimately true that in relation to His infinite reality our actions may be minuscule and meaningless; nevertheless, He has created a realm in which every aspect of our lives is significant and impactful. Simultaneously, on the level of "sod," the hidden depths of the ultimate existence, there is nothing we can do which is contrary to God's consummate unity, and there is therefore never an occasion in which He experiences frustration or displeasure. This dynamic of the conflicting reality of sin can be seen in a section of the Torah which is known as the "tochacha/rebuke." In the book of Leviticus, in the portion of "Bechukosai," God lays out a lengthy list of punishments that will result if the people choose to violate His will. He begins:

> If you will not listen to Me and you will not fulfill all of these commandments.
> (Leviticus 26:14 - 15)

He then proceeds with a litany of curses that will ensue from this disobedience. But He begins these consequences with a very strange verse:

> *V'nasati panai bachem v'nigaftem lifnei oyveichem.*
> I will set My attention against you, and you will be smitten before your enemies.
>
> (Leviticus 26:17)

What is odd about this statement is the literal translation of the Hebrew words. Though the first part of the phrase is commonly rendered, "I will set My attention against you," the literal meaning of the words "v'nasati panai bachem" is, "and I placed my face in you." This language confounds the sages. How is it that God's 'placing His face in us' is a consequence for our disobedience?

The Maharal,[57] in his classical commentary Gur Aryeh, points out in response to this anomaly that the expression "God's face" is always positive. "Kol 'panim' hu l'tova/all reference to God's face is for the good," he asserts. Therefore, he changes the word "פָּנַי/panai," which means "my face," to "פִּנַאי/pinai," which means "my attention." As such, he explains the verse to mean "I will set my attention against you," as it is commonly understood. Rashi, the primary expositor of the Torah's "pshat," or plain meaning, concurs with the Maharal's suggestion that the intention of the verse is that God will focus His attention on those who transgress His will. He adds that the word "panai/my face" also shares the root of the word "poneh" which means "to turn." The verse, according to Rashi, is thus indicating that God will turn (poneh) His attention (pinai) to those who disobey Him in order to punish their misdeeds.

While these interpretations suit the context, they rely on a maneuvering of the language in order to do so, and they do not address the text's literal meaning. They fail to do so because the literal translation of the words provides us an insight that goes far beyond the surface of the Torah to its very depths. Rashi establishes early on in his commentary on the Torah that his purpose is only to explain the simple level of the text:

> I have come only [to teach] the pshat/simple meaning of Scripture.
>
> (Rashi on Genesis 3:8)

---

[57] Rabbi Yehuda Loew, sixteenth century Kabbalist from Prague.

While Rashi's intent is only to explain the surface layer of the Torah and not its deeper mystic implications, the verse itself reveals a "sod/secret" that is mind-blowingly profound. As we saw from the Gur Aryeh above, "all reference to God's face is for the good." Therefore, if we do not change the word from "panai/my face" to "pinai/my attention," and we read the verse precisely as God Himself actually wrote it, then we realize that even when one transgresses God's will, He still "places my face in you." This brings us to the shocking and counterintuitive conclusion that ultimately, *even our negative actions will only bring us positive results*!

The illogic and seeming injustice of such a conclusion is what led the sages to alter the language for the sake of the simple understanding. However, the deeper truth is that God, at His essential level, is not compelled by logic or motivated strictly by justice. It is true that within the realm of "pshat" and the limited structure of the "olam/world" in which we live, logic and justice are paramount. However, beyond this realm of "helam/hiddenness," *when God's essential nature is revealed, His love, forgiveness and unity transcend the rules of reason and judgment.* At such a level, whether we go in God's ways or we turn away from His commandments, ultimately His response is the same! Either way, "v'nasati panai bachem," He has placed His face within us. **Regardless of our actions and our conduct, we are Godly at our core and nothing can change that!**

It is essential to reiterate that this does not mean that there are not laws or consequences for our actions within this temporal realm in which we currently exist. But it means that in our ultimate reality, all of these distinctions and repercussions cease to exist. God's love for us is not dependent on our compliance. He "turns" to us, and "faces" us regardless of our conduct. He cannot help but face us because His "panim/face" is lodged in our "pnimyus/core." The only real question is whether *we* are facing *Him* or turning away - whether we are conscious of His love and unity, and thus responding to it with love, or we are unaware of His existence at the base of our existence, and therefore turning away from Him to pursue other avenues that we mistakenly believe to be in our best interest.

Obstruction

The choice is ours!

We can choose which layer of existence we prefer to inhabit and manifest. We can opt to live in a world of "pshat," where justice and judgment reign supreme, and where compliance is rewarded and defiance is penalized. Or we can decide to peel back the layer of the "pshat/ simple level" to uncover the "sod/secrets," thereby dwelling in a reality where God's infinite love and unity transcend the superficial distinctions that subject us to division and valuation. This is not to say that we can rest exclusively in the layer of our choosing and ignore the others or pretend that they don't exist. We have, after all, been placed in this world with a mission and a purpose to fulfill here. We can, however, determine whether we are going to remove the veil and expose what is beneath, or add to the coverings that conceal our essence and confine us to the surface.

This brings us back to the beginning of the chapter. There we explained that the first garment in which we were enclothed and concealed was fashioned and applied by God, but the additional layers that have been added over that initial covering were created by us. Rather than working to reveal our core, we have labored to further obscure it for the variety of reasons that we went on to discuss (shame, fear, etc). This, we will now come to understand, is the true nature of what we refer to as "sin." Commonly understood as an evil deed or a crime, we conceive of sin as an affront to God, a disrespecting and disobedience. We feel guilt for having broken His law and His trust. We feel fear for having exposed ourselves to His wrath and punishment. We feel remorse for having proven ourselves weak and flawed. We beg for forgiveness and mercy, knowing that though we are unworthy, He is nevertheless compassionate. We admit our wrongdoing, and we appeal to His tolerance. He chastises us, repays us with the consequences of which He had given us more than ample warning, and then He forgives us and grants us another chance to grow and do better. In this "pshat" dynamic, God is just. He has forewarned us; He is disappointed by our failure, and saddened at least, and perhaps even angered, by our disobedience. He disciplines us, but He is forbearing and does not hold a grudge.

However, according to our new "sod" perspective and the awareness that ultimately God is neither offended, nor even affected, by our misdeeds (as we explained above, "if you sin what effect do you have on Him"), then we must refine this understanding of transgression. What is sin truly, and what is its impact if it does not ultimately impact God? We can find an answer in the words of the prophet Isaiah:

> Your iniquities have separated between you and your God.
>
> (Isaiah 59:2)

The prophet seems to suggest here that our sins cause us to be separated from God. But this raises an obvious question: how is it possible for anyone or anything to be separate from God?! If He is One, and thus He is everywhere and everything at once, then how can we be distinct or distant from Him? In truth, we cannot. And in fact, we never were. At the level of "sod," we know that "A-donai echad / God is one" - there is nothing but Him alone. Sin, therefore, does not, and cannot, separate us from God from His vantage. It can, however, create an obstruction from our perspective and in the realm of "pshat." Understood this way, *sin is the layer of interference and concealment that we create between ourselves and our Creator. As such, sin is that which renders us less perceptive of, and receptive to, God.* It is the curtain or barrier that we erect 'between' us and Him which makes it more difficult for us to perceive and reveal the truth of His infinite light. Though we are ultimately no more 'distant' from God after we have sinned than before - because God is everywhere equally - nevertheless, each sin encrusts us in another layer that makes us less capable of seeing the Godliness within us and around us.

Why do we sin? Why do we create these barriers? Because we believe ourselves to be separate already. We have forgotten what we truly are, and each "sin" takes us further and further from ourselves. As the verse from Isaiah quoted above continues:

> And your sins hide the face from you.
>
> (Isaiah 59:2, end)

The first half of the verse indicates that our sin separates us from God. This second half adds that sin hides "the face/panim" from us. It does not indicate whose face is hidden - is it our face or God's face that sin hides from us and makes it more difficult for us to sense? The answer is both. Our misdeed creates an additional layer of covering that we drape over our own "panim/inner essence;" and since the "Pnei Hashem/ face of God" is embedded within our "pnimyus," therefore when we further obscure our own essence, we increase our separation from Him as well.

Seen in this light, sin is not an "evil deed" for which we deserve punishment. It is rather a self-defeating act for which we deserve sympathy. God desires to avail us of His light and of the peace and bounty that comes with the revelation of His infinite presence. We can choose to accept and receive that or to refuse it. When we choose the latter, it is not because we are wicked, but because we are misguided and unaware of what we have spurned. No one would intentionally trade infinite benevolence and abundance for the limited and ephemeral delights of this world unless s/he were incapable of clearly seeing and understanding the comparison between the two options. It is God Himself who has obscured our vision, and as a result of our myopia we have made decisions that are not in our best interest, further diminishing our ability to see and choose properly. God's reaction to our errors and our predicament is therefore not anger or righteous indignation, but rather compassion and the desire for us to "see the light" that is within us. He knows our weaknesses - He created them - and yet He believes in us nonetheless. He does not want to do the work for us, but He provides us His Torah so that we can utilize its wisdom to delve inward, remove the coverings, and thereby allow His blessings to flow freely and abundantly.

When we come to God in prayer, therefore, it is with remorse, but not shame or self-flagellation. We are sorry not because we have harmed or hurt Him - He cannot be harmed or hurt - but because we recognize that we have denied ourselves His love and denied Him the opportunity to fully express that love. We ask for forgiveness, but what that means is not that He was angry at us or distanced from us and we want to be reconciled. ForGIVEness means that we want to remove the barriers that have temporarily interfered with His GIVing. We ask Him to help us to clear away the blockages that we have created, and to help us to refrain from erecting these blockages again in the future. Help me to open to You, we pray. Help me to peel off the many layers that I have clad myself in, and to access and uncover the channels through which You give Your infinite benevolence to me, and through me to all of Your creation.

———◆———

Unveiling

Once we understand the nature of the obstructions that we have placed between our surface and our core, we are now ready to remove them. This removal will enable us to:

a) answer the first question that God asked humanity, "ayecha/where are you,"

b) comply with the initial command that God made to Abraham the first Jew, "lech lecha/go to yourself," and

c) fulfill the mission that was assigned in the opening words of Torah, "Breishis bara Elokim/the primary thing is to reveal God."

It will also enable us to transition our reality from a state of hiddenness and darkness to a state of revelation and light, and thereby to be a true "light unto the nations." This divesting of the layers that "separate between you and your God" and that "hide the face from you" is precisely the process of "teshuvah/return" that we are working on daily and throughout our lives. While "teshuvah" is commonly understood as repentance for sin, with our new understanding of "sin" as the layers we place over our essence and the face of God that is hidden within us, we will now recognize "teshuvah" as the efforts we make to unveil and shed those layers in order to expose what is beneath them. When we accomplish this "teshuvah/return," we will reveal the level of "sod/secrets," which is the ultimate truth of God's unity. At this level, our sins are meaningless and there is only divine love. In such a reality, we will align ourselves with God's will not because we are coerced to or because we fear to do otherwise, but because God's unconditional love arouses within us a reciprocal love. In other words, we cannot help but love the one who loves us so completely. Finally, we will come to understand that we are nothing other than Godliness, and therefore it is our very nature to act Godly.

In closing this discussion on the true nature of sin, it is important to note that the ability to reach this place of guiltlessness and to be absolved of all past wrongdoing is one of the Torah's deepest and most sensitive secrets. There is the possibility, of course, that there will be those who view this accessibility to instant forgiveness and faultlessness as a license to ignore or transgress the laws that God has established within the world. It is for this reason that many sages fought against the proliferation of the teachings of Kabbalah and Chassidus and insisted that the Torah's mystic secrets should remain confined to a select few.

However, the Baal Shem Tov and his followers knew that the awareness of God's limitless love, along with one's inherent accessibility to the boundless realms beyond this world, would ultimately be positive. Our recognition of God's unity and of our complete inclusion in that unity will not lead to distance from God. On the contrary, it will activate alignment with His will in the recognition that it is truly our very own will. When we recognize our Godly potential and essence, we respond to the divine teachings and edicts not with obedience and acquiescence, but rather with communion and consocation. *We perform God's will not in hope of reward or for fear of punishment, but in love of the One who loves us infinitely, and in recognition of the reality that we are each intricate instruments of His expression and simple portions of His being.*

Chapter 6: BEING GODLY

Revolution

At this point, we have established that the destination of our journey is within, and we know that in order to continue this journey and reach the face of God where all impurity, darkness, and plurality cease to exist, we must remove the coverings that we have amassed over our center and open a path in order to penetrate to our inner depths. We know that when we access this space, we will avail ourselves of a constant flow of Godliness and goodliness that will not only provide us everything we need, but will also enable us to endow the entire creation around us with everything it lacks. The next question, then, is how specifically we can remove these coverings. Fortunately, Torah provides us an intricate practice in order to help us do so. As a matter of fact, this is precisely Torah's purpose and intent, and we will explore this subject in chapter seven.

However, before we do so, we must pause on our path and return to the question that we began to address in chapter five. There, we introduced the question "how are you," and we touched on the self-esteem that comes with the recognition of the Godliness within. We explored the Torah's conception of the "Adam/human" as one who is not only from the "adama/earth," but is also "adameh l'Elyon/similar to God." We explained that what we are seeking is therefore not far from us but already in our inherent nature and in our grasp. We saw that this tremendous sense of self-worth lightens our load and brightens our journey through the darkness of this world. In chapter five, we then went on to analyze the coverings that obscure the light within us, the reasons they exist, and the ways in which we reinforce them rather than divest ourselves of them. Before moving onward, it is worthwhile to backtrack a few steps and further discuss how illuminated one becomes, and how beautiful life can be, when we are opened and our inherent Godliness is expressed.

As we deduced earlier, the answer to the question "how are you" will depend on our answer to our first question, "ayecha/where are you" and its corollaries "what are you" and "why are you." If we locate ourselves in this physical realm - if we identify ourselves as the body that fumbles around in the darkness, and if we conceive of our purpose as the accumulation of material possessions and the satisfaction of our body's passions and urges - then most certainly our answer to the question of "how are you" will be not well. It is not possible to be well in the long run in a realm of entropy where everything decays other than the appetites which consistently grow. If, on the other hand, we locate ourselves within, if we identify ourselves as the "Pnei Hashem/face of God" that is hidden in our "pnimyus/inner core," and if we realize that our purpose is the revelation of our Godly light within the darkness, then we will answer "how are you" with the humble recognition that "I am great." I am great because that which I truly am is pure and unadulterated Godliness.

This is a profound and potentially life-altering concept, but how do we take it out of the realm of the conceptual and bring it into the actual so that we truly feel great and we truly actualize our greatness? If I read this book and then put it down and move onward with some vague intellectual notion that God is within me, what have I really gained? Has my life truly changed in any significant way? Do I feel different? Do I act differently? Do I treat the people around me differently? The recognition of one's inherent Godliness is not simply a nice idea, or an inspiring spiritual insight. It is a revolution. It is a complete transformation of one's life from a condition of limitation, mortal frailty, and fallibility, to a brand new reality of vastness, transcendence, and boundless potential.

The ramifications of God's complete unity compel us to admit that not only is God within me and the ultimate essence of what I am, but He is similarly the core and ultimate reality of all else. In other words, not only are we ourselves nothing but Godliness, but furthermore everything we encounter is nothing but Godliness. Even the darkness and the layers of concealment that disguise this truth are nothing but Godliness! Imagine if you were conscious of this reality at every moment. How would your life be different? How WILL your life be different when this becomes your constant mindset?

Self Image

The first thing that will change with the awareness of God's absolute unity is the relationship one has with her/himself. It is no secret and no surprise that the vast majority of us dwell in a state of constant insecurity, self-consciousness, and self-critique. For some of us, our relationship with ourself is even more problematic. We tend toward self-loathing, displaying consistent behaviors that are self-defeating and self-destructive. Some of this negativity in our self-concept can be attributed to the shame that we discussed in the previous chapter. This shame is partially derived from a misunderstanding of our origins, and a misinterpretation of the concept of sin and Adam and Eve's "fall from grace" in the Torah's opening chapters.[58] Even those who are not interested in theological issues or religious involvement are subject to the pervasive cultural conception of the inherent sinfulness of the human being. This is perpetuated, in part, by those who have always sought to exploit our discontent in order to keep us under their control. Regardless of the sources and perpetrators of this toxic self-regard, its ultimate cause is the basic unawareness of what we are and why we exist.

---

[58] See section entitled "Shame" in chapter 5

Have you ever felt okay? Be honest. When was the last time you had a sense, deep down inside of you, that you are completely acceptable just as you are? Have you ever in your adult life experienced the conviction that you are fine and good and there is nothing wrong with you? Do you ever feel an absolute guiltlessness, a confidence that there is nothing you should be doing or being at this moment that you are not? This is not to say that you are perfect or complete - because we are not perfect or complete in this realm - but that you are complete in your incompleteness? Such a sense of worth and self-acceptance is extremely rare. Even those whom we deem to be "successful" and "accomplished" rarely exude the kind of contentment and serenity that would characterize this type of self-assurance. Accomplishment in our modern societies is usually identified with the amassing of material assets, the acquisition of power, and/or the achievement of renown. But all of these are generally the result of a drive for validation and recognition. Their possession usually only increases the appetites and renders the self more hungry and restless, and less satisfied and calm. How many people have you met in your life who truly seem to be fulfilled and happy with who and what they are?

Because we don't know who or what or where we are, we are constantly questioning our existence and calibrating our worth. This incessant self-evaluation and critique leaves us anxious and insecure. We feel judged and dissected, and the 'self' that we view in the mirror is flawed and blemished and unable to stand up to such persistent and excruciating scrutiny. The judgment comes from those around us, but even more frequently and damningly, it comes from ourselves. Most damagingly, we believe that the perpetual critique comes from God, the One who created us and who is ashamed of how far we are from what He had intended us to be. This assumption of God's criticism and ire is the very root of so much unhappiness and heartache, and it is so heartbreakingly unnecessary, because it is simply untrue! *God does not disdain us. He does not focus on our faults or look for opportunities to judge and condemn us. God IS us!* He therefore relates to us, understands us, appreciates us, roots for us, and loves us completely. Simultaneously, He challenges us, He hides Himself from us, and He allows us to be unaware of His absolute unity and His absolute love. But this concealment and its challenges are, as we have explained throughout this book, only a function of His love. Without it, we could not exist as seemingly separate beings, and He would have no "other" to whom He could express His infinite desire to give.

God's desire to overlook our faults and His disinterest in judgment and censure is stated explicitly in Torah:

> He (God) does not look at sin in Jacob, and He has not
> seen crookedness in Israel.
> (Numbers 23:21)

Here, the wicked prophet Balaam is forced to declare that not only does God not *seek* faults in His children, but furthermore, He does not even *see* our shortcomings. It is not merely that He is not looking for opportunities to blame and shame us, but that even if He were, He would find none. This is because He does not view our acts as sin at all. This is reinforced by a verse from Psalms which states:

> *Ashrei adam lo yachshov A-donai lo avon.*
> Happy/fortunate is man, God does not consider His sin.
> (Psalms 32:2)

On the simple level, this verse is commonly translated as "happy is *the* man whose sin is not considered by God." However, the literal reading of the verse reveals a deeper and more internal truth. It does not say "ashrei *ha'*adam/happy is *the* man" but rather "ashrei adam/happy is man." On the level of "pshat/simple understanding," the verse seems to refer to a certain type of person who is deserving of God's overlooking of His sins. But according to its "sod/secret meaning," it refers not to a particular person or people whose sins are not considered, but rather to mankind in general - all people - for God does not consider our sin. Why does He not do so? Because, as we discussed in the previous chapter, our misdeeds do not affect Him. They only create another layer of covering that obscures our view of Him and our recognition of His presence within our core. Ultimately, "lifnei A-donai/before God," or at the level of God's face, we are not judged. And as we find and experience this level of our essential reality, we need not judge ourselves. We can actually begin to experience life, and experience ourselves, without constant self-re-crimination and critique.

If we conceive of God as one who is constantly counting and accounting our sins and merits, and we want to emulate Him and be Godly, then we too will perpetually be judging everything around us and within us. But we must pause and ask ourselves if God is truly so, or if we are making Him in our image. Did He create us with this tendency and imperative to be constantly judgmental? Is this what He wants from us, to be always on guard, always tense, always afraid that we will fall or fail and then be punished? As we have quoted previously, Torah tells us "serve God with joy."[59] How can we possibly serve with joy if we are always afraid? We can perhaps serve Him with fear, but is it truly possible to be joyous when we are incessantly critiquing our performance and dreading our inevitable failure?

God knows that we are fallible. He created us imperfect and He situated us in the dark. He not only accepts our imperfection, but establishes it as a condition of our existence. It is what distinguishes us from Him and enables us to be the "other" that He desires. Therefore, we can accept our imperfection and strive for improvement without hating our deficiency. We can feel motivated to grow without feeling inadequate. *We can act Godly because we are Godly, and not simply because we want to avert retribution.*

If we view God as a strict and exacting judge who sits above and eternally assesses His creation, then our lives will be focused on right and wrong, good and evil, reward and punishment. We will view ourselves and our surroundings through this lens, and we will feel guilt when we err, and pride when we comply. We will judge and critique and forever struggle to negotiate this duality that bifurcates our existence. But if we view Him as the sole existence and the very essence of our being and all being, then we will stop evaluating ourselves and believing we are deserving of consequence and rebuke. Then we will stop struggling with life, and we will learn to navigate the currents without being angry that they don't always flow the way we wish. We will trust in God and know that He is here always; that everything is so because He makes it so; that I am so because He has made me so; that I can accomplish anything with His help when I stop limiting myself and limiting Him.

---

[59] Psalms 100:2

When we focus on the divisions that God has created, we live in division and limitation. When we focus on His unity, we unite with Him and transcend all of our constraints. Torah refers to God by multiple names which, as we have mentioned, allude to various aspects of His being. He is both "A-donai" and "E-lohim." "E-lohim" is His judgment, His manifestation within the world of division and plurality. "A-donai" is His infinite transcendence, His aspect beyond limitation and delineation. We and the world exist on multiple levels simultaneously: the physical reality and the spiritual essence. The question is not which aspect of God, of us, and of the creation is true, because they each have their truth. The question is in which aspect we choose to exist. We can dwell in the realm of limits, physicality, and judgment, or we can choose to transcend this space and live a life of expansiveness, patience, and infinite growth.

A recognition of our Godliness and the love that God feels and displays for us will revolutionize our self-image and transport us from an outlook of self-consciousness to one of God-consciousness. It will carry us from a state of self-judgment to one of intense self-esteem. When we recognize that the "Pnei Hashem/face of God" is lodged in our "pnimyus/inner core," then we can finally love ourselves and treat ourselves with the patience and kindness that we deserve. Even as we recognize that the casing that encrusts and conceals our ultimate self is less 'lovable' per se, we are aware that that exterior is not what we essentially are; therefore, we needn't be self-critical because that is not a representation of our truest "self" at all. Yet because "A-donai echad/God is One," we understand that even this bodily shell is Godliness, serving His purpose of allowing each of us to exist. With this awareness, we can come to value that part of ourselves as well.

We can begin to appreciate every aspect of creation, even as we work to refine it, transform it, and reveal it for what it truly is. We can love even those things that we must battle, even those things that have no awareness and no manifestation of their Godliness. If so, then we can certainly know that we are okay and fine, even as we are imperfect. I have work to do, but that need not hinder me from having genuine sympathy toward myself. Equipped with this self-directed sympathy, I can then sympathize with the entire creation. With this perspective, our angst and shame will begin to melt away, and we will begin to experience a buoyancy, clarity, and serenity that will transform our lives and our world completely.

<hr />

Peace

After one's self-image changes, everything else begins to change as well. With the abandonment of self-consciousness and self-critique comes a tremendous release of pressure and tension. The transformative potential of this release and relief cannot be overestimated. It is the difference between a life of subtle, but endless anxiety, and an experience of liberation that many of us cannot even fathom because we are not conscious of our captivity or the possibility of its cessation. The stress in our lives is like an incessant, irritating hiss that we fail to hear or address because of its constancy. It is like a chronic ache that we eventually resign ourselves to because we become convinced that it is inevitable. It is a sad reality that the vast majority of us accept this type of torment, unaware that there is an alternative.

It is difficult to describe peace to one who has not experienced it. It is perhaps like trying to describe color to one who is blind. Yet it is important to explain this state to the best of our ability, because it is incredibly precious, and it is freely available despite the fact that it is so lacking in common experience. The hope is that we will work harder to seek and discover it if we grasp even some vague sense of its profound value and its attainability.

If we would be asked to define peace, we might characterize it as the absence of battle or conflict. By such a definition, much of the world today can be said to be "at peace" in that the zones of war and regions of armed conflict are relatively few. But it would be difficult to contend that most places in the world today enjoy true peace. We would be hard pressed to find many places where the majority of its inhabitants (or even a minority for that matter) would honestly assert that they are at peace. Real peace is a rare commodity in this world. It is not simply a matter of an absence of physical violence. What then is it?

We might suggest that peace is the absence of not only tangible and material violence, but also emotional and psychic conflict. One who is at peace would therefore not be plagued by thoughts and feelings that are troublesome or confounding. Yet while this may be true of someone at peace, it would be hard to argue that peace is merely the lack of challenge, contention, and variance. If that were the case, then could we say that anyone or anything that is not challenged is experiencing peace? Would we suggest that a cow is at peace, for example? Or a boulder? Or one who has suffered a brain injury and is no longer in touch with her/his mental and emotion faculties?

Peace would seem to be more than a simple lack of conflict. Furthermore, the absence of conflict tells us nothing of one's ability to maintain composure and tranquility if and when conflict does inevitably present itself. Genuine peace will not only precede discord, but it will even preclude it. It will enable one to endure challenges and stress without panicking or crumbling or responding to disturbance with reciprocal disturbance. Peace is therefore not merely the absence or avoidance of tension, but rather it is something that provides us the ability to tolerate and abide the vicissitudes of life with a state of equanimity, acceptance, and constructiveness. What is this magical or mystical thing called peace that affords us an almost superhuman stability and poise?

As we work toward an understanding of this concept, it will be useful to point out something that peace is not. In Torah, peace is not a goal in and of itself. In some spiritual systems, the attainment of peace is the end game. Life is not considered to have significance beyond its experience, and therefore the objective is to attain a level of surrender and acceptance which can make our existence not only tolerable, but even beautiful. Peace, in such a framework, is not simply a tool to enable one to achieve some other aim, but it is the aim itself. There are certainly worse things to aim for, and one cannot be blamed for setting something as wonderful as peace as her/his target. But doing so, according to Torah, will not fulfill one's potential or discharge the holy duty that s/he was created to perform.

Similar to this idea is the concept of happiness in Torah. Happiness, or "simcha" in Hebrew, is not merely a Torah ideal, but it is a commandment, as it is written "ivdu es Hashem b'simcha/Serve God with joy."[60] Yet while Torah requires happiness and stresses its necessity, the objective is not the happiness itself, but the service that it facilitates and

---

[60] Psalms 100:2.

engenders. The verse from Psalms is not only telling us to serve God joyously, but it is instructing how we can achieve the service of God: "Ivdu es Hashem/serve God" - how do we do so? - "b'simcha," with, and through, simcha/joy. Without happiness, it is difficult to focus on anything but our own quandary or misery. When we are happy, however, we are able to move beyond ourselves and focus on how we can be of service to others and to the world around us.

Similarly, peace is a means to a greater end. The goals in Torah, as we have mentioned repeatedly, are to find oneself - "lech lecha/go to yourself" - and to reveal God in the realm of darkness and concealment in which He has hidden Himself - "breishis bara E-lokim es hashamayim v'es haaretz/the primary thing is reveal God in heavens and the earth." Peace is both a mechanism to help us reach these goals, and a product of their accomplishment. If we do not have peace, then we will be in constant turmoil, whether we are conscious of it or it afflicts us subconsciously. We will be occupied with so many ancillary battles that we will be unable to focus on the task at hand. Life presents us with endless diversions and enticements that heighten our tension and rob us of the ability to be in touch with what is truly important and significant. Peace is the clarity that comes with the elimination of these distractions, and it is the ability to ignore all of those things that vie for our attention. In one sense then, peace is the capacity to focus on what we are here to do.

Focus is the discipline to direct consciousness on a designated thing and shut out the many other things that surround it and compete for one's attention. It is the peeling away of all extraneous and superficial factors and details in order to pinpoint what is principal and essential. This is both the path to peace, and the essence of what peace is. When we succeed in shucking away all of the layers that cover our core, we will arrive at a place within us that is untouched and imperturbable. It is a dimension of incredible light and lightness. There is no tension there or conflict, because there is nothing else there at all. It is a mere point, but it is endless. Once we touch it, it envelops us. We find that it is not merely within us, but we are within it, and we always have been. It is the face of God, and God is One and all.

Oneness is the basis and foundation of true and ultimate peace. The Hebrew word for peace is "shalom," which derives from the root "shalem," which means "whole." Peace, quite simply, is the awareness that we are whole, and the eradication of all those deceptions in our lives that swarm around us and try to convince us otherwise.

The torment and angst of life is disconnection, division, and individuality. We feel alone and alien. We see ourselves as small and insignificant, hopelessly flawed, and irreparably broken. "Shalom/Peace" is the consciousness that God is within us and that we are within Him; that He is the fundamental and solitary truth of us and of all creation. The "world/olam" that we inhabit is a realm of "helam/concealment" that hides the reality of God's wholeness for all of the reasons that we have already discussed. Our task is to penetrate the concealment, to illuminate and eliminate the darkness. When we do so, we will experience the peace and euphoria of reuniting with everything we thought we had lost and lacked. The sense of alienation, the agony of not belonging in a cold world that does not know you or care about you, all of this will suddenly fade away, and we will experience the ecstatic intertwining of the billions of souls that are ultimately singular and undifferentiated.

When we realize that we are whole and one, there are no boundaries or limitations. We flow through and with everything as we are all kindred and synergistic. There is no fear, or trepidation, or bias. There is no need to explain oneself, or justify, or beautify. We need nothing, and we lack nothing, because we have everything, and we are everything. There is no tension or awkwardness, no self-consciousness or defense. There is no need to find the right words or wear the right clothes. There is no vanity, or jealousy, or envy. There is only amity, and empathy, and community in its truest sense.

On the subject of community and the interrelation of its members, there is a well-known Talmudic phrase:

*Kol Yisrael **areivim** zeh bazeh.*
All Israel is responsible for one another.
(Talmud, Shavuot 39a)

The word "areivim" means "guarantor," and the simple understanding of the verse is that we must all guarantee each other's well-being. However, the word "areivim" also means "mixed" and "intermingled." On a deeper level, we therefore glean that the reason we are responsible for others is not merely because we have a duty to them, but because we are inextricably co-mingled with one another. We are one soul, one being. Peace is not simply an alliance between us in which we agree to do no battle; it is the recognition that we are fundamentally one, and that any conflict between us is only a battle with oneself.

Ultimately, words will do this no justice. The peace that we are trying to describe here is more than simply the communion of all human souls. It is the absolute unity of all existence. This cannot be adequately transmitted in black ink on a white page. It must be experienced with a sense that is not visual or tactile or sensible. This is why one closes her/his eyes when s/he recites the Shema prayer: "Shema Yisrael, A-donai E-loheinu, A-donai echad/Hear Israel, the Lord our God, the Lord is One!" To attain this complete and euphoric oneness we must remove ourselves from the constraints of our six senses and our intellect, and we must shut out everything we know and think we understand. It is supra-rational, and supra-sensual, but it is palpable. You can feel it if you reach for it deep within you. And when you feel it, even a tiny twinge of it, it will send a type of spiritual shudder throughout the entirety of your being. There will be a tickle at all of your edges, a subtle pins-and-needles sensation in your toes, and your fingers, and your scalp, and then your entire skin, as all of your extremities begin to give way. You will feel a sudden weightlessness, and gravity will momentarily release its hold on you. You will wonder if you are about to float away or dissolve. And if you don't panic, if you resist the urge to grasp on to something solid in order to anchor yourself to the familiar, then you will eventually be overcome with the ecstasy of the harmony, integrity, and unity of all things.

It will require focus and concentration to attain this consciousness and this level of peace, but each of us is capable of doing so. This is one of the primary goals of Jewish prayer - to reconnect to the essence and unity of all things. As we have explained previously,[61] prayer is commonly relegated to the simple requesting of one's needs, but the concept of "tefilla/prayer" according to Torah is more about reuniting with one's source. The rich tradition of Jewish meditation has been an integral aspect of Torah practice for millennia. One of the primary focal points of meditation in the prayer service is the recitation of the Shema, which focuses us on the reality of God's sole existence. Unfortunately, many are accustomed to rushing through the prayer service, fulfilling their duty of

---

[61] See chapter three, section "Inward Bound"

pronouncing the proper words and phrases, but failing to take advantage of the profound transformation and liberation that is available through even a short but devoted meditation on the words and concepts they utter.

To experience the sense of oneness and the peace that meditative prayer can offer, try the following: Find a quiet room and sit in a chair. Close your eyes and breathe in through your nose and out through your mouth. Imagine that each inward breath brings cleansing air down into your abdomen and up into your mind. In your abdomen it collects tension, and in your mind it collects extraneous thoughts. When you exhale, allow yourself to feel the tightness drain from your body as the commotion slips from your brain, and begin to relax in the chair. Feel your weight in the chair and your feet on the floor, and let everything else go - the room and all that is in it, the house or building and the environment in which it is situated, let it all slowly vanish. It is now just you sitting in a chair, which rests on the ground, in an open expanse with absolutely nothing around you as far as the eye can see.

Keep breathing in and out, and now let the ground fade away. It is now just you on your chair, floating in space, with nothing around you, or below you, or above you. There is only a dull light or a glowing darkness that surrounds you as you sit comfortably on your floating chair. As you continue to breathe, slowly and calmly inhaling and exhaling, you realize that there is nothing holding the chair, and the chair is not holding you, so you let the chair go as well. And now it is just you, floating, weightless, alone but not lonely.

There is a stillness and quietness all around you that makes you feel calm and at rest. You realize that the body does you no good here, and so you let it disappear just like everything before it. And you are still here in the space, but you cannot be seen. You are not missing or lacking, you are everywhere now that there is nothing to confine you to one part of the space. You no longer struggle to be seen, to be recognized, to be special, because the "you" that yearned for those things was so small, and this everything which you are now suffused within is so complete and full and infinite. The tension that coursed within you is released, dispersed, and set free. The static that was in you has become ecstatic, an energy that uplifts you and enthralls you. You feel it, but you don't contain it. You share it, and you can move with it across the expanse and back. You are here and there and everywhere at once. You are free. There is no in and no out. You breathe, but it is not you breathing, it is the universal breath moving like a great tide in the expanse. You move with it because you are mingled with it. There is no resistance, no fear of drowning, no struggle to float. There is no surface and no depths. It is all depth, and you are deep within it, and around it, and of it. You are of everything, "in Of" with it. Love is when you desire to bond with something separate from you. "Of" is when you understand that there is nothing separate from you. You lack nothing, and desire nothing. You are whole and holy. You are "in of" - at one, and at peace, with everything.

This is the "shalom/peace" and "shleimus/wholeness" that we can experience when we access the face of God within us and we shed all of the layers that clothe, surround, and conceal it. It is not easy to do so, because the default of this "olam/world" is "helam/concealment," and the crust that divides and individualizes us does not stop growing on us for a moment. This is why peace is so rare and fleeting. And this is why we must seek the face of God constantly, as it says in the "Hodu" prayer at the beginning of the daily service, "seek His face always."

Peace will never come of its own or settle on us without effort. It is not the lack of work or a state of rest. In Torah, peace is not a passive affair. It is the labor of consistently delving inward and penetrating the barriers that alienate us from our essential self and the identical essence of all things. We must make peace with exertion and challenge, conscious that all of the trials and obstacles we face are also elements of God's infinite oneness. There is nothing that blocks or hinders us, because the blockages and hindrances are composed of precisely the same stuff that we are. With the consciousness that we are whole and one, we can alleviate the tension and stress that pervades and surrounds us, and thereby completely transform our lives and our world.

Bittul

There is a term that the mystics use for this concept of 'being one with everything' which we have described above. It is "hitkallelut/inter-inclusion." The root of the word is "k-l," which means "all," and the term "hitkallelut" thus means to be included in all. But interestingly, the root "k-l" also means "expiry," as in the word "**kil**ayon/annihliation." We can understand this duality of meaning because if something is subsumed in everything, then it no longer maintains its own individual existence. Like a drop of water that falls into the ocean, it no longer exists as an individual drop as it becomes mingled with the entirety of the sea. This duality exists in the term "shalem" as well. As we have seen above, "shalem" means "whole," but it can also be translated as "complete" or "finished." From this linguistic nuance we can approach another subtle level in the concept of "shalom/peace." Peace, we will find, can be achieved not only by seeing one's greatness and perfection in the enormity and entirety of the whole (as we discussed in the previous section), but also on the contrary, by letting oneself go completely. By releasing the pressure of striving to exist and individuate, one can thereby allow oneself to relax into the reality of her/his ultimate "nothingness."

This is known in chassidic teachings as "bittul," which literally means "nullification," but is often translated in this context more specifically as "self-nullification" or "self-abnegation." At first glance, this notion of self-nullification does not seem desirable or productive, as it is completely contrary to the instinct for self-preservation. But while the body, or animal aspect of humanity, strives for self-preservation and self-aggrandizement, the soul knows that its greatest accomplishment is not asserting itself, but rather giving itself completely. The soul is not concerned with itself because it is not a self; it is a component of the all-encompassing and exclusive reality of God. Therefore, by surrendering itself, it simply reunites with the infinite. "Bittul/self-nullification" is the end of the self, but it is not the end of the soul. For the soul there is no end. Its only limits are when it is individualized, so to speak, and confined to the physical restraints of the body. The more it gives itself - through acts of self-sacrifice and surrender even as it remains within the body - the more it is united with its infinite reality.

The sacrifice of one's self does not truly result in nothingness therefore, but rather in "everythingness." One does not become nothing through self-nullification; rather s/he becomes unified with everything. Individuality is not what makes me something, it is what separates me from everything. I do not cease to exist when I let go of my boundaries, I cease to be small and limited. I begin to truly exist when I stop insisting on my individual existence. In this sense, the choice is not the existential quandary of "being or nothingness," as Jean Paul Sartre phrases it; it is rather being or "everythingness." Shakespeare's classical dialectic in Hamlet's soliloquy, "to be or not to be," is not the authentic question. In our framework, the option would be "to be or to truly be." In other words, one can decide whether to be small by insisting on one's particular being and thus holding on to finitude, or to be limitless by letting go of one's self and thus entering eternity and infinity. Surrender and self-nullification, therefore, will lead to both "nothingness" and "everythingness" simultaneously. What is nullified and eradicated is not the true self, but those wrappings and trappings that we erroneously believe to be the self. These wrappings actually conceal the "Pnei Hashem/face of God," which is our ultimate self and the essence of all things. With "bittul/self-nullification," these coverings become nothing, and then it is revealed that we are truly everything.

Though it is known as "self-nullification," this negation of the self does not mean that one has no sense of dignity or worth and therefore allows the world to mistreat and trample her/him. On the contrary, through "bittul" one is conscious of her/his infinite worth as a veritable part of God. One knows that the truest expression of her/his value and preciousness is the transcendence of the ego and its self-concern. This secret of the inestimable value of nothingness is identified by the mystics in several places in Torah. In the book of Job, we find the following:

> V'chochmah me'**ayin** timatzei?
> And wisdom, **from where** will it be found?
> (Job 28:12)

Simply translated, the verse is read as a question, asking where wisdom is to be found. The word "ayin" is rendered in this reading as "where." However, the term "ayin" also means "nothing." Therefore, the verse can simultaneously be read as a statement rather than a question: "and wisdom from nothingness will be found." True wisdom, the chassidic masters teach, is the awareness that we are "nothing" in and of ourselves, and we are only expressions of Godliness. In fact, the very word for "wisdom" in Hebrew, "chochmah," is an articulation of this understanding. "Chochmah," the Chasidic masters teach, is a compound of two words, "koach/power" and "mah/what." Wisdom is thus "the power of what." In other words, wisdom is the enlightened capability to ask 'what am I' - what is my ultimate essence and ultimate worth - and to recognize that I am nothing in and of myself.

The value and power of nothingness is also articulated in Psalms. There, King David exclaims:

Me'*ayin* yavo ezri?
From **where** will my help come?
(Psalms 121:1)

On the simple level, once again reading the word "ayin" as "where," David is asking where is the source of his help. However, on a more subtle and mystic level, reading "ayin" in its translation of "nothing," the verse is David's statement of precisely where his help will originate: "from nothingness will my help come." What does this mean? How does one's help come from nothing? David is informing us that through accessing the lofty level of "bittul/self-nullifcation," he will no longer be subject to the perils of which he has been afraid. By recognizing that he is truly and ultimately "ayin," i.e. nothing other than Godliness, and furthermore that there *is* nothing other than Godliness, he realizes that there is therefore nothing to fear. If I exist and I am a substantial and solid target, then I am subject to attack. But if I don't exist, because I am one with the infinite, then the blows and projectiles that are launched at me will fail to land and will move right through me. When I am not trying to assert and establish myself because I am nothing in my own estimation, then nothing can harm me because there is no 'me' to be harmed.

Fearlessness

One of the most significant impediments to peace is fear. Even if one is not at war or in battle, if s/he is afraid, then s/he is certainly not at peace. Previously, we had discussed the fact that self-consciousness and self-condemnation are obstacles to an experience of self-worth and contentment, and that the discovery of the face of God within us would bring us to the realization of our wholeness and integrity and a resultant mindset of peace. In the case of fear, it is the recognition of our immateriality which will enable us to overcome any worry of attack or violence. There is nothing to fear because there is not only no object of attack - for I am nothing substantial and therefore all aggression will move right through me - but furthermore there is no attacker - for just as I am "ayin/nothing" so is my assailant "ayin/nothing." Therefore, anything and everything that is hurled in my direction has no substance either. There is not only no target, but there are no arrows. There is no bow and no archer, no aggressor and no victim.

The pervasiveness of fear in our lives is not surprising. For as we have discussed from the very first pages of this book, we have been created in a realm of darkness, and we are lost from the moment we are born. In addition to this, Torah characterizes life as a constant battle. In his work *Tanya*, the Alter Rebbe describes the conflict between the Godly and animal aspects of our soul as two rival armies which are fighting for control over a city.[62] Each of us is the "city," and our two opposing inclinations - our Godly nature and our animal nature - vie for dominance over our being. With this battle raging perpetually within us and around us, it is no wonder that we are ravaged by fear. The Zohar similarly depicts our spiritual reality as a battle:

> With the dawn, one should cleanse himself of everything, and then arm himself for battle.
> (Zohar III, 260a)

Each new day, the Zohar tells us, confronts us with a series of skirmishes as the various aspects of our existence wrestle with one another. Even seemingly simple daily processes present us with constant conflict and confrontation:

> A time of war is the time of prayer.
> (Likkutei Torah, Ki Teitze)

---

[62] *Tanya*, Likkutei Amarim, chapter 9

Prayer, which is allegedly to be a time of peace and calm, is in fact a time of war. As we attempt to focus and clear our mind, we are barraged by distractions and temptations, and our quietude and clarity are perpetually challenged. Even things as mundane and simple as consuming food present us with friction and contention:

> The time of eating is a time of battle.
> (Zohar III, 188)

The act of eating inflames our animal instincts and provokes our baser nature. In effect, every moment of life is a struggle between our hidden inner essence that wants to express itself, and our outer material housing which wants only to further sate and pleasure itself, and therefore strives to keep its Godly origins suppressed.

Because of the nature of this ongoing conflict between the spiritual and physical forces of our existence, we are constantly confronted with the violence and cacophony of battle. However, our response to this warfare need not be fear. The question is how we prepare for the battle, and how we engage the "enemy." If, as the Zohar states, we begin the day with the battle of prayer, then we can glean from the prayer service the strategy and methodology with which we should face the combat that threatens us.

Most soldiers and forces prepare for war by girding their bodies in protective armor and readying their weapons. They cover themselves with gear that will reinforce and guard their flesh so they will not be harmed and their ranks will not be diminished. The more shielded and impenetrable they are, the greater their chance of victory. However, Torah prayer prepares for battle in a diametrically opposite manner. The daily service begins with the recital of "karbonos/sacrifices," in which one reads verses that narrate the order of the animal sacrifices that were offered in the Temple. The intention of these sacrifices was the consumption of the flesh and the eradication of the animal casing that conceals the spirit within. Through meditating on this act in the beginning of the daily prayers, the Godly essence that is hidden beneath the flesh is empowered and prioritized.

Yet this is counterintuitive. As the enemy fortifies itself in armor and equips itself with weaponry, Torah urges one to take her/his flesh, her/his animal and physical strength, and place it on the fire. As the enemy approaches in full regalia, one burns away her/his garments, armor, and all of her/his material might. One does so with the realization that these trappings make one vulnerable, not secure. We come to understand that muscle and metal don't protects us, but rather they contain us. They isolate us and make us small and frail. Beneath them, within them, free of them, we are only light and fire. We are spirit, which is impenetrable and untouchable. We are one with the spirit all about us, and therefore we are unified and infinite. We enter the battle unencumbered and unafraid. We move through the field undetected. We leave the skirmish unharmed. The weapons of mankind destroy the flesh, but we have shed the flesh and can be neither felt nor felled. "Me'ayin yavo ezri" - from nothingness will come my help. If I am nothing to myself, then who can get to me?

The battle is over when there is no one here to fight. When we give up our animal, our fleshy and material self, we become invincible, and the enemy ceases to exist. Prayer is meditation on this self-transcendence and its subsequent oneness. Through prayer, we peel off the garments that constantly grow on us like a crust. Our daily experience in the world convinces us that our physical individual reality is paramount - that I am the center of the universe, and that the weight of the world presses on me every moment. We pray to disentangle ourselves from this lie, to disrobe from this costume, to remind ourselves that we are united with everything else. The struggle then ends, and the fear melts away. Our blood pressure stabilizes, and we face the day with peace and confidence. The war does not end, but we are at peace even in the midst of the battleground.

Peace, and the transcendence of all fear, are possible when we become aware that the two enemy forces clashing within us are not truly enemies, and are not truly 'two' at all. The Godly and animal aspects of our being are not, in fact, opposites, because there are no opposites, and there is no opposition at all. There is only one. The goal is therefore not to overcome, to conquer, or to vanquish. It is rather to unify. It is to recognize that we are all inter-included, and to lose ourselves - and thereby find ourselves - in the uncompounded infinity that is hidden within our core.

Spiritual growth, Torah teaches us, is thus a lifelong process of disrobing. We begin naked, vulnerable, and afraid. We spend our days seeking shelter and acquiring garments. We lose ourselves inside our clothing and structures. With Torah's wisdom, we will come to understand that the fortifications we have constructed around us do not protect us, instead they imprison us. We will then work to dismantle and discard these structures in order to uncover what we have buried within them. With God's help, we will finish and once again find ourselves "naked," but now we will be unashamed, untouchable, and unafraid.

Letting Go

Inner peace, we have seen, is achievable through a process of release and surrender. Surrender is a term that is generally misunderstood in our culture. It connotes a sense of weakness and loss in a world that is concerned primarily with strength and victory. But Torah's conception of surrender is related to the concept of "bittul" that we have been discussing above. It is a positive nullification, if such a thing can be said. It is the result not of frailty or cowardice, but of tremendous power and fortitude. It is a liberation rather than a submission, and an accomplishment rather than a failure.

Surrender in this context is not giving up, but rather we can refer to it as "giving in." We are giving expression to what is within us, opening a path to the "Pnei Hashem/face of God" that is in our "pnimyus/inner core" and allowing it to become manifest. We are relinquishing not our true self, but the external construct that contains and restrains our true self. We are not submitting to some foreign force, but we are sloughing off the alien force that has been controlling and limiting us. We are thereby allowing our authentic essence to finally be expressed. This surrender is not a defeat but an overwhelming victory. In a sense, it is a victory over the need to be victorious. While the ego desires to fight and win, the "Pnei Hashem" has no ego, and it surrenders to One because it is One. There is no struggle, no fear, and no shame. There is only release and realignment, reunification and peace.

To achieve such a surrender, along with the serenity and bliss that it engenders, seems to be a prodigious task that is beyond the grasp of the vast majority of us. It is the spiritual masters and mystics who can attain such lofty levels, we convince ourselves. But what if we are all capable of reaching such heights? What if doing so is not a matter of scaling precipitous peaks or spending decades learning to decipher the most abstruse and esoteric texts, but simply learning to let go? We touched on this idea earlier in chapter four[63] where we cited God's insistence that "the thing is very near to you; it is in your mouth and in your heart so that you can fulfill it."[64] The peace and bliss of unifying with His presence is therefore not something that we must chase or create, but it is something we can simply allow.

The question that we must ask ourselves is whether it is easier to continue living on the surface of this existence and contending with all of the stress and tension that is found here, or to relinquish our hold on this superficial layer in order to experience a more authentic and sublime reality. It would seem to be easier to remain here - otherwise why would the vast majority of us do so our entire lives? Why would we allow ourselves to be freed from this realm of conflict and anxiety only when we die? It would seem that most of us don't have the strength, the wisdom, or the ability to transcend our current circumstances and embrace our Godly truth. But what if we are actually holding on to this realm rather than being held by it? What if the effort we are expending in grasping who and what we believe ourselves to be is much greater than the energy it would take to relinquish our grasp and let go? What if we are hanging on to our lives - and hanging on *for* our lives - so intently that we don't even realize that we can simply stop and set ourselves free?

Imagine, for a moment, releasing that tight grip that you constantly maintain on being you - that tension that begins somewhere behind your sternum or beneath your shoulder blades which exerts incessant gravity on all of the particles that distinguish you from everything that is not you. Imagine letting it go, and dissolving. Imagine the relief of ceasing to pull everything inward in a desperate attempt to be you as long as possible; ceasing to protect all that you perceive to be you from

[63] Section "Not In Heaven"

[64] Deuteronomy 30:14

all that you believe to be not you. Imagine the ecstasy of unwinding after being so tightly wound; of finally being unguarded and unafraid; of coalescing with everything and clinging to nothing. What if you release your hold and find that you won't actually fall apart or fall to pieces? The world will not actually tear apart at the seams, because there are no seams. There are no parts or pieces. It is all one, and it's all fine, and it will all be fine.

This incredible relief cannot be described in words. It must be felt. The feeling is utter relaxation. It is the rest that comes when you set down a tremendous weight that you have been straining to hold your entire life. You are so accustomed to the strain that you have come to ignore it, but you can release it. You can put it down and sit down and let every ounce of pressure drain from your body.

Prayer is precisely this process of letting go. As we discussed earlier in the chapter, prayer is pausing from our daily routine to reconnect to what we truly are, and to disconnect from what we are not. When we begin each morning with prayer, we literally begin anew. We let go completely of who we were the previous day. We abandon all of our worries and thoughts and suppositions, allowing ourself to be completely emptied. As we begin reciting the order of the "karbonos/sacrifices" in the Temple in Jerusalem, we allow our flesh and body to be burned away in the fire on the altar. With them, all concerns and responsibilities melt away - if they are important, they will be there when we return after our prayer. Thoughts will try to impose themselves, insisting that they are urgent, but we will not let them. We challenge our suppositions and the weight we lend to things. How dire is it? How grave and important? What will happen if I let this feeling go? Does it really matter if this person thinks this of me, or if I don't win this argument, or if I don't have this item? What if I release these worries and needs - will I not be okay? Will I not, in fact, be more okay? What if I don't satisfy this urge or desire? What if I just let them go? What if I let go of all the anger and tension and desire - will I fail to be as great or strong as I was, or will I simply be lighter and more nimble and less tethered?

When we allow everything to dissolve, we can experience the bliss of weightlessness and stillness and timelessness. We will not die when we stop striving to exist and accomplish. We can experience moments of non-being, bathe in those moments, and then come back. All of the things that we need to do and be will be here waiting for us when we return. But those few, precious moments of nothingness and everything-ness and oneness will make the world we return to less onerous and op-pressive. We will know that all of these things that press us and stress us are not as solid and absolute as we had imagined. We are not defined by them or grasped by them. We can let them go whenever we choose.

This is not to shirk or abandon our responsibilities. Nor is it to suggest that there are not significant duties and issues in our life - our job, our relationships, our financial concerns - which may not be easy. But they are all one with us. They are all part of God, as are we. Seen in this light, they need not trouble us or worry us. It's not that we ignore them or wish them away, but we train ourselves to release them at vari-ous times throughout the day in order to remind ourselves that they do not own us, control us, or define us. We re-contextualize them, uniting with them and knowing that they are all elements of something univer-sal and benevolent and mysterious. Through this, we can approach one of the most profound secrets in all of Torah: "hishtavus/equanimity."

<hr />

Equanimity

In his 16th century work "Shaarei Kedusha/Gates of Holiness," Rabbi Chaim Vital[65] tells the story of a sage who wanted to join one of the mystic circles in order to study the deep secrets of Kabbala. Induction into such esoteric societies was granted only to those who had already mastered the revealed and exoteric teachings of the written and oral Torah. This was a prerequisite because a fluency in the common ways of the world was necessary before delving into the mysteries of the uni-verse. Therefore, when the sage approached the head of the society and asked to be admitted to his inner circle, the Kabbalist administered a thorough test of the sage's Torah knowledge. After the sage answered all of the questions posed to him, the Kabbalistic master confirmed to him that he had indeed amassed an impressive understanding of Torah, and

<hr />

[65] 1543-1620. Renowned Kabbalist from Safed who was the foremost disciple of the Arizal.

that he must answer only one more question: one person honors you, and one person insults you, how do you respond to them? The sage answered that he would respond to them no differently, though his feelings for the one who shamed him would admittedly be less favorable than for the one who showed him honor. The master did not admit him to his circle, instructing him to go continue his learning and return when there is no difference to him whatsoever between being honored or shamed.

This lofty level of spiritual development is known as "hishtavus," which in English is translated as "equanimity." The root of the Hebrew word is "shaveh," which means "equal," and the idea of "hishtavus/equanimity" is that all happenings and eventualities in one's life are valued equally regardless of their apparent benefits or detriments. This attitude and quietude is a result of one's ability to recognize the divine unity that underlies all things. In spite of surface and temporal differences, each and every experience is understood to be a facet of a Godly reality that is not only universal and infinite, but is also indispensable and beneficent. The Baal Shem Tov[66] expounds on this concept through a deeper understanding of a common phrase from Psalms:

> *Shiviti* A-donai l'negdi tamid.
> I place God before me always.
> (Psalms 16:8)

This verse is often identified as a fundamental tenet of the Torah lifestyle. On its simple level, it alludes to one's constant awareness of God and the necessity to consider Him and His ways before deciding how to act in any given situation. But the Baal Shem Tov explains that the word "shiviti" in this verse, translated traditionally as "I place," shares a root with the word "shaveh/equal" which we identified above. The first word of the phrase can therefore be rendered "it is equal to me," and the Baal Shem Tov thus reads the verse on the level of "sod/secrets" as follows: "all is equal to me, (because) God is before me always."

When one becomes aware that everything "before me" is simply another manifestation of Godliness, and that all of the multifarious aspects of creation are not only connected, but actually unified in purpose and essence, s/he will no longer be afraid, agitated, or confused. S/he

---

[66] Tzavaas HaRivash, 2

will rather be confident, content, and resolute, and all will be equally good in her/his estimation. This "hishtavus/equanimity" is one of the highest levels of spiritual development. It can be attained only by consistent meditation on God's unity and the awareness of God's presence within everything.

When one reaches this elevated consciousness, life transforms completely, and one can experience a state of freedom and tranquility no matter what challenges confront her/him. In such a context, the story is told of a man who once approached the Maggid of Mezeritch with the question of how it is possible to fulfill the Torah's edict to thank God for everything that happens to him whether it is good or bad, as it is written "a person is obligated to bless upon the bad just as he blesses upon the good."[67] The Maggid told the man that in order to find the answer to such a question, he should travel to the home of the chassid Reb Zusha of Anipoli. The man followed the Maggid's directions through the forest and came eventually to a ramshackle cabin. He knocked on the door and was warmly greeted by Reb Zusha, who invited him in. The shack's interior was even more shabby than it had appeared from outside. There were no furnishings other than a crude wooden table and bench, and few supplies other than some basic necessities. Nonetheless, Reb Zusha's demeanor was warm and upbeat, and he offered his guest everything he had. After observing the poor chassid for some time and realizing that he had never met anyone so destitute, the man posed his question. He explained to Reb Zusha that the Maggid had recommended he travel here to ask him how it was possible to be grateful to God even in the face of severe suffering. Reb Zusha considered, and finally responded that it was an excellent question, but he couldn't understand why the Maggid had sent the man to him, as he had never suffered a day in his life.

This type of acceptance and serenity in the face of hardship and deprivation represents a sublime level of faith. Yet the chassidic masters describe even greater heights of equanimity in which the experience of adversity is not simply tolerated or even unnoticed (as in the case of Reb Zusha), but rather overturned or transformed completely. The Lubavitcher Rebbe distinguishes in this context between the concepts of faith and trust. Faith, "emuna" in Hebrew, is the belief that God controls everything and is capable of anything. If circumstances present them-

[67] Mishnayos, Brachos 9:5

selves in a given way, then that is precisely as God wills it, and therefore there is no reason to worry or complain. God can, of course, change the situation if He chooses to do so, and so it is reasonable to request His assistance if one desires a different outcome. However, recognizing that all is in God's hands, one therefore never despairs and accepts everything that comes to him with patience and tolerance.

In contrast to this attitude of "emuna/faith," the Lubavitcher Rebbe defines trust, "bitachon" in Hebrew, not merely as the awareness of God's omnipotence, but furthermore as the certainty of His complete benevolence and the resultant assuredness of only positive outcomes. In other words, "emuna/faith" is the awareness that God CAN effect salvation and will do so eventually, while "bitachon/trust" is the knowledge that He WILL do so in a revealed way now.

This subtle difference may seem academic. The "emunah/faith" and simple acceptance of Reb Zusha is a tremendously high level of spiritual development which one can spend an entire lifetime working to achieve. However, the Rebbe teaches that even the extraordinary level of "bitachon/trust" is accessible to each of us, and we can truly live a life in which all of our experiences are positive in the moment. This consummate degree of equanimity is not simply a matter of accepting and enduring the bad now, and believing that its benefits will eventually be revealed either later in this life or at least in the next. It is rather the ability to assure that the good that God intends for us will be manifest now. This attitude was expressed by the Tzemach Tzedek[68] in his mid-19th century yiddish saying:

Tracht gut vat zein gut.
Think good and it will be good.

Referencing Torah wisdom from millennia prior, this ancient (and generally unattributed) source and precedent of modern theories of "the law of attraction" asserts not only that positive thinking will result in positive outcomes, but it also provides an explanation for why this is the case. *"Positive thinking" in the Torah context is not merely a matter of envisioning, and thereby manifesting, something that one desires. It is*

[68] 1789-1866, Rabbi Menachem Mendel of Lubavitch, the third Rebbe of the Chabad/Lubavitch chassidic dynasty.

meditating on the ultimate reality of God's complete oneness and abso-lute benevolence. "Tracht gut vat zein good/think good and it will be good" does not mean visualizing personal goals or rewards, but rather ruminating to the point of complete internalization on the truth of God's utter goodness and oneness. It is living with the constant awareness that every single thing that one experiences is simply another expression of Godliness. When one "tracht gut/thinks good" in this way, then it will necessarily "zein gut/be good" because s/he will have broken through all of the barriers that conceal the face of God within her/him and around her/him. The darkness that conceals the light will give way, and there will only be radiance and warmth and peace. This is the equanimi-ty that we can achieve when we recognize the "Pnei Hashem/face of God" in our "pnimyus/inner core." This is the power that each of us possesses to remake our reality and transform the universe.

Radiating Love

We began this chapter with the assertion that the recognition of the face of God within us could, and must, change our lives completely. The first shift, we noted, will be a revolution in the way we perceive our-selves as we move from guilt and self-recrimination to dignity and self-sympathy. From here, we begin to experience peace and fearlessness. Releasing our hold on the limited versions of ourselves and our world that we have previously clung to, we become acquainted with the trans-formative power of equanimity. With it, we are able to not only accept our reality, but to embrace it, and ultimately to shape it and actively par-ticipate in the process of "tikkun/transformation" for which we were created. Yet beyond all of these seismic life-shifts which we have ex-plored throughout this chapter so far, there is an even greater revolution that occurs.

As one allows her/his Godliness to be manifest, there begins to well within her/him something even more ineffable, overwhelming, and phenomenal than self-acceptance, contentment, and peace. S/he begins to experience an extraordinary synergy and affinity with everything s/he encounters. Where there was once a pervasive air of separateness and alienation, one now begins to feel a stunning sense of belonging, empathy, and intimacy as s/he recognizes that the essence within her/him is identical with the essence of everything around her/him. With the revelation of the "Pnei Hashem/face of God" in one's "pnimyus/inner core," one will suddenly access a rapturous sensation of love that is unlike anything s/he has experienced before.

Love is the most powerful force in the universe. It is also, perhaps, the most misunderstood. It is desired by all, and apprehended by few. It is abundantly available, but it is tragically lacking in the lives of so many. The concept of love has been so distorted and misrepresented that we don't have any idea how to find it or hold onto it. It slips through our fingers though it is right there in our grasp. We have become so confused about what love is that as we struggle to attain it, earn it, or fall into it, we don't realize that it is, and always has been, nestled in our core. Love is not something to be found or to receive. It is entrusted to us at our creation. It is the essence of what we are, and it is waiting to be tapped, released, and shared.

This reality is expressed in the Hebrew word for love, "ahava," the root of which is "hav," which means "to give." From this derivation, we glean a profound insight about the nature of true love. It is not simply a yearning we have for those to whom we are attracted, or an affection for those from whom we have received kindness or other benefits. Love, in the Torah's sense of the word, is an intrinsic desire to give to an other. This jibes with the concept of God's love that we have discussed repeatedly. He created the world because He desired to give - "it is the nature of the good to do good."[69] He gives to His creations because He loves, and He loves His creations because we enable Him to express His giving nature. His creations, in turn, desire to give. The more in touch we are with the Godliness within us, the more we yearn to express our giving nature.

In addition to the comprehension of a term that is reflected by its etymology, the Hebrew language provides additional insight to a term's meaning from its *numerology*. Referred to as "gematria" in Hebrew, the numeric value of Hebrew words is based on the fact that each letter of the aleph-bet is also a number. The first letter, "א/aleph," is one, the second letter, "ב/beis," is two, and so on. The tenth letter "י/yud," is ten,

---

[69] See chapter two, section "Good Nature"

and then each of the subsequent eight letters represent multiples of ten - the eleventh letter, "כ/chof," is twenty; the twelfth letter, "ל/lamed," is thirty etc. The nineteenth letter, "ק/kuf," is 100, and then the subsequent and final three letters represent hundreds, so that the twenty-second and last letter, "ת/tav," is 400. Based on the numeric value of words, which are determined by tallying the values of their letters, we can find correspondences with other terms of equal value, and thereby deduce additional meaning and relevance.

The letters of the word "אַהֲבָה/ahava/love" equal the number thirteen: "א/aleph/1" + "ה/hei/5" + "ב/beis/2" + "ה/hei/5" = 13. Thirteen is also the value of the word "אֶחָד/echad," which means "one": "א/aleph/1" + "ח/chet/8" + "ד/daled/4" = 13. The "gematria/numerology" of terms is a more hidden and esoteric expression of its meaning, and from the numerical equivalence of terms we can learn their deeper implication. The parity of the terms "ahava/love" and "echad/one" inform us that love, at its essence, is a unity that eliminates all distinction between lover and beloved. The profound secret is not that we become one with that which we love, but that we love those things with which we are inherently one. In other words, true love does not cause unification, it is rather a result of the fact that we are already and always united. When we recognize God's absolute oneness and our consequent unity with all things, an adoration for every aspect of our reality wells and radiates from within us.

This explains one of the Torah's most well-known, but least comprehended, verses:

> You shall love your fellow as yourself.
> (Leviticus 19:18)

So fundamental is this verse that it has been identified by Rabbi Akiva, one of the most renowned Torah sages, as the "all-inclusive principle of Torah."[70] Beyond Jewish tradition, this concept has been referred to as "the golden rule," an ethic of kindness and empathy which urges generosity of spirit. It is said that every major religion or philosophy contains some version of the golden rule. But while the Torah verse is equat-

---

[70] "Klal gadol baTorah." Torat Kohamim 19:45

ed with similarly themed statements in other traditions, these comparisons fail to identify nuances which differentiate the Torah's specific language and which reveal an additional layer of meaning that provides us not only ethical guidance, but also a profound mystic truth.

The ancient Greek admonition "Do not do to others that which angers you when they do it to you;"[71] the Christian "Do unto others as you would have them do unto you;"[72] the Hindu "One should never do that to another which one regards as injurious to one's own self;"[73] and the Muslim "As you would have people do to you, do to them; and what you dislike to be done to you, don't do to them"[74] - all of these bear thematic similarities to the Torah's verse from Leviticus. However, they are more similar to a line from the Talmud in which Hillel the Elder responds to a man who asks him to teach him the whole Torah while standing on one foot:

> That which is hateful to you, do not do to your fellow.
> That is the whole Torah; the rest is the commentary; go
> and learn.
> (Talmud, Shabbat, 31a)

The statement from Leviticus - "you shall love your fellow as yourself" - differs from all of these in that a) it refers specifically to "love," which they do not, and b) it is a commandment, not a maxim or even an ethical advisory. This raises two obvious questions: First, how can one be commanded to love? While it is understood that actions can be legislated - for example, treat others, or do not treat others, in such and such a way - it is difficult to comprehend how an emotion like love can be mandated. Secondly, how is it possible to fulfill such a commandment? Can one truly love another as much as one loves her/himself?

---

[71] Isocrates

[72] Matthew 7:12

[73] Mahabharata Book 13

[74] (Kitab al-Kafi, vol. 2, p. 146)

One who takes these questions seriously must conclude that "love your fellow as yourself" is more than a simple directive. As the Chassidic sages point out frequently, the word "torah" is derived from the term "horaah," which means learning or instruction. Though Torah is often viewed primarily as a book of law, it is in fact an instrument of development and connection. Therefore, it is not only impossible that the Torah would issue an edict that we would be unable to fulfill, but additionally, as a book of instruction, the Torah would not require us to do something without providing insight into how that requirement can be satisfied. "Love your fellow as yourself," therefore, is not merely commanding us to love, but it is furthermore revealing the deep secret of love's nature and essence. The verse tells us not only *that* we should love our fellow, but also *why* we should do so and *how* we can do so.

Why should one "love your fellow" - because s/he is "as yourself." How can one "love your fellow" - by recognizing that s/he is "as yourself." The key here, and the key to love in general, is to understand that "as yourself" in this verse does not merely mean 'similar to you,' or even 'identical to you,' but also 'one with you.' On the simple level, the verse may be exhorting us to love others because they are just as desirous, or deserving, of love as we are. On a somewhat deeper level, it is encouraging us to love others just as generously and forgivingly as we love ourselves. But on its deepest level, the verse is instructing us that it is possible to *truly* love an other only when we recognize that that other is not simply *like* ourself, but that s/he is veritably the same as oneself because in essence we are one!

Just as our ultimate self is nothing but Godliness, so too, our fellow is only Godliness as well. "Ahava/love," as we have explained previously, is equivalent to "echad/one." When we recognize that the other is truly one and the same as myself, then love will arise effortlessly. It is not difficult to love another as oneself when we identify that the other is undifferentiated from oneself. In fact, this is the only way to achieve love in its most true and ultimate sense. We can desire an other. We can sympathize and empathize with an other. We can even give altruistically to an other. But the Torah is teaching us that *we can only truly love, in the most profound and divine sense of the term, when we understand that the other is not in fact an other at all.*

The commandment of "love your fellow as yourself," therefore, is not compelling an emotion, for you cannot demand one to *feel* a certain way. It is rather obligating us to meditate on the reality of our unity and to cultivate this awareness so that love will arise naturally and constantly. This is one of the primary functions of prayer. We have discussed previously that the Torah's concept of prayer is not merely requesting our needs from God, but rather reconnecting with Him through deeply contemplating our essential Godly nature. This contemplation similarly enables us to reconnect with one another and with the entire creation when we meditate on God's oneness and the inter-inclusion of all things. It is for this reason that the daily prayer service begins with the very verse that we have been discussing. After the morning blessings, at the very opening of the morning service, there is a line in the prayer book that reads:

> It is proper to say before prayer: I hereby accept upon myself the positive commandment of 'you shall love your fellow as yourself.'
>   (Siddur Tehillat Hashem, p.12)

As one commences the morning prayer, which is to set the tone for everything s/he will do throughout the coming day, one is instructed to meditate on this verse and to accept it upon ourself. Why this particular verse? It is certainly an important commandment, and it is, as Rabbi Akiva declared, an "all-encompassing principle of Torah." But this is not a time of learning Torah, it is a time of prayer. What does this verse have to do with prayer, and why is it established as the very first line of the prayers? It is so because the essence of prayer is moving inward to find the "Pnei Hashem/face of God" within our "pnimyus/inner core," and recognizing that this Godly face is likewise within the "pnimyus" of everything that we will encounter in the day ahead. With this, love will surge from our depths and will radiate from us to embrace and enflame all of those around us.

One Voice

Prayer, according to Torah's conception, is thus our opportunity to remind ourselves of what we ultimately are, to find the infinite Godliness that is hidden in our essence, and to allow it to suffuse us and emanate outward. With this, we will understand another powerful, but often overlooked, nuance of the daily prayer service. Just prior to beginning the standing silent prayer ("amida") that is the culmination of each of the three daily services, one is instructed to utter under her/his breath the following words:

> Lord open my lips and let me declare **Your praise**.
> (Siddur Tehillat Hashem, p.50)

On the simple level, this phrase is a request to God to assist us with our prayers. On a deeper level, it is an acknowledgement that it is not we who open our lips, but rather it is God who provides us the ability to do so, just as every capability we have is from Him and in His hands. On an even more esoteric plane, it is an expression of the profound awareness that the words that one is about to speak are actually *God's* words - "*Your* praise" - which He communicates through our lips. We are not simply asking for the ability to praise Him; we are inviting Him to express the praises that He wants to offer through our vocal chords. While "Your praise" is simply understood as 'praise *of* You,' it can also be interpreted as the 'praise that You express.' As we discussed earlier,[75] God does not need our praises. The word "tehilla/praise" is from the root "hil" which means to light or ignite, as in the phrase "be-HILo nero/He lit his candle."[76] When God expresses praise, therefore, He is illuminating the darkness with His light. When we allow Him to open our lips and vocalize *His* praise through our mouth, we are participating in the process of enlightenment and revelation for which He created us. The ultimate meaning of this verse then is that we are asking God to let us be the vessel for the message and the light that He desires to deliver into His creation. Let me be conscious of the fact that this is all

[75] Chapter three, section "Halleluy-ah"

[76] Job 29:3

that I am. Let me align myself with Your will so that You can flow through me without obstruction or resistance.

This understanding will lead to the awareness that the God that moves through me is the very same God that moves through everyone else. There is only one voice, but it is intoned through many throats. There is only one wind, but it blows through many vessels. We are all instruments plied by the same hand, and played with the same breath. We are the same stuff, expressed through various forms. We are one soul that has been temporarily divided into "pieces" and dressed in different clothes.[77] In our deepest essence, there is no distinction between us - we are "echad/One."

Imagine how different life would be if we lived with this awareness; if we could transcend our limited perspective of me and you and understand that you are only another manifestation of what has manifested in me as me. This has been described as water that has been poured into different containers, or light that shines through different shades of glass. Though it is the same water or the same light, it appears and exhibits differently depending on that which contains or conveys it. If we can understand each other this way, then would it not be foolish to resent one another, or envy one another, or harm one another? We would only be hating or hurting ourself. It would be as if one accidentally smashes his finger while hammering a nail, and then grabs the hammer with the injured hand and smashes the hand which held the hammer first.

Each of us often does things that are imperfect. Sometimes we berate or hate ourselves for doing so, but we generally forgive ourselves or at least make excuses for our errors. When we understand that the other is our same self expressed in a different vessel, then we will similarly grant that other the benefit of finding reasons for her/his actions. Think of the person that you like least in the world, someone with whom you have had an ongoing feud or who is currently making your life difficult. Now put yourself in her/his shoes, literally. Imagine that it is you in that body, the very same you that is in your body, but with a completely different set of traits and experiences. How did you become you and s/he become her/him? Is there a different soul in each of you, or is there simply a different framework for precisely the same soul?

---

[77] See chapter two, section "Good Nature" where this analogy was explained.

Is it possible that the identical essence, placed in a vastly different context and environment, could produce such distinct and conflicting individuals? It is not only possible, it is precisely what has happened! If we trace us both back to our beginning, prior to our lifetime of experiences and challenges, there is no difference. If we peel back the surface, all the way down to the life force that vivifies and animates us, we will find absolutely no distinction. It is the same face of God within each of us.

When I see the me in you and the you in me, I cannot hate you. I can only love. As the superficial and temporal exterior falls away, all of my anger melts away, and I see only what unites us rather than all of the surface elements that divide us. Being Godly thus begins with seeing God within all of us and within everything. This is what the mystics see, and this is what each of us will see when we hone our vision. Everything opens, all of the veils fall away, and our world is suddenly filled with great light. When we come to the awareness that we are all limbs of a single being, our feelings of resentment, competition, and antagonism fade away. What remains is a remarkable sense of consonance, harmony, and love that will radiate from us and ignite all of those with whom we come in contact.

Acting Like God

Throughout this chapter, we have discussed the various ways that one's life will transform when s/he recognizes the face of God within her/him. S/he will find self-respect and peace. S/he will recognize the good in all things. S/he will feel and exude tremendous love. But the ultimate outcome of recognizing one's Godliness is more than experiencing positive emotions. It is becoming Godly. By this, we do not mean acquiring power or obtaining all of one's needs or desires (though this all becomes possible, as we have discussed). Being Godly in this sense is a matter of becoming a truly positive and productive force in the universe. It is dwelling constantly in a divine consciousness which perceives the underlying harmony and resonance of all things. It is shaping and refining reality instead of being shaped and confined by it. When we realize that we are Godly, we will act Godly. This means that we will allow our highest nature to become our daily conduct.

This shift will indeed change everything if we allow it. It will not be a sudden and instant transformation, but with the constant awareness of our Godly essence, we can begin to infuse every decision and reaction with the patience, clarity, and generosity that characterizes the Godly perspective. Rather than responding to daily circumstances from the limited, vulnerable, and self-protective attitude of a "merely human" individual being, we will remind ourself that we are not small and powerless. We are rather a vessel for God's expression, and we need not be afraid and self-concerned. As soon as we begin to feel reactivity welling within us, we will learn to pause and to consider how God would act in such a situation. Though the tension and stressors of life may not abate, we will become habituated with breathing deeply and reminding ourself that God is in there, and that we can let Him out, so to speak. Don't keep Him hidden and unexpressed, we will whisper inwardly. Don't mistake yourself for the frail and needy organic matter that conceals your essence. Don't let that guide you and roil you and destabilize you. Rather be what you ultimately are. Let your Godly soul pervade you, steady you, and project through you.

In this way, we will become exceedingly giving and forgiving. We will find ourselves willing to give and forgive far beyond what we previously considered comfortable. We will constantly transcend our "normal" human tendency to be strict and exacting. Even when we are wronged and outrage is justifiable, we will overcome justice with kindness, as God does. Just as we ask Him to continually forgive us, so we will continually forgive others. Is this superhuman? Perhaps. Is it more than should be expected of us? No, because we *are* superhuman. We are Godly. We can choose to ignore or suppress our essence and be "only human," but we will choose rather to express our Godly reality.[78] When

---

[78] To be clear, this does not mean that we will allow others to trample on us or violate our dignity. Generosity and forgiveness do not mean self-neglect or being permissive of abuse. They mean the transcendence of ego. We can, and must, distinguish between being insulted or offended and truly harmed. If it is only our ego that is being bruised, we can tolerate this because we have let our ego go. Yet we will not tolerate danger or abuse. Being Godly is not being naive or sacrificing our dignity. It is knowing our true value and worth and letting unimportant things pass through us.

we choose to do so, the world will not buffet us. We will disarm all triggers, and we will no longer be prone to all of the provocations that have traditionally set us off. All of the many stimuli that used to infuriate us will no longer have any effect. We are even. Our breath is a constant and steady flow. Nothing can harry us or disturb our rhythm. We remain centered, which means that we are constantly conscious of what exists in our center and the center of all things.

With such an attitude, even small things begin to take on meaning and value. Every moment is precious, because it is a Godly moment, an opportunity for us to express our Godliness. Every action is carried out with intentionality and dignity - not only "important" or public activities, but even private and ordinary things like the way we eat, the way we speak, the way we dress. There is nothing mundane because it is all Godly, and therefore holy. We begin to appreciate and savor everything. No longer a hamster wheel of banal and meaningless moments, life becomes a series of sacred encounters. The taste and texture of this food on my tongue; this chance and momentary interaction with a stranger on the bus; the dance of leaves in the wind. When we come to see all of these as a reflection of God and an element of the same holistic unity of which we are a part, life then becomes a constant meditation. We begin to move more carefully and deliberately, considering each step and each outcome. We treat nothing as if it is extraneous. We value each person, and we make it our business to help her/him recognize the dignity within her/him as well. Suddenly, each interaction has a purpose and a meaning. If we don't perceive it, then we pause to find it. Why am I in this particular situation now? What is awaiting me in this moment that I am here to extract and beautify? Each experience offers tremendous significance and worth, and we approach every moment as an opportunity, a mission, and a gift.

We may know few people who truly live this way, but we have all heard stories of those rare individuals who exude an almost otherworldly aura of peace and generosity and wisdom. They are often humble servants who are not seeking notoriety or power. Yet on account of their rare insight and dignity, there have gathered around them those who seek their guidance and crave their leadership. In spite of their formidable influence and their ability to lead legions and move mountains, they are gentle and sensitive. They speak quietly, displaying remarkable patience, and espousing empathy and nonviolence even in the face of brutal opposition. This is because they do not confuse force with power. They know that the most potent energy in the universe is love, and that the most effective means of achieving one's goals is through peace and union rather than conflict and compulsion. Therefore, they have no need to demonstrate their strength, because they are confident that if they simply allow their Godliness to radiate, it will stimulate the Godliness of those around them.

These remarkable people are referred to as "tzadikkim," or "saints," or even "angels," but they are human like the rest of us, and they are not as distant or different from us as we may believe. The distinction is that they can see the Godliness within them and around them, and therefore, they radiate clarity, love, and acceptance. They provide a beam of light in the darkness, and people flock to them because we are all attracted to light. Each of us is capable of similarly discovering our essence and unmasking it. It is not only the few or the select who have the potential to manifest their divine reality. Every one of us has this potential, and therefore every one of us has the responsibility to do so. This is our life goal and our assigned task.

We "reveal God in the heavens and the earth" when we unleash the Godliness that is embedded within us. We are all "saints." We are all God's agents and emissaries in the truest sense of the terms, because we are all fragments of God which He has disseminated throughout His creation. The question for each of us is not "am I truly Godly," but rather "am I expressing my Godliness?" Am I revealing it or concealing it? Is the "Pnei Hashem" broadcasting and irradiating through me, or is it obscured by all of the garments and barriers that I have imposed over it? If I am wracked with self-doubt, disharmony, and enmity; if I am reactive and I find myself battling life rather than embracing it, then I have not yet fully accessed or released the Godly essence that animates me and awaits me. When I am able to do so, I will begin to experience all of the sublime transformations that we have discussed throughout this chapter.

Chapter 7: PRACTICE

Liberation Practice

We are far enough along our journey now to know where we want to go and why we want to go there. We are traveling inward to discover the infinite truth of God - His "panim/face" - that is hidden within our "pnimyus/inner core." We do so because that is our mission - "lech lecha/go to yourself" and "bara Elokim/reveal God" - and also because, as we have discussed at length in the previous chapter, the awareness of our inherent Godliness transforms our lives completely and brings us profound joy, peace, and love. The question for us at this point is "how."

We began our journey with the question "where are you?" We then moved on to "how are you?" We now continue with "how *can* you?" How will you be able to continue onward and penetrate the many veils and impediments that block your inward progress? A consciousness of our goal, direction, and potential is a valuable first step. An understanding of the barriers that we have erected and a desire to remove them will aid us on our path. Awareness of God's unbounded love for us and of the infinite and reciprocal love that wells within us will inspire us with enthusiasm and tenacity. But the obstructions are thick and persistent. They will not vanish simply because we want them to. Furthermore, they regenerate quickly from one moment to the next on account of the coarseness and darkness of the world we inhabit. Therefore, even if we are able to succeed in making meaningful progress beyond our limitations today, we may find ourselves right back where we started tomorrow.

Fortunately, Torah provides a holistic and integrative practice that enables one to remove the barriers consistently and cumulatively. This, in fact, is the very goal and essence of Torah. Recognizing that the blockages that we have erected are the root of all of our confusion and misdirection because they conceal our essential Godly reality, Torah offers a systematic approach to the identification and elimination of these boundaries in every aspect of our lives. This approach combines both consciousness and action, both awareness of the nature of our current reality and practical procedures that will enable us to transcend and transform it. *Torah practice is, in essence, a series and system of rituals and reminders to keep us conscious of what we truly are - pure Godliness - and to help us remove the darkness and crust that conceals this truth.*

To understand Torah properly, we must recognize that it is simultaneously a work of philosophy and a book of law. What Torah imparts to us is not only profound ideas and insights which plumb the very depths of our existence, but also detailed directions on how to apply its wisdom and manifest its truths in a realm where they are concealed. Throughout Torah, six hundred and thirteen "mitzvos/commandments" are legislated which provide detailed guidelines of conduct for every aspect of one's life. The Torah lifestyle is thus highly regimented and minutely regulated. From a superficial perspective, the many "mitzvos," along with the many more customs and behaviors that Torah observance promotes may be viewed as excessive or even oppressive. However, we will come to understand that every one of the many rituals and regimens that are mandated by the Torah are elements of an intricate **liberation practice**. Each of these picayune details and behaviors are mechanisms through which the practitioner can peel away another layer of darkness and dismantle the fortifications that block her/his inward progress. This vital work is not relegated to particular periods of each day, certain days of each week, or special observances each year. It is the purpose of every moment of life, and therefore it is a discipline that one engages in constantly. Through this practice, one infuses consciousness of her/his mission and potential into every mundane activity, whether it is the way s/he dresses, the way s/he eats, sleeps, bathes, conducts business, interacts socially and interpersonally, etc.

Many spiritual systems concern themselves primarily with consciousness, i.e. the focusing of one's thought on the nature of her/his existence through meditation and retreat from the hustle and bustle of daily life. Torah practice, on the contrary, intends to instill that consciousness into every action and into a complete engagement with the world rather than a removal from it. The question, of course, is whether one will infuse the Torah's many actions, rituals, and practices with the mindfulness that will provide them their power to transcend and transform one's reality, or whether s/he will simply go through the motions. In the latter case, the mitzvos are reduced to a series of restrictions rather than a system of liberation. The mindfulness that is meant to underlie every mitzvah is called "kavana/intention." Though one can fulfill a mitzvah without the proper "kavana/intention," in doing so s/he has not exploited its full potential, nor has s/he performed it as it was intended by God to be a tool for our emancipation. Without "kavana/intention," each mitzvah is like a body without a soul, or a shell that is lacking its contents. With the proper "kavana," however, the Torah's directives will enable us to open and to connect to our innermost dimensions. The most basic "kavana" for each mitzvah is thus that it is an exercise which God has provided us to train us in the process of opening and moving beneath and beyond the surface. With this general consciousness in mind, we can then explore each aspect of Torah practice to understand how it contributes more specifically to that project and mission.

Torah's liberation practice includes a) a system of routine mitzvos that are to be performed throughout the course of each day, b) calendrical observances that mark the weekly, monthly, and yearly phases, as well as c) milestone rituals that span the duration of the entire life-cycle. One is thus provided opportunities to open and delve inward each day, each week, each month, each year, and throughout the complete term of her/his life. For the purposes of our introduction to these concepts, we will focus in this volume on the lifecycle events, which will give us an overview of Torah's lifelong approach to the process of opening and revelation. We will find that each of the observances that mark the birth, development, and major transitional periods of the soul's journey in this world are focused very clearly on this theme of removing the veils that cover our core and expressing the Godliness that is hidden within.[79]

Bris Milah

The very first ritual that a male engages in after birth is "Bris Milah," or circumcision, which is the removal of the foreskin that covers the head of the male reproductive organ. It is no coincidence that the lifecycle begins with an action that is so clearly and graphically connected to this concept of opening and uncovering. Birth itself is an act of incarnation, which literally means to infuse and contain something within a covering of flesh, and from this moment on, every aspect of life is part of the process of revealing what has been enclosed and enclothed inside the body. For this reason, we begin life with the removal of flesh in order to signify that this new being will be devoted throughout his time in this world to this sacred process of uncovering his inner essence, just as his forebears have been before him. Throughout his life, he will bear the sign of the covenant on his body, and in particular on his sexual organ, in order to remind him that it is not the world of the flesh that is most important, but rather what lies beneath it.

While circumcision is practiced throughout much of the modern world for hygienic reasons, the Torah ritual focuses more on one's spiritual integrity and well-being than his physical health. For this reason, the practice is not referred to in Torah simply as "milah," which means 'circumcision,' but rather as "bris milah," which means "*covenant* of circumcision." A "bris/covenant" in Torah is something that transcends all con-

---

[79] A detailed exploration of the other aspects of Torah's liberation practice - ie. the daily mitzvos, as well as the weekly, monthly, and yearly calendrical observances - is included in our more comprehensive book, *Pnei Hashem*. See Postscript.

siderations and conditions. It is not a simple agreement or contract that can change based on fluctuating circumstances. It is a bond that is entered into which is unbreakable and everlasting. It transcends the vicissitudes of time or fortune or mood. Parties enter into a "bris/covenant" when they wish to signify the eternality and essentiality of their relationship. This is the implication of this ritual at the very beginning of life - it conveys that while the lifespan in this casing will be finite, and while the body will change and eventually fail, that which is beneath the flesh is infinite and immortal. While the bond between the soul and God may be hidden temporarily, it will never be broken. No skin, no matter how thick, can ultimately interpose between the soul and its source. They will always be united even if they are seemingly divided.

This unity and immutability, which is reflected in the word "bris/covenant," is also expressed in the fact that circumcision, according to Torah, is not to be performed immediately at birth, but on the eighth day:

> And at the age of eight days, every male shall be circumcised.
> (Genesis 17:12)

The number eight represents the supernatural realm, which is the realm beyond nature, or the divine. Seven denotes the natural order - as evidenced from the fact that there were seven days of creation and correspondingly seven days in a week, earth has seven continents and seven seas, there are seven colors in the rainbow, etc. Eight is that level which is higher than nature. By performing circumcision on the eighth day, one acknowledges that the "bris/covenant" is not subject to the limits and laws of the natural world that the soul has now entered. One cuts away a layer of skin to indicate the impermanence of the flesh and, as we stated above, to begin the lifelong process of exposing the essence that lies beneath it.

The term "circumcision" is not employed in the Torah only in reference to the removal of the foreskin of the male reproductive organ. It is mentioned also to refer to a concept known as the "circumcision of the heart." In Deuteronomy, God instructs Moses to command the nation:

You shall circumcise the foreskin of your heart.
(Deuteronomy 10:16)

Later in the book, Moses repeats the phrase:

> And the Lord, your God, will circumcise your heart and
> the heart of your offspring, [so that you may] love the
> Lord your God with all your heart and with all your
> soul.
(Deuteronomy 30:6)

The sages explain that the circumcision of the male foreskin and the circumcision of the heart are two components of the same mitzvah. As we explained in the last section, every mitzvah has two dimensions - the physical action and the spiritual intention, or "kavana." The "circumcision of the heart" is the inner dimension of the act of "bris milah." The spark of God, which is the innermost point of our soul,[80] is contained within our heart, so to speak.[81] But the heart is closed, and the spark is thus concealed within. Throughout our lives, we must therefore work to circumcise the heart, to remove the "flesh" that encloses the spark in order to allow it to become manifest.

The Alter Rebbe takes this concept one step further. He explains that the Torah's two references to the circumcision of the heart refer to two different stages of circumcision. In the physical circumcision of the male organ, there are two layers that must be removed. The first is the thick foreskin, and the second is a thin membrane that adheres to the glans. In both ritual circumcision and medical circumcision, both of these coverings are removed. In ritual circumcision, if the foreskin is excised but the membrane is left in tact, then the "bris milah" is not deemed kosher and the child is not considered to be circumcised. The Alter Rebbe relates these two physical layers to two stages in our spiritual development. First, we must eliminate the coarse and obvious impediments that hinder the expression of our Godly essence. Afterwards, we must seek

---

[80] As discussed in chapter three, section "The Face Within You"

[81] We are speaking here not of the physical organ of the heart, but the spiritual concept of the heart as the core of our being.

and peel away the subtle blockages that garb and inhibit our soul like a thin and almost imperceptible membrane.

Significantly, the Alter Rebbe points out, the first reference to the circumcision of the heart states "**You** shall circumcise the foreskin of your heart," while the second indicates that "**the Lord, your God,** will circumcise your heart." From this distinction, he explains that our task is to work diligently throughout our lives to eradicate the thick foreskin, i.e. the daily challenges that suppress our spiritual growth and expression. When we do so, God will then respond to our efforts at self-refinement by assisting us in dissolving the more subtle forces which are difficult for us to perceive and uproot.[82]

It is important to note that the circumcision of the heart is as applicable to females as it is to males. If so, then why is it that females do not require the physical act of circumcision? This is not because they lack the male reproductive organ, but on the contrary - the fact that they do not have a male organ is because they are not in need of physical circumcision. The male is more directed to the external, physical, and superficial - this is reflected by his sexual organ which protrudes from his body and extends to the outside. The female is born with a greater connection to the interior and less susceptibility to becoming mired in the coarseness of the material world around her. Her sexual organ is within her, and through the intimate union, she draws even the male externality inward.

We can see the greater spiritual sensitivity of the female in the relationship of Abraham and his wife Sarah. When Abraham is instructed by Sarah to send away his son, Ishmael, who was attempting to harm his brother Isaac, Abraham objects. However, God instructed Abraham:

> Whatever your wife Sarah tells you, listen to her voice.
> (Genesis 21:12)

The sages note from here that Sarah was greater than Abraham in prophecy, and that women possess a spiritual sense that men do not. Because of their inherent natures, the male is in need of circumcision and the female is not. Nevertheless, the "helam/hiddenness" of our "olam/world" affects even the more spiritually attuned female. Although she does not require the "bris milah" at the outset of her life in this world,

---

[82] Torah Or, Lech Lecha, B'etzem Hayom Hazeh Nimol Avraham

she is charged with the circumcision of the heart, and she, too, will spend her life working to peel back the layers of concealment that cover the face of God within her.

———◆———

Shearing And Shining

Like circumcision, the subsequent major life-cycle rituals designated by Torah mark significant phases in the development of the soul's relationship to this world and its embodiment and expression within the physical realm. Birth, as we mentioned, is the induction of the soul into a corporeal form. But Torah teaches that this coupling of the body and soul is not a single event. It is rather a process that plays out throughout the span of several decades, and in some ways, throughout one's entire life.

The soul, according to Torah, is a completely singular entity, as we have discussed previously. But as it descends into this world of multiplicity, it takes on various dimensions and becomes a compound of a variety of parts. As we mentioned in chapter three,[83] there are a number of different names for the soul in Hebrew - "nefesh," "ruach," "neshama," "chaya," and "yechida" - and these refer to various levels and functions. Additionally, it is taught that each being is comprised of two different soul components, the "nefesh Elokis/Godly soul," and the "nefesh habehamis/animal soul." The animal soul is also referred to as the "the vitalizing soul," and it is the force within us that makes us live and drives us to perpetuate our existence within this physical world. It therefore includes our impetus to eat, to procreate, to protect ourselves, and all of the other natural instincts that are common to all forms of sentient life. The Godly soul, on the contrary, is unconcerned with physicality and self-preservation on an ego level. It is focused on the spiritual reality that exists beneath and beyond the physical. It exists before and after the soul's connection to this particular body.

As we mentioned briefly in the previous chapter, the Alter Rebbe describes life as a constant battle between these two aspects of our soul. They are like two rival armies, he teaches, which are fighting for control

---

[83] Section "The Face Within You"

over a city. The city, and thus the prize, is our body and being within this world. If the divine soul is victorious, then our body will perform Godly actions and engage in activities that promote a revelation of Godliness within the world. If our animal soul conquers the city, on the other hand, then our body will be utilized for the pursuit of its more base and animalistic urges and tendencies. This battle rages constantly for most of us, and the tides of war are constantly turning. Sometimes the Godly soul gains control of the city, and at other times the animal soul surges and takes over.

In context of the human lifespan and the Torah's rituals that mark the major life-cycle events, it is essential to understand that these two aspects of our soul do not introduce themselves into our body at the same time or at the same pace. The animal soul arrives within the person from the moment of birth. Without it, one could not live. It is like the electricity that turns a machine on and enables it to function. The Godly soul, however, does not reside within us immediately. This is evident from the actions and behaviors of an infant, which do not differ significantly from other newborn species. It eats, it sleeps, it excretes waste. It pursues its desires and instincts and does not display any complex intellect or morality. The Godly soul begins to introduce itself into the person later, and its investment is gradual. Unlike the animal soul, it does not enter all at once, but it takes many years from the time it begins to present itself to the time it is fully incorporated. Just as we saw earlier,[84] light comes after darkness - "it was evening and it was morning."[85] First the stage is set, with all of its limitations and concealment. Then the light emerges from the darkness to reveal itself with blinding brightness in comparison to what preceded it.

The life-cycle events that the Torah marks with special rituals correspond to the various stages in the Godly soul's infusion and embodiment. The "bris milah/circumcision" on the eighth day is the moment when the Godly soul begins its entry into the child. While the first seven days represent the natural world, as we explained above, the eighth day activates the supernatural aspect of existence. It is therefore at this point that the Godly soul initiates its affiliation with the physical realm. The

---

[84] Chapter 2, section "Night And Then Day"

[85] Genesis 1:5

removal of flesh at this point, in addition to all that we stated above, can signify the weakening of the animal force as its rival enters the fray and the battle for control of the "city" begins.

The next life-cycle ritual is when the child reaches the age of three. For the boy, the third birthday is marked by an event called the "upsherin," which is yiddish for "shearing" because on this day, the child is given his first haircut. A girl's third birthday marks the beginning of her lighting of the shabbat candles every Friday before sundown. Both of these practices represent a new phase in the life of the child and her/his induction into the rituals of Torah observance. By this time, there has been an investiture of the Godly soul that enables the child to begin to express it through the performance of divine physical actions, or mitzvos. The girl's lighting of candles is an explicit demonstration of her ability (and therefore her concomitant responsibility) to begin to transform the darkness around her. For the boy, the cutting of his hair is, like the "bris milah/circumcision," another physical symbol of the work he will have to do throughout his life to remove the coverings that continually grow over him to conceal his core. While the majority of the hair on his head is cut short, the "peyot," or earlocks, are left slightly longer (or significantly longer in some sects), and additionally, he begins to wear a "yarmulke/head covering" and "tzitzis/ritual fringes" full time. All of these practices are reminders that even as we shear away the barriers, there remain coverings which we must be conscious of constantly if we are to fulfill our worldly mission.

Taken together, the rituals of "upsherin" and candle lighting represent the work that we have been discussing and which each of us is tasked with throughout our lives: to remove the superficial layers and to reveal the Godly light that radiates from within. As we will soon see, the efforts of the male and female will eventually fuse in order that they will provide each other assistance in that life work. But before we can achieve the fusion of the male and female in the ritual of marriage, there must first be the completion of the investment of the Godly soul in each of them individually.

Bar/Bat Mitzvah

It takes over a decade for the Godly soul to become fully incorporated in the body. To be more precise, it is a twelve year process for a girl and a thirteen year process for a boy. It is at this point, on the girl's twelfth birthday and the boy's thirteenth, that the "bar/bat mitzvah" is celebrated and one transitions from the Torah's definition of childhood to adulthood. A child in this sense is one who is not fully invested with its Godly soul, and adulthood is reached at the moment that the Godly soul completes its embodiment. Until now, the animal soul has maintained its advantage. But now the Godly soul culminates the process that it had begun at the "bris milah/circumcision" for the boy and at birth for the girl. "Bar mitzvah" literally means "son of mitzvah", and "bat mitzvah" means "daughter of mitzvah." "Mitzvah," means "commandment," and one who reaches the age of bar or bat mitzvah is now a son or daughter of the commandments. What does this mean, and why is this happening now?

On the simple level of "pshat," the "bar/bat mitzvah" is the moment when the new "adult" becomes liable for the fulfillment of the commandments. Prior to that time, s/he was a child, too young, immature, and inexperienced to bear the responsibility for the mitzvos and the culpability for their violation. Throughout the past decade, it has been the parents' responsibility to teach the child how to perform the mitzvos properly. Now the training wheels are removed, so to speak, and the young adult is deemed mature enough to take responsibility for her/his actions.

On a deeper level, we understand that it is not simply time and practice which have brought one to this new status. If that were the case, then there would be those children who, through either their inherent refinement or their diligence and/or the diligence of their parents, would be ready to reach this level of preparedness before they arrive at this age. Conversely, there would be those whose immaturity could persist for years beyond their twelfth or thirteenth birthday. Furthermore, we might expect to find differences in the timing of "bar/bat mitzvah" between those who were raised in homes that were steeped in Torah and those whose families and forebears knew nothing of the Torah's teachings and could therefore not prepare them. Nevertheless, the fact is that the timing of bar/bat mitzvah is not determined by one's knowledge, experience, or maturity, but simply by arriving at the designated age. This is because, as we stated above, there is a spiritual evolution which has now reached a tipping point in the life of this person. S/he is now fully equipped with the ability to counter the animal soul and to express the Godliness that is hidden within. This is facilitated through the fulfillment of the mitzvos, and this is why it is at precisely this moment that one becomes responsible to abide by them.

Mitzvos, as we have discussed,[86] are not simply "commandments," or actions that we are required to fulfill for the sake of some other being who rules over us. They are not labors that we are assigned in order to enrich some master and/or to simply demonstrate our allegiance. They are exercises that we have been provided which enable us to open the pathway inward and connect to our infinite essence. While the word "mitzvah" is indeed derived from the word "tzivui/command," it also relates to the Aramaic "tzavsa/bond." A "bar/bat mitzvah" is therefore not only a 'son/daughter of the commandments,' but a 'son/daughter of the bond.' Understood in this sense, the "bar/bat mitzvah" celebrant is one whose essential bond with God has reached a new level of revelation.

Of course, we are all bound with God from the moment of our creation. "God is one," and there is nothing other than Him. However, at birth, the spark of God that is our soul descended into this realm of concealment and buried itself within a casing of flesh. Our life work, as we have discussed at length, is the revelation of that spark and its unity with all of the other sparks that have likewise embedded and obscured themselves. There are times in our life when our ability to express that unity is augmented. The "bar/bat mitzvah" is the moment that one is now granted the full strength of her/his Godly soul so that s/he can begin to make it manifest. The method through which s/he can do so is the mitzvos - they are the actions that one can perform within this physical world that enable her/him to tear open the camouflage and transform concealment into revelation. Now that one has arrived at the completion of her/his Godly soul's embodiment, s/he is granted the full complement of the mitzvos in order to perform her/his earthly task of transformation and revelation. The "bar/bat mitzvah" can therefore be understood as the

---

[86] Chapter three, section "Inward Bound"

induction of the individual into the ranks of the special corps for which s/he was created, and the moment that s/he is endowed with the treasure chest of riches, resources, and implements with which s/he will pursue and accomplish the mission ahead.

Marriage/Fusion

The soul, we have seen, is comprised of many different components. There are the five levels of the soul - "nefesh," "ruach," "neshama," "chaya," and "yechida" - which refer to various functions and degrees of engagement of the Godly force within the body. There are also the two inclinations of the soul, the "nefesh Elokis/Godly soul" and the "nefesh habehamis/animal soul," which oppose each other and battle constantly for control of the body. Yet all of these pieces together still do not constitute a complete soul. A complete soul, according to the Zohar, is not contained by any one individual. Each person represents a half of a soul, and it is only through marriage that the two halves, which had been separated prior to birth, are reunited. The evolution of the soul that we have been discussing, therefore, is not completed at the stage of "bar/bat mitzvah," though that was the moment when the Godly soul finished its transmission into the body. The "bar/bat mitzvah" marks, on the contrary, a new beginning, the formal commencement of the person's mission and journey. But s/he is still incomplete, and there is another beginning ahead. At marriage, one rejoins the other half of her/his soul in order to embark on the lifework of self-discovery, self-transcendence, and procreation that can only be accomplished in partnership with one's "zivug" or soul-mate.

As we saw earlier, the male and female souls are not identical. They develop differently and they reflect various qualities. When they join, they complement one another and they are able to accomplish far more than either could accomplish individually. We might wonder why God established it this way. Why was each soul unit divided into two and invested in separate bodies only to reunite later? Could God not have left the soul intact and embedded it into a single body that incorporated all of its qualities and potentials? In fact, the Midrash tells us that it was not only possible for God to do so, but this is precisely what He originally did.

> Said Rabbi Yirmiyah ben Elazar: In the hour when the Holy One created the first human, He created him **androgynous**, as it is said, '**male and female He created them**.' Said Rabbi Shmuel bar Nachmani: In the hour when the Holy One created the first human, He created him double-faced and sawed him and made him backs, a back here and a back there.
> (Breishis Rabba, 8:1)

The Midrash here informs us that Adam was not created first followed by Eve's subsequent creation. Adam and Eve were created simultaneously in the form of one being with both genders and two faces or fronts. Subsequently, God split this single being into two, each with its own gender, and its own front and back. This secret is revealed in the very text of the Torah itself, which the Midrash cites:

> Male and female He created them, and He blessed them, and He named them Adam on the day they were created.
> (Genesis 5:2)

The simple reading of this verse from Genesis seems to indicate that God created both male and female beings. But the Midrash reveals that the deeper meaning of the verse is that this was a single being that was created both male and female. "He named *them* Adam," the verse states, indicating that Adam, the first human, was not merely a "him," but rather a "them" that included both genders and all of their various capacities. This condition did not last long however. Soon after the creation of Adam, God separated 'them' into Adam and Eve, him and her, and thereby established two complementary individuals who would partner together.

What is the meaning of all this? Why did God create a single, androgynous being and then cleave it into separate male and female parts? Was His original creation an error?

In the first chapter of this book, we asked a similar question about the other seeming "errors" of our origin story. Did God not know that we would sin and therefore be exiled from His garden? If not, then what does that tell us about His wisdom and His control? If He did know, then why would He have allowed us to sin, setting us up for failure and exiling us with the shame of our 'original sin'? We have answered these questions at length, both in the first chapter[87] and the fifth.[88] As we have explained according to the central Torah doctrine of "hashgacha protis/divine providence," God does not make errors. There is no force that competes with Him, and there is nothing that occurs in the universe that is contrary to His will. Therefore, there is a precise intentionality in every aspect of the process of our creation, and just as there are powerful reasons that we were first created in the garden with diaphanous skin only later to be garbed in opaque flesh and exiled from Eden, so too there is a profound lesson for us to learn from the fact that we were originally one androgynous being that was then divided into separate genders and forms.

We can begin to understand this with the concept that God created Adam "in His image." The verse quoted from Genesis above, "male and female He created them," is immediately preceded by the phrase "in the likeness of God He created him."[89] God is neither male nor female. He is one. He comprises all qualities, including both genders, and He is limited by none.[90] Creating humanity in His image thus necessitated that it included both male and female form. Just as Adam/Eve's translucent skin and placement in the Garden of Eden were indicative of their original perfection, so too their androgyny was a symbol of their wholeness and integrity. However, perfection and unity were not the conditions for the world that God would now create. This was to be a realm of concealment and division. Why? In order that there should be the existence of others to whom God could express His love, as we have ex-

---

[87] Section "Intentional Error"

[88] Section "Shame"

[89] Genesis 5:1

[90] We utilize the male pronoun "He" only as a matter of grammar, and not to indicate any gender designation or limitation.

plained previously in chapter two.[91] There, we quoted a verse from Genesis in which God contemplates Adam's solitary condition and decides upon the creation of his mate.

> And the Lord God said, "It is not good that man (ha'adam) is alone; I shall make him a helpmate opposite him.
>
> (Genesis 2:18)

We explained that while on the surface this verse is referring to Adam, the first man, on a deeper level the word "ha'Adam/*the* man" alludes to "Adam Kadmon," primordial man. This is the image of God Himself that precedes the creation and in the likeness of which the earthly Adam is fashioned. This verse is therefore a statement of God's reason for the creation - it is not good for *God* to be alone. "Good" is defined by the bestowal of kindness or caring from one to another. If God is alone, as He was prior to the creation, there can be no "good" because there is no one to whom He can express it. Just as this verse therefore explains why God decided to make divisions in His infinite unity in order to create otherness (so that there would be an outlet for His essential goodness), similarly it provides His rationale for splitting Adam below and forming male and female from the single being that He had originally created. It was not "good" for Adam to be alone, i.e. all one. "Good" would be effected only if there were separate beings who could express love and kindness to one another. Therefore, God hewed Adam in two:

> And the Lord God caused a deep sleep to fall upon man, and he slept, and He took one of his sides, and He closed the flesh in its place. And the Lord God built the side that He had taken from man into a woman, and He brought her to man. And man said, "This time, it is bone of my bones and flesh of my flesh. This one shall be called ishah (woman) because this one was taken from ish (man)."
>
> (Genesis 2: 21-23)

---

[91] Section "Good Nature"

These verses describe the surgery that God performed on both Adam and Eve. Prior to this, they were both referred to as "Adam," as we saw above, "He named *them* Adam." He then determined that they should be individuals who would later reconnect. Therefore, He put them to sleep and performed the surgical procedure that severed them, and then healed the flesh where they had been conjoined.

Marriage, we see from this, is the allegory for the entire purpose and project of creation! God divided His unity to create the semblance of multiplicity in order to express His love to one who believed itself to be separate and distinct from Him. Ultimately, His beloved, in response to the love that God bestowed upon her/him, would recognize that s/he was not truly separate from her/his lover at all. Their unity would be revealed even within the framework of their seeming diversity. God's limitless light would thus glow within the darkness of this world. So too, God formed a single being in His likeness, and then divided it into pieces that would consider themselves independent. Eventually, these two beings, who seem to be individual and distinct, would come together and overcome their differences to fuse and coalesce. Through this process, they would recognize the transient and illusory nature of the flesh that confines and divides them, and they would become aware of the inner reality that unites them and ultimately defines who and what they are.

We have been detached and dispersed in order to reassemble and reunite. When we do so, we find the essential adhesive that is at our core. That is the face of God which is within each of us. It binds us to one another, to our Creator, and to every aspect of His creation which is only another disguise in which He hides Himself.

Wedding

Many more pages, and indeed chapters, could be devoted to the Torah's conception of marriage and the many opportunities it provides us to uncover the layers that encase us and to find the face within. Torah teaches that the marriage between husband and wife is an allegory for the relationship between God and humankind. Therefore, the exploration of the dynamics of the marriage bond will bring us as close as we can come to understanding the interconnection of our soul and its Creator. However, to explore this subject in the depth that it deserves is beyond the scope of this book. Nevertheless, before moving on, it is worthwhile to shift from the concept of marriage more generally and focus briefly on the protocol of the wedding itself. As we have been discussing, Torah provides not only a conceptual arena for inward exploration and spiritual growth, but also an intricate practice that promotes and supports self-discovery through very specific actions which carry profound meaning and significance. As such, the wedding rituals convey the aforementioned themes and ideas of marriage through the performance of very particular physical procedures and customs.

The wedding ceremony is incredibly rich with rituals and symbolism. The process begins long before the "chosson/groom" and "kallah/bride" walk down the aisle. One week prior to the wedding day, the couple separates and will not see one another until a very special moment just before the formal ceremony begins. The wedding is divided into two parts, known as the "kabbalat panim" and the "chuppah." "Kabbalat panim" is translated as "reception," but it literally means "receiving faces." "Chuppah" means "canopy" or "covering" in reference to the bridal canopy under which the couple stands throughout the formal ceremony. It is no coincidence that these terms, and the rituals that they name, relate to the concepts of 'face' and 'covering' which we have been discussing in this book. For the wedding, like all of the milestone events throughout one's life, is a practice designed to assist us in the process of uncovering our "pnimyus/inner core" and finding the "Pnei Hashem/ face of God" that exists there.

On the surface level, the term "kabbalat panim" is rendered simply as "reception," and this is a more informal phase of the wedding where the bride and groom are situated in separate rooms as guests begin to arrive and are "received" (the meaning of "kabbalat") or greeted. Various legalities are performed at the groom's reception, including the signing of the "ketubah/marriage contract" by the officiating rabbi and two witnesses, and the reading of the "tena'im," or the conditions of the engagement. Following the completion of these legal documents, together the mothers of the couple break a plate to symbolize the irreversibility of the contracted terms. At this point, the "badeken" takes place - a powerful ceremony that will provide a far deeper meaning to the term "kabbalat panim."

"Badeken" means "covering" in Yiddish, similar to the English term 'bedeck,' which means to adorn or dress up. The groom, followed by his guests, proceeds from his reception room to the hall where the bride is seated on a throne, and the couple comes face to face for the first time since their separation a week prior to the wedding day. Throughout this week, the bride and groom have had no contact. It is therefore at this very emotional moment when the couple greets one another that we understand that the "faces" (panim) which are "received" (kabbalat) during this stage of the wedding are not simply those of the arriving guests, but more particularly the faces of the bride and groom themselves. It is a brief, but profound and often tear-filled moment, and then the groom places a veil over the bride's face in preparation for the "chuppah," the formal marriage ceremony which will shortly commence. The derivation of this custom is from the first meeting of the matriarch Rebecca and her intended husband, the patriarch Isaac.

> And Isaac went forth to pray in the field towards evening, and he lifted his eyes and saw, and behold, camels were approaching. And Rebecca lifted her eyes, and saw Isaac, and she let herself down from the camel. And she said to the servant, "Who is that man walking in the field towards us?" And the servant said, "He is my master." **And she took the veil and covered herself.**
> (Genesis 24:63-65)

As the story goes, Abraham had sent his most trusted servant, Eliezer, to the land of his birth to find Isaac a bride from Abraham's relatives. When Eliezer returns with Rebecca, she and Isaac see one another from a distance for the first time, and at this moment, Rebecca immediately covers her face with her veil. This act of veiling herself when she first encounters Isaac has been expounded on many different levels. In one sense, it is an expression of her modesty. In another sense, it is the declaration that now that she has met her betrothed, her beauty will be reserved for him exclusively. On a deeper level, it is Rebecca's statement to her future husband that it is not her superficial beauty which he marries, but the tremendous worth within her which cannot be seen with the physical eyes. On an even more esoteric level, it is explained that just as Moses was forced to cover himself with a veil when he descended from Mount Sinai because of the beams of Godly light that radiated from his face after his intimate interaction with God,[92] so too the bride emits the glow of her divine essence at the time of her wedding.

In this last explanation, we see that as marriage is an allegory for the relationship between God and humanity, so too the wedding is represented by the events at Mount Sinai. Moses, as a representative of the entire nation, is the bride, and God is the groom. When the bride and groom come face to face and unite - in other words when there is a "kabbalat panim/receiving of faces" and they truly receive one other's "pnimyus/inward essence" - there is an inevitable overflow of the divine light that dwells within them. It beams from the bride's face so blindingly that it must be covered in order for the "olam/world" of "helam/hiddenness" to continue to exist.

After the "badeken," which again means "covering" in Yiddish, the ceremony continues with the "chuppah," which also means "covering" in Hebrew, and in this second phase of the wedding this symbolism continues. The groom proceeds first to his place under the bridal canopy, or "chuppah," which is generally a prayer shawl (tallis) or other embroidered cloth that is held aloft by four poles. The bride then follows, and when she arrives, before standing at his side, she first walks around the groom seven times. He then places a ring on her finger, encircling her reciprocally. The marriage contract is read, a series of seven blessings is recited, and at the end of the ceremony, the groom stomps on a glass that will shatter beneath his foot. The bride's veil is removed, and the couple proceeds from under the "chuppah" to great rejoicing from the guests.

From even such a quick and cursory overview of the rituals associated with the wedding ceremony, we see a consistent focus on the dynamics of concealment and revelation with which God created, and creates, the universe. The separation of the bride and the groom for the week prior to the wedding mirrors the division that God has created within His unity in order for the creation to be formed. The "kabbalat panim/meeting of the faces" of the bride and the groom at the "badeken" is the beginning of the reunification that is not only the goal

---

[92] See Chapter three, section "Halleluy-ah"

of each marriage, but of the creation as a whole. The veil with which the groom covers his bride at the "badeken" ceremony parallels not only the veil with which Moses covered the "horns of light" that projected from his face, but also the veil of this physical universe with which God has shrouded His own face and buried it within our flesh. With the veil, the groom acknowledges that it is not the surface or physical beauty of his bride that he embraces, but the spiritual core that is deep within her. The two then proceed to the "chuppah" where the canopy above them alludes not only to the home that they will build together, but also to the reality that they dwell beneath a cloak that God has spread over them, and that the holiness of their union lies beneath it. They encircle one another - she with seven revolutions around him, and he with a single ring around her finger - both representing the fact that they are enveloped and contained. He then shatters a glass, which commemorates the destruction of the temple in Jerusalem but may also allude to the shattering of the barriers that divide them and conceal their Godly core. Her veil is then lifted, and they go forward together from under the "chuppah" as a married couple.

In summary, we find that the dominant and repeated images at the wedding are faces, coverings, circles and breakage (the plate after the reading of the "tena'im," and the glass at the end of the "chuppah" ceremony). The marriage will later be consummated with the act of intercourse, which once again enacts this process of encircling and covering, penetrating, opening, and revealing. Intimacy is fusion. The woman opens to the man and draws him inside. They reconnect after having been separated before birth. Together, they are able to then touch the divine. The ultimate outcome of this process is procreation, in which the process of God's creative project is mimicked, and the miracle of new life results from the act of enclosing and concealment.

Death/Completion

The soul, as we have discussed, finishes its investiture in the body at the "bar/bat mitzvah," and then reunites with its other half at marriage. For the remainder of its time in this body, it will be working to answer God's question "ayecha/where are you," and to fulfill its task of "bara Elokim es hashamayim v'es haaretz," revealing God within this realm of hiddenness. The time it is allotted to do so will depend on a variety of factors, and it will remain here, ideally, until its mission is accomplished. While birth, according to Torah, is the moment that God has determined that the world requires this particular soul's service, death is the moment that its service in this particular incarnation is complete. This does not mean that the soul's journey is over. The soul does not, and cannot, die; it only detaches from the casing in which it was temporarily infused. It will now continue its process either in the spiritual realms, or it may require additional incarnations in this physical world in order to finish the task that it is called upon to perform here.

Death, according to Torah, is nothing to fear. We fear death because it is unknown and because it seems to be the end. But it is not the end. It is the culmination of one progression and the beginning of another. We tend to view death as a punishment, a consequence for misdeeds. It is commonly seen as the threat that God holds over us to keep us subservient, and the vengeance He administers when we step too far out of line. But where does this conception come from? Why do we imagine God as this temperamental, hostile force? This is certainly not the view of Torah, which declares:

> No evil descends from above.
> (Breishis Rabba 51:3)

And:

> His kindness is eternal.
> (Psalms 136:1)

As well as:

> The world is built on lovingkindness.
> (Psalms 89:3)

God, as we have seen, does execute judgment in His creation, and there are indeed consequences for improper action within the framework of this world. But the notion of a punitive, vengeful God, and the perception of death as nothing more than a penalty for disobedience, are only products of a superficial and unsophisticated reading of the Torah's text which is inconsistent with its inner spirit and essence.

The first time death is mentioned in Torah is in the second chapter of Genesis soon after the creation of Adam and Eve. They are still in the garden of Eden, and God informs them of the prohibition of eating from the fruit of the tree of knowledge of good and evil:

> And the Lord God commanded man, saying, "Of every tree of the garden you may freely eat. But of the Tree of Knowledge of good and evil you shall not eat of it, for on the day that you eat thereof, you shall surely die."
> (Genesis 2:16-17)

On the simple level, this can be read as a warning and a statement of punishment: if you eat the fruit, I will penalize you with death. Alternatively, it can be read as a statement of fact: if you eat the fruit, you will surely die *at some point*. In other words, you will be susceptible to death if you eat the fruit, whereas if you do not eat the fruit, death cannot affect you. With either reading, God forbids the eating of the fruit; but in the first interpretation, death is utilized as a threatened retribution, and in the second interpretation, death is offered as an explanation for the prohibition. Why were Adam and Eve liable to death following the eating of the fruit? In the simple reading, it seems to be because they were sinners who were now deserving of execution. But if so, why were they not executed upon eating the fruit and merely exiled instead? The "threat" indicates that they would die "on the day that you eat thereof." But they did not die on that day, and as a matter of fact, they lived for nearly a millennium afterwards. Therefore, we can understand that what God is conveying to them in this verse is that through the consumption of the fruit they would become, on that very day, *liable to death*. Somehow the act of eating the fruit altered their nature in such a manner that death was now a possibility for them at some time in the future. In other words, it's not that Adam and Eve *should* die because they ate the fruit, but rather that they *could* die because they ate the fruit. How and why did the fruit create this new dynamic?

The tree of the knowledge of good and evil represents dichotomy - good AND evil - and eating its fruit internalized duality within humanity. It brought us down into the world where there is differentiation - good and evil, light and darkness, life and death. Had we not eaten the fruit, we would have remained in the Edenic realm beyond all of these dialectics and oppositions. Eden was an intermediate space between the heavens and the earth. It is a way station between the ultimate reality of God's complete unity, and this world of division, concealment and multiplicity. Adam and Eve existed in Eden as "others," distinct and individualized from God, but they were not conscious of their otherness and individuality until they ate the fruit. They were not conscious of themselves at all - therefore they were not aware of their nakedness - but immediately afterwards they were self-conscious and ashamed. Ingesting the fruit introduced the existence of a self within them. When one is united with God, s/he is infinite and cannot die. But as soon as one exists independently, then s/he is finite and susceptible to death. This is what it means to be "mortal," the root of which is "mort," which is Latin for "death."

As we have discussed repeatedly, a realm of Godliness beyond all duality is not what God intended for this world. This was what existed before the creation, and therefore, if this was His desire, then there would have been no need for the creation at all. On the contrary, He wanted us to live within a world of darkness in order to enlighten it. In such a finite and superficial dimension, death is not a punishment, it is a simple reality. In fact, it is an act of mercy without which one might be consigned to darkness for eternity. After Adam ate the fruit, God removed him from the garden "lest he stretch forth his hand and take also from the Tree of Life and eat and live forever." Living forever within the framework of duality is not desirable, and not what God wants for us. Existence within this realm that is known as "olam hasheker/world of falseness" is only to be temporary. What would truly be a punishment would be to condemn us to this darkness forever. Death is actually a release, a liberation from the confines of good and evil, and a re-entry into the "olam ha'emes/world of truth" where one can once again experience God's oneness.

If this is so, then perhaps life itself is a punishment. Perhaps one could imagine that s/he would be better off ending her/his life as soon as possible in order to avoid the illusion of separation and thereby exist within the more ultimate truth of unity with God and all. Indeed, the Chassidic masters explain that the soul does in fact yearn to be free of this world so that it can return to the place from which it came. In this sense, they explain the expression from Proverbs:

> The soul of man is the candle of God.
> (Proverbs 20:27)

The human soul is like the flame of a candle. If we observe a flame, we see that it is always reaching upward no matter what direction the candle is oriented, and it is never still but always flickering. This flicker represents its constant striving to leap from off the wick that holds it, in order to reunite with the source of fire above. So too, the mystics teach, the soul is constantly flickering upward, yearning to free itself from the 'wick' of the body and to reunite with the source of all souls in the heavens. Nevertheless, it knows it has a job to do here in this world. It was placed into the body in order to discover itself and its creator and to illuminate the darkness. Therefore, though it longs for the realm of light from which it came, it simultaneously recognizes the reason and necessity for its being here. With this, we can understand the saying of the sage Rabbi Elazar Hakapor:

> Against your will you live, and against your will you die.
> (Pirkei Avos 4:22)

The soul does not want to come down to this world of darkness and concealment where it will be confined and deluded. However, once it is here and it becomes enwrapped in the body, it becomes entangled in the life of the flesh and doesn't want to leave. On a deeper level, it doesn't want to leave because it knows it has a job to do here, and it is so devoted to God that it does not want to abandon its post until the job is complete.

All of this will enable us to understand a strange verse in the prayers of Rosh Hashana, which is the Jewish new year and is also known as "Yom hadin/the Day of Judgment." The new year is not simply celebrated as the beginning of a new cycle and a time of renewal and resolution; it is a time of deep introspection when one considers her/his conduct throughout the past year and refocuses her/himself on the purpose for which s/he was created. It is a time of contemplation and evaluation for God as well, and on the first day of each new year, He reconsiders His creation and decides how He will conduct it going forward. The prayers of the day therefore focus on "teshuvah," returning to a consciousness of who we are and why we are here. We recognize our failings throughout the past year, and aware of God's great love and mercy, we ask for another opportunity to do better. We request life and sustenance and all of the things that will make the coming year more successful than the past. God is then said to inscribe each of us in the book of life, writing precisely what will happen to us in the year ahead. In one of the central prayers of the day, the following is recited:

> Remember us for life, King Who desires life, and inscribe
> us in the book of life **for Your sake** God of life.

What do we mean to say that one is asking for life for God's sake? To be honest, is it not that one begs for life because s/he loves life and fears death? To suggest that the prayer is for God's benefit seems to be disingenuous. However, at this holiest time of the year, one is speaking from the deepest level of her/his soul. When one accesses her/his "pnimyus/inner core" and finds the "Pnei Hashem/face of God" within, s/he knows that s/he is completely one with God, that s/he is simply a piece of Him hidden within the illusion of plurality. What one desires then is only to do God's will, to make Him revealed in the darkness. Therefore, one asks for life not because s/he desires it for her/his sake, but rather for God's sake; in order that s/he can complete the task that God assigned her/him. With such consciousness, one is not worried about death. One doesn't beg to be signed in the book of life because s/he fears the alternative. One requests more time to do her/his work for the sake of the "King Who desires life."

For our own sake, death seems to be an elevation. It is an end to the groping in the darkness that life in this world represents. Yet we do not request death. Ironically, it is with self-sacrifice that we request life. 'Please allow me to stay here,' we ask, 'in spite of the darkness and confusion and struggle that I face here daily, because I know that you want me here. Though I seem to be distanced from You here, and I flicker upward constantly because I would much prefer to exist in a realm where there is no apparent separation between us, yet because I love You, I will remain attached to the wick as long as You require my service here.' We therefore remain in this world, and we work daily to reveal the reality that God is here just as He is above.

From this brief exploration and comparison of the roles and functions of life and death, we can appreciate that death is not a punishment. It is rather a completion of the soul's work in this particular body and a transition from this "olam/world" of "helam/hiddenness" back to a realm where the truth of God's unity is apparent. This is not to say that death cannot also be a consequence for deviant action in this world. Clearly this is the case in a variety of circumstances when one transgresses severely and is sentenced by Torah law to the death penalty. Yet even in such an event, we can understand this not simply as a penalty, but as a removal of the soul from the situation in which it will continue to be led astray by its inability to see its truth. The soul is taken from this world not because it is evil, but because it has been unable to penetrate the physical veil in which it is garbed and to thereby express its essential Godliness. It is therefore extracted from the darkness that has overwhelmed it in order to be reunited with the light from which it originates and of which it is comprised.

While most souls are not liable to such drastic measures, the vast majority do not complete within one lifetime the revelation and transformation that we have been assigned. As such, death comes as a respite and a completion of this particular phase in this particular incarnation. The soul reunites with its source to refresh its connection before it is sent back again to continue the work that is incumbent upon all souls throughout history. Eventually, through our collective work across the millennia, this world will be transformed from darkness to light, from concealment to revelation. At this point, we will no longer require death in order for our unity with God to be manifest.

Funeral

Now that we have a better understanding of Torah's conception of death, we can explore the rituals that Torah prescribes to mark this final phase of the life-cycle. As we saw with the rituals of "bris milah," "upsherin," "bar/bat mitzvah," and the wedding, we will find that the funeral rites include very specific practices that focus us on the lifelong process of opening and the revelation of our innermost core. Several of the observances of the funeral bear striking resemblance to the rituals that we have described previously, and this is a reflection of the constancy of these themes of inward exploration and disclosure that underpin every stage and aspect of our existence. In particular, the procedures and ceremonies of the funeral resemble those of the wedding. From this we will see that death is, in many ways, another form of marriage.

Just as the male and female halves of the soul were separated at birth and then reunited at marriage, so too our soul is severed from its revealed union with God when it is sent down into this world at birth, and then it is reunited with its source when it leaves the body at death. As we have discussed at length, there can be no true separation from God as He is one and there is nothing other than Him. It is the mission of the soul to confirm this ultimate reality while it is within the body. But on the revealed plane, birth represents distance and division, and death releases the soul from its perceived detachment and therefore resembles the reunification of souls at the wedding. For this reason, it will not be surprising that one of the Hebrew scriptural terms for death, "כְּלוֹת הַנֶּפֶשׁ/ klot hanefesh," which literally means "expiry of the soul," shares the same root as the word for bride, כַּלָּה/kallah. The root itself, "כַּל/kal," means "all."[93] The linguistic correspondence of these terms reveals their conceptual connectedness. Just as at marriage, the husband and wife fuse to become one and cease to be the individuals that they were previously, so too at death, one ceases to be the distinct individual that s/he had been while confined to the body, and s/he returns to the inter-inclusion ("hitkallelut" in Hebrew) within all. Each of the life-cycle events, as we have seen, represents a stage of progression in our process of moving from individuality to oneness.

---

[93] As we saw previously, in chapter six, section "Bittul."

Like the wedding, the end of life ceremony is divided into parts. The first ritual after death is called "tahara," which literally means "purification." The second phase is called "levaya," which means both "escorting" and "joining." The "tahara" is the ritual washing of the body, and the "levaya" is the formal funeral service. Following the service, the body is buried and the process is complete. These three phases parallel the phases of the wedding that we discussed earlier. Prior to the wedding, both the bride and the groom customarily immerse in a "mikvah," a ritual bath. This bathing is not a cleansing of the body, but a purification of the soul in preparation for its coming unification. Similarly, the ritual washing of the body after death is not a matter of hygiene, but a spiritual cleansing that readies the soul for its transition. Prior to the burial, the soul is still attached to the body though it is no longer contained within it. It is in an intermediate stage where it is no longer incarnate, but it cannot yet proceed on its journey back to its incorporation in its source. For this reason, the funeral and burial are conducted as soon as possible after death. After the body is washed, it is wrapped in a shroud. It is not dressed in finery, and nothing is to be placed into the casket other than the body and the shroud in which it is wrapped. The casket is to be made of simple wood with no metal. This will enable it to decompose more quickly. Just as the soul reunites with its source, so too the body is to reunite with the earth - "you will return to the ground, for you were taken therefrom, for dust you are, and to dust you will return" (Genesis 3:19).

While the washing of the "tahara" service resembles the immersion in the "mikvah" prior to the wedding, the subsequent shrouding of the body parallels both the veiling of the bride at the "badeken" and the covering of the couple at the "chuppah." Once again, the theme of covering and enwrapping is central. This is then compounded when the shrouded body is placed into the wooden casket prior to the "levaya" ceremony. At this point there is a body, which itself was a cloak for the soul, wrapped in the secondary layer of cloth, which is then housed in the casket, another layer of containment. As we know, the purpose of enclothement and concealment of the soul within the body was for a subsequent revelation in which the extraneous layers would be pierced, the barriers would be broken, and the inner essence would manifest. It would then be able to permeate and transform its surroundings. At the wedding, this was symbolized by the breaking of the plate, the shattering of the glass, the removal of the bride's veil, and the couple's emergence from under the "chuppah." Similarly, at the funeral, the formal ceremony begins with a ritual called "kriah/tearing," in which the immediate family of the departed soul rips their clothing near the area of their heart. On one level, this represents the fact that their loved one has been torn from them and they are left with a hole in their heart which their loved one used to fill. In the context of our discussion, however, this tearing alludes to the rupturing and removal of the layers that obscure what is underneath. The soul is now ready to be freed and unencumbered from the veil of the body so that it can rejoin its source.

This phase of the funeral which begins with the "kriah" is therefore called "levaya," which, as we have mentioned, means not only "escorting," because we escort the soul as it begins the next stage of its journey, but also "joining," because the soul is now able to reconnect to the unity from which it had been sundered. The breakdown of the barriers and the shedding of the concealing layers will continue with the burial. Just as the married couple embraces intimately and thereby unites after the wedding, so too the body penetrates into the ground in order to decompose and become nullified and incorporated into its source. The soul remerges with its origins in the spiritual realm.

There are further parallels between the wedding and the funeral, like the seven days of celebration known as the "sheva brachos" which follows the wedding, and the seven days of mourning known as "shiva" which follows the burial. Similarly, there is the special status of the bride and groom for one year after the wedding known as "shana rishona/first year" and the year long period of "aveilus/mourning" after the burial in which the mourner recites the "kaddish" prayer and is restricted from certain activities. All of these similarities reflect the thematic correspondence in these transitional phases of the soul. The customs and rituals that Torah has assigned to them enable us to remain focused on the essential concepts of inner discovery and Godly reunion that define every phase of our existence.

We thus see that the lifecycle rituals that Torah assigns are not simply regulations that govern one's behavior, or even cultural traditions that provide a rich and unique ethnic character. Ultimately, each of the customs and ceremonies are essential components of the intricate liberation practice that God has granted in order to help one peel away the veneer and find His face within. Just as this is the case with these milestone observances, so too will one find that Torah's daily rituals (including daily prayer, daily Torah study, and daily mitzvos), as well as its weekly, monthly, and annual calendrical rituals (including the sabbath and holiday observances) all express these themes of uncovering and uniting.[94] We see that Torah provides not only a map, but also an elaborate regimen of exercises or practices that enables one to see through the darkness and peel away the veils that obscure each of the openings through which s/he must progressively pass on the journey ever inward.

---

94 As mentioned in footnote 79, a detailed exploration of these other aspects of Torah's liberation practice - ie. the daily rituals and the weekly, monthly, and yearly calendrical observances - can be found in our more comprehensive book, *Pnei Hashem*. See Postscript.

Chapter 8: END GAME

Yemot Hamashiach

We have been on a journey. We began with the question of "where are you," establishing that by virtue of our creation in a world of darkness, we are inevitably lost and in need of being found (chapters 1 and 2). We then set out to find ourself, determining that the direction of the search must be inward because our "panim," our face and essence, is hidden within our "pnimyus," our inner core. We established that it is not only our face that we will find there, but also "Pnei Hashem," the face of God, for "Anochi nosein lifneichem," He has placed His deepest self in our deepest recesses (chapter 3). As we proceeded on our inbound expedition, we addressed a second question, "how are you," exploring the notion of our hidden potential and our ability to feel great if and when we do discover the greatness that is at our core (chapter 4). From there, we moved on to examine the veils and blockages that keep us from tapping this infinite potential (chapter 5), as well as the tremendous spiritual heights and depths that can be achieved if we manage to penetrate these barriers (chapter 6). Having determined that there is great incentive to persevere in our search in spite of its difficulties, we then asked a third question, "how can you" - how can we succeed in this search in spite of all of the pitfalls and obstacles that impede our progress. In response, we began to explore how Torah's rituals and observances are a liberation practice that empower us to move ever further inward (chapter 7).

As the book draws toward its end, our journey continues. Though we now know precisely what we are searching for (the "Pnei Hashem/Face of God"), where it is awaiting us (in our "pnimyus/innermost core"), and how to get there (by following the intricate liberation practice that is established in Torah), the journey may not end in this life. Nor, for that matter, will it necessarily end when this life is over. It may continue into our next life, and perhaps multiple future lives. Though it is not widely known or understood, reincarnation is very much a Torah concept. It is referred to in Hebrew as "gilgul," which literally means "wheel." The soul's cycle keeps spinning even after one particular life-cycle is over.

It is said that a soul must return to this world repeatedly until its task is fulfilled. That may be a task that is specific to a particular soul, or it may be the task of fulfilling all of the mitzvos, which is common to all souls and takes longer for some than others. As we have discussed from the first chapter on, the ultimate task that is incumbent upon each of us individually, and all of us collectively, is "Breishis bara Elokim es hashamayim v'es haaretz," to make God revealed throughout His creation. Every mitzvah one performs is a contribution to this effort, another shell broken and another fragment of light revealed. Though the process may not be completed in a single lifetime, or even in a series of reincarnations, every life is contributing to the task.

There is, however, an "end" to the journey, so to speak. That is when the revelation that we have been working toward will be accomplished. It is when the "Pnei Hashem/face of God" is manifest throughout the creation. When the "pnimyus," or ultimate reality, of all things will be visible through the veil of physicality that had previously concealed it, all will be conscious of God's exclusive unity, even amidst the multiplicity of this lower realm. This time of revelation and fruition is referred to in Torah by a variety of names, among them "olam haba/the world to come" and "yemot hamashiach/the days of the messiah." It is one of the Torah's thirteen principles of faith that one is to expect this messianic revolution every single day. We long for it, and we therefore labor tirelessly to precipitate its occurrence. While the Torah's concept of the messiah is complex, and a thorough treatment of the subject is beyond the scope of this book, for the purposes of our subject it will suffice to understand that "Mashiach/the messiah" will come when God determines that the time of darkness and concealment is complete. His coming will usher in a new age of "enlightenment," in which the conduct of the world will be transformed completely because we will all be able to see what was hidden from us until now.

In one of the most renowned and idyllic descriptions of this future time, the prophet Isaiah proclaims:

> And a wolf shall live with a lamb, and a leopard shall lie with a kid; and a calf and a lion cub and a fatling [shall lie] together, and a small child shall lead them. And a cow and a bear shall graze together, their children shall lie; and a lion, like cattle, shall eat straw. And an infant shall play over the hole of an old snake and over the eyeball of an adder, a weaned child shall stretch forth his hand. They shall neither harm nor destroy on all My holy mount, for the land shall be full of knowledge of the Lord as water covers the sea bed.
> (Isaiah 11:6-9)

Isaiah here describes the peace and camaraderie that will envelop all of the world's creations. In the final phrase, he explains what will cause this new state of affairs to arise. There will be no violence or conflict because "the knowledge of the Lord" will permeate the creation. This does not simply mean that because all of the beings of the world will come to *believe* in God, therefore they will resolve to live in peace. Indeed, throughout history there have been many who have waged violent wars precisely because of their belief in God. The mere awareness of a Creator and a divine ruler of the world has certainly not precluded conflict until now. Why, then, would we assume that it would do so in the future?

As we have explained previously, the word "daas/knowledge" also means "fusion" or "intimacy," as in the verse "Adam *knew* Eve his wife."[95] What Isaiah is informing us, therefore, is that with the advent of the messianic age, God will be "known" throughout His creation not simply in the sense of an intellectual cognition. Rather, His unity will be revealed throughout the creation, as everything will perceive its inherent oneness with Him. In other words, all of the various creatures of the world will recognize that they are simply varying manifestations of Godly expression. We will see through the materiality that distinguishes and individualizes us, and we will therefore perceive the common Godliness that pervades and unites us. With such awareness, conflict will cease because there will no longer be any "other" with whom to battle or contest. Even the animals will possess this inner vision, and the erstwhile predator will coexist peacefully with its former prey.

Eyes To See

As we have discussed many times, the nature of this "olam/ world" is "helam/concealment." This is a realm of darkness and obfuscation. We have little ability to perceive the truth, and in fact it is so dark that most of us are not even aware that it is dark.[96] We have become so accustomed to blindness that we don't even realize that we are blind. Yet the Torah is a torch, and it sheds light in the darkness. It enables us to see - at least with our mind's eye, even if not with our fleshy eyes. We are therefore able to be aware of the truth even if we cannot clearly perceive it. We have described this state of affairs in chapter three,[97] explaining that we may "modeh/acknowledge" and admit the ultimate reality, even though it is not yet "baruch/brought down" and revealed. Yet it is our goal to make it "baruch," to manifest the truth so clearly that it is not

---

[95] Genesis 3:1

[96] As we described in chapter two, section "Double Darkness"

[97] Section "From Knowing to Showing"

only an inner awareness, but an outward perception. This palpable vision will be available to all of us in the time to come.

In his final days on earth, at the end of the forty years throughout which he led the nation in the desert, Moses alludes to, and distinguishes between, the vision that the people have had and the vision that they will eventually gain.

> You have seen all that the Lord did before your very eyes in the land of Egypt, to Pharaoh, to all his servants, and to all his land; the great trials which your very eyes beheld and those great signs and wonders. Yet until this day, the Lord has not given you a heart to know, eyes to see and ears to hear.
> (Deuteronomy 28:1-3)

You have seen miracles and wonders, Moses tells the people, but "until this very day" you have still not been given "a heart to know, eyes to see and ears to hear." In other words, there are varying degrees of clarity and perception. The Exodus from Egypt was the first redemption from exile, and thus the beginning of the process of illumination. Prior to that great liberation, one's vision and understanding of her/himself and the world was so limited that s/he believed in her/his ability to be enslaved by the forces of concealment and constraint. God took the people out of there with signs and wonders, granting them the capacity to see beyond the natural world. Their eyes were opened as the sea split open and then the heavens opened over Mount Sinai when the Torah was delivered. This granted them far greater perception than they previously had, but even this vision was not yet true and permanent. The heavens closed after the Sinai experience, and one was once again subject to the myopia of physical sight within the world of darkness that was created specifically to conceal the truth of God's oneness.

Even as miracles followed them throughout the forty-year journey in the desert - manna raining down daily from heaven, Miriam's well following the nation to provide water, the clouds of glory providing shelter and protection from the elements - still the people did not have "eyes to see" the ultimate truth. This condition persists until today. Therefore, we might have moments of clarity, but they are fleeting and unsustained. They do not infuse our being permanently and completely, and we are thus able to "see" and embrace God at one moment, and then revert to our brute egocentrism the next moment. This, as we explained in the very first chapter, is not our fault, because the very existence of a finite creation depends on our inability to perceive God's infinity.

"You have seen all that the Lord did before your very eyes in the land of Egypt," Moses says. God had granted this glimpse and glimmer of the truth. But He had still not given one the capacity to fully see. He provided the Torah, which would enable us to train our eyes and hone our vision throughout millennia of additional exiles ahead. But true vision will come only with the final redemption. This is alluded to by the prophet Michah, who augurs the following in God's name in regards to the onset of the messianic era when this final exile will end:

> Like the days of your going out of the land of Egypt, I
> will show them wonders.
> (Michah 7:15)

The sages debate the meaning of this verse. Does it indicate that the miracles that will be performed at the time of the final redemption will be similar to the miracles that were performed at the exodus from Egypt - "like the days of your going out of the land of Egypt"? Or does it mean that just as the miracles in Egypt were totally unprecedented and beyond all experience, so too the future miracles will be so wondrous, that in comparison, those previous miracles from the Exodus will no longer seem wondrous at all? After all, if the future redemption is only comparable to the former redemption, then what is its advantage? And if there is no advantage, then what is the reason for all of the hardship and suffering that we have had to endure in the interim?

The Lubavitcher Rebbe[98] proposes that one of the keys to understanding this verse is the word "arenu/I will show." The prophet does not say that God will "perform" wonders, as He did previously, but rather that He will "show" wonders this time. What is the difference between "performing" miracles and "showing" miracles? The Rebbe explains that there are miracles that God has performed throughout history which we have not recognized as miraculous, because He has garbed

---

[98] In his discourse "Kimei Tzeischa MeiEretz Mitzrayim."

and hidden them in the framework of the natural world. These hidden miracles, the Rebbe says, are even loftier than the obvious miracles that have abrogated the laws of nature. This is because they come from such a high level of Godliness that they cannot be perceived within the confines of the world. Therefore, they go unnoticed, seeming to be merely natural, though they are in fact so subtle and ethereal that they are completely imperceptible to our dull and insensitive physical senses. Miracles like the splitting of the sea are beyond the nature of the world, but they are able to come down into the world and interrupt its regular functioning. Yet miracles like the conception of new life and the constant creation of matter from nothingness are so profound and sublime that they are not even recognized as miraculous. With the ultimate redemption at the end of this current and final exile, God will *show* us the wonders. He will enable us to see Him in everything and to understand that everything is miraculous. The ultimate reality to which we had previously been "modeh," aware but not perceiving, will finally become "baruch," clear and palpable.

Eye To Eye

Based on the above, we can say that the sum of human history has been an "eye-opening experience." We begin with severe visual challenges, and throughout our spiritual evolution, we become increasingly percipient. As we have explained, the redemption from Egypt was the beginning of the process of eye opening, and the redemption from this final exile will complete the process and grant us perfect vision.

Just prior to the Exodus from Egypt, God promises Moses "now you will see." Moses had approached God in confusion. In their first meeting (at the burning bush), God had instructed Moses to go down to Egypt and to command Pharaoh to "let my people go." Moses did so, but the immediate result was not liberation. On the contrary, his demand was met with further oppression. Pharaoh responded that the people were not working hard enough if they had time to daydream about going to serve their God. He would therefore make their work more difficult so that they would have no time for these types of idle thoughts. He ordered his taskmasters to stop supplying the slaves with straw with which they made their bricks. The quota of bricks would not be reduced, but now the slaves would have to go find and gather the straw themselves. The people were obviously upset by this outcome, and they railed against Moses for making their situation worse. Moses subsequently returns to God and asks Him to explain Himself:

> Moses returned to the Lord and said, "O Lord! Why have You harmed this people? Why have You sent me? Since I have come to Pharaoh to speak in Your name, he has harmed this people, and You have not saved Your people."
> (Exodus 5:22-23)

God responds:

> **Now you will see** what I will do to Pharaoh.
> (Exodus 6:1)

A new vision would be introduced to Moses and the people as a result of the Exodus. What was this vision? On the surface, it was "what I will do to Pharaoh." They saw the miracles and wonders of the ten plagues and then the splitting of the sea. But the greater vision came just afterwards at the time of the giving of the Torah on Mount Sinai. Then, God informed the people of who and what they truly are:

> Face to face God spoke to you at the mountain.
> (Deuteronomy 5:4)

As we have discussed previously,[99] the significance of the phrase "panim b'panim" - literally "face IN face" - is that God made us aware of the fact that His face - the "Pnei Hashem" - is embedded in our "pnimyus/innermost core." This was true from the time of our initial creation, but this essential truth had been hidden from us until the Torah was given on Sinai. It was with the Torah that we were granted the ability to "see" the face of God within us, at least with the power of our men-

---

[99] See chapter three, section "Face In Face"

tal eye. This is expressed further by the verse "Reeh Anochi nosein lifne-ichem hayom/see I place before you today."[100] As we discussed in chap-ter three,[101] the "sod/deeper understanding" of this verse is that the transcendent level of "Anochi" is "nosein lifneichem," placed into our "pnimyus/inner core." This new vision is alluded to by God's promise to Moses "now you will see."

Yet there is a level of vision that is even greater than this concept of "panim b'panim/face to face," and that is the level of "ayin b'ayin/eye to eye." While the vision of "panim b'panim/face to face" was grant-ed at the time of the Exodus and the giving of the Torah, the vision of "ayin b'ayin/eye to eye" will be granted at the time of the ultimate re-demption, as the prophet Isaiah declares:

Ki **ayin b'ayin** yiru b'shuv A-donai Tzion.
Eye to eye they shall see when the Lord returns to Zion.
(Isaiah 52:8)

Quoting this verse, the Alter Rebbe comments that the quality of vision in the messianic age will be:

To a greater extent and with greater strength than at the
giving of the Torah, for then they did not see eye to eye,
but rather they heard what was visible.
(Torah Or, Vaeira, Vayidaber)

The perception at the time of the giving of the Torah, the Alter Rebbe informs us, was like hearing as opposed to seeing. Sound is a less powerful, clear, and definitive form of perception than sight. It provides us a sense and impression, but it is not certain and unmistakable. The level of "panim b'panim/face to face" that we acquired at the giving of the Torah was like this type of 'hearing' vision. As the Alter Rebbe states, we then "heard what was visible." We became aware of the fact that the "Pnei Hashem/face of God" is lodged in our "pnimyus/inner core." However, we could still not see this reality clearly. With the coming re-

---

[100] Deuteronomy 11:26

[101] Section "In Your Face"

demption, we will see "ayin b'ayin/eye to eye" - the existence of the "Pnei Hashem" within us and within all things will not simply be conceptual, but it will be plain for all to observe.

This is expressed in another prophesy of Isaiah, when he claims:

> And the glory of the Lord shall be revealed, and all flesh
> together shall see that the mouth of the Lord spoke.
> (Isaiah 40:5)

On this verse, the Alter Rebbe[102] comments on the specificity of the wording "all *flesh* shall see." Not only will there be a spiritual or intellectual knowledge of God in the time to come, but His omnipresence will be perceptible to the flesh itself. Furthermore, not only will this vision be applicable to our physical, fleshy eyes, but "*all* flesh shall see." In other words, this perception will not be limited to optics, but we will be able to "observe" the face of God with every one of our senses and every aspect of our being. We will feel, smell, taste, hear, and see God constantly. This is because it will be revealed to us, finally, that there is nothing other than God, and therefore everything we experience with any and all of our senses, is simply and exclusively divine.

Seers

While the vast majority of humanity is yet unable to see the "Pnei Hashem/face of God" "ayin b'ayin/eye to eye," there are those in every generation who already possess this capacity. The great Torah scholars in general are referred to as "**einei** ha'eida/ the **eyes** of the congregation."[103] But the greatest visionaries, those who have immersed themselves in the Torah's deepest secrets, have been granted by God the perception that the rest of us will acquire only in the messianic age.

---

[102] In Torah Or, maamar Vayoshet Hamelech

[103] A phrase borrowed from Numbers 15:24.

In this light, there is a story recorded in the book "Toras Shalom" about the Rebbe Rashab.[104] Once at a chassidic gathering, the Rebbe Rashab was explaining to his disciples the existence of God in everything. He said, "bring me a plate and I will show you the power of God within it." The precise phrase he used was "hislabshus koach hapoel b'nifal/ the clothing of the power of the Creator within the creation." His followers eagerly brought him a plate, anxious to witness the promised wonder. But at the last minute, the Rebbe changed his mind. He explained that he was worried that if he revealed the Godliness within the plate, then the observers would begin to worship the plate. They would be so overwhelmed by the Godliness in the plate that they would forget that it is Godliness and think that it is the power of the plate itself. Such is the nature of the concealment of this world - even if we were to be shown the vitality that animates the material garments, we would attribute the power to the garments themselves and forget that they are merely the outer trappings of a more essential and underlying reality. It is therefore not only sight that we are lacking, but also the capacity to properly translate and integrate the wisdom that clear vision imparts. Through their tremendous devotion to plumbing the depths of the Torah's secrets, the great mystics and tzadikkim have acquired both sight and vision.

Another story is recorded about two of the Rebbe Rashab's predecessors, the Alter Rebbe and the Mitteler Rebbe.[105] One Rosh Hashana, after the morning prayers, the Alter Rebbe approached his son Dov Ber (who would later succeed his father and become the Mitteler Rebbe, the second Rebbe of the Lubavitch dynasty) and asked him "with what did you pray today." His question, in other words, was what was his son's "kavana/concentration" focused on throughout the holiday prayers. The Mitteler Rebbe responded with a very deep and esoteric kabbalistic idea about the souls standing before their Creator. He then asked his father the same question - with what did you pray today? The Alter Rebbe responded "I prayed with the shtender." A "shtender" is the wooden lectern or stand that many are accustomed to rest their prayerbook on as they

---

[104] Rabbi Shalom Dovber Schneersohn, fifth rebbe of the Lubavitch Chassidic dynasty. 1860-1920

[105] Rabbi Dovber Schneuri, second rebbe of the Lubavitch Chassidic dynasty. 1773-1827

pray. Throughout his prayer, the Alter concentrated deeply on the idea that the wooden "shtender" that held his prayerbook was constantly being recreated by the word of God that comprises and vitalizes all matter. What everyone else saw merely as a structure of lifeless wood, the Alter Rebbe was able to perceive as a form of condensed divine energy. What he expressed to his son and future successor here is that Godliness is not to be found only in abstruse and esoteric dimensions, but it is here, in this lowest world, in even the most seemingly base and lifeless creations.

It is related that just before his death, as the Alter Rebbe lay on his deathbed, he stared up at the wooden ceiling and said that he no longer sees the wooden beams, but only the holy letters. As we mentioned previously, all physical matter is ultimately composed of Hebrew letters which were spoken by God in order to effect the creation, as it says in Genesis "And God *said*, let there be...". In the final moments of his time on this earthly plane, the Alter Rebbe was not only able to see the Godliness that exists within all matter, but he was no longer able to see the matter at all. So refined and elevated had his vision become at that point that he could detect only the "Pnei Hashem/face of God," and not the veils that concealed it.

It is true that few of us are on the level of such mystics, but we all have the potential deep within us to see what they have seen. It is therefore incumbent upon each of us to train ourselves, to the extent of our ability, to perceive the Godliness that underlies everything. But we need not travel this journey alone. There are guides who have been blazing trails through the darkness for generations. They may not transport us directly to our destination, for each of us must conduct her/his own search and must carry her/his own weight. But as we make our way and hone our vision, it behooves us to attach ourselves to those who can already see.

Helping Others See Themselves

In addition to seeking out and learning from those whose vision is sharper than our own, there is another way that we can precipitate the promised time of vision, peace and unity. And that is by helping those whose vision is duller than our own. Each of us is a guide, and each of us holds a torch. Wherever we may be along the journey through the darkness, it is certain that there are others who are behind us, or who haven't yet begun. Hopefully, through this book, we have now at least identified the fundamental human task and have taken, at least, the first few steps along the path. We understand that we are here to "lech lecha/go to yourself" and to "bara Elokim es hashamayim v'es haaretz/reveal God within the heavens and the earth." We know where the "lecha," our true self, is hidden - deep within our "pnimyus/core." We are aware that when we arrive there and find it, we will also find the "Pnei Hashem/the face of God," which is the innermost foundation of us and of everything else that exists. Unlike so many who are searching for meaning and fulfillment in external physical possessions or far-flung destinations, we are therefore aware that the direction we must travel is within. We can point to the scriptural sources that clearly lay out these ancient and eternal truths. We may feel like we have just begun the journey ourself, but equipped with all this, we are ready to share our light and help others delve inward through the darkness. This is why we are here, and this is the gift that we have been given in order to give it others.

What each of us must know is that everyone, no matter who they are or where they're from, wants nothing more than to see and reveal the "Pnei Hashem/face of God" within them. This desire itself may be hidden from them, but were they aware of the infinite goodness that is embedded in their core, they would stop at nothing to access and manifest it. Often, it is easier for others to recognize our inherent goodness than for us to identify it ourselves. This is especially the case with those of us who have stumbled in the past and have become convinced of our depravity or worthlessness. Our essence is so encrusted that we have come to identify ourselves with the crust rather than that which it conceals. Yet those who love us unconditionally can see through our veneer.

We find this in Torah with Abraham, whose first son, Ishmael, had become corrupted and began, at the age of fifteen, to worship idols like the Canaanites around him.[106] When his brother Isaac was born, Ishmael would shoot arrows at him, pretending to play, but putting the boy's life at grave risk. Sarah, Isaac's mother and Ishmael's step-mother, informed Abraham of Ishmael's degenerate behavior and urged her hus-

---

106 Shemot Rabbah 1:1

band to send Ishmael away. "But the matter greatly displeased Abraham, concerning his son."[107] He was aware of his son's shortcomings, and he knew that Sarah was right that Ishmael would need to be sent away for the sake of Isaac's safety. Still he was pained, not only because he loved his son in spite of his shortcomings, but because he believed in Ishmael's potential to do and be better. Years earlier, when he had been informed that Sarah would give birth to Isaac, and that Isaac would be his spiritual heir, he immediately prayed to God on his first son's behalf:

> *Lu Yishmael yichyeh lifanecha.*
> Would that Ishmael will live before you.
> (Genesis 17:18)

Why is it that upon hearing the news of Isaac's forthcoming birth, Abraham prays that Ishmael will live? Is there some reason to believe that Isaac's birth might be related to Ishmael's death? If we examine Abraham's request carefully in its original Hebrew, we see that it is not merely Ishmael's survival that Abraham is concerned with, but something deeper. He does not simply pray "Lu Yishmael yichyeh/would that Ishmael will live," but he adds the word *"lifanecha."* As we have seen repeatedly already, this term is plainly translated as "before you," but it literally means "in your face." As such, what Abraham prays for at this moment is that Ishmael should live at the level of God's face, the "Pnei Hashem" that dwells deep within him. He realizes that it will be his son Isaac who will carry his inheritance as the patriarch of the Hebrew nation, and he recognizes the failings of his son Ishmael that render him unfit for this responsibility. Yet he beseeches God to assist his first son in accessing the divine light that is hidden in his "pnimyus."

Though Ishmael is unconscious of that light himself, his father perceives it clearly and wants nothing more for his child than that he should find it and reveal it from within him. Indeed, the sages teach that though he struggled with his corrupt tendencies throughout his life, "Ishmael did teshuvah/return in Abraham's lifetime."[108] His father's recognition of his essential goodness certainly aided him to manifest it.

---

[107] Genesis 21:11

[108] Bava Basra 16b

Jacob And Esau

Similar to his father Abraham, we find that Isaac also had two sons with vastly divergent natures. While his son Jacob was an "an innocent man dwelling in the tents" of Torah learning, his son Esau was "a man of the field who knew how to hunt."[109]   Rashi comments on this verse that "as soon as they became thirteen years old, this one (Jacob) parted to the houses of study, and that one (Esau) parted to idol worship." As he grew older, the sages teach, Esau indulged in every type of transgression, from murder to theft and adultery. Yet when Isaac neared his death and it came time for him to pass on the birthright that he had received from his father to one of his own sons, he chose Esau instead of Jacob. His wife Rebecca knew that it was Jacob who deserved the blessing - like her forebear Sarah, it is once again the mother who has clarity on such things - and she devised a plan whereby Jacob would dress in Esau's clothes and "trick" Isaac into blessing him. Yet the question remains, how is it possible that the wise and holy Isaac could make such an error?

The mystics teach that Isaac was able to perceive the root of Esau's soul, which derived from a heavenly realm so lofty that it was beyond this lowly "olam/world" of "helam/concealment" and limitation. He believed that if Esau were granted the additional power of the birthright "bracha/blessing," he would be able to harness his otherworldly potential and channel it into the world. After all, "bracha/blessing," as we have discussed in chapter three,[110] means to "bring down," and therefore Isaac believed that his "bracha/blessing" would enable Esau to bring his lofty essence down into manifestation. Rebecca also recognized her son Esau's hidden power, but she knew that some energies are too lofty for certain souls to bring down on their own. She understood that it would require a "partnership" of sorts between her two

---

[109] Genesis 25:27

[110] Section "Blessed Are You"

sons in order for this intense holiness to be accessed. She therefore instructed Jacob to dress himself in Esau's clothing. On the surface, the reason for this masquerade was so that Jacob could deceive his father Isaac, who was blind, and convince him that he was in fact blessing Esau as he originally intended. But the chassidic masters explain that when Jacob dressed in Esau's garments, it was as if the two brothers' energies were combined.

What was the incredibly lofty Godly source of Esau which his parents and his brother were trying to access and manifest? It was, as the text explicitly records, the "Pnei Hashem":

Haviah li tzayid v'asei li mat'amim v'ocheila v'avarechecha
lifnei A-donai *lifnei mosi.*
Bring me game and make me tasty foods, and I will eat,
and I will bless you **before the Lord** before my death.
(Genesis 27:7)

The Alter Rebbe[111] addresses the significance of the words "lifnei A-donai/before the Lord" in this verse. Could it not have said simply 'I will bless you before my death,' without adding the phrase "before the Lord"? The Alter Rebbe explains that the blessing needed to come from a level "lifnei/before,' or higher than, the name "A-donai." This name of God represents the realm of worlds, and Esau's soul root was higher than all of the worlds. In order to reach it and bring it downward, Isaac would have to go "lifnei A-donai," beyond the worldly plane. And as we have explained multiple times already, in addition to "before" or beyond, "lifnei" literally means "to the face." Isaac could see the "Pnei A-donai/face of God" in his son Esau, though Esau could not see it himself. He wished to bless Esau "lifnei A-donai" - that he should be able to access this lofty level within himself. As his own father before him, who prayed that Ishmael should be able to see God's face within him - "Lu Yishmael yichyeh *lifanecha*/would that Ishmael will live before You" - Isaac wished nothing more for his son Esau than that he could also find and reveal the "Pnei Hashem" at his core.

Unfortunately, in spite of his father's efforts, Esau would be unable to do so. Unlike his uncle Ishmael, Esau did not return to the path of

---

[111] Torah Or, maamar Reeh Reiach Bni

righteousness and "teshuvah." Nevertheless, though he was unable to allow his essence to fully manifest through the thick veils of his base animalistic nature, there were instances throughout Esau's life when his ultimate Godliness momentarily broke through. One of these moments occurred in the immediate aftermath of Isaac's bestowal of the blessing on Jacob. Unaware that Jacob had already secured the blessing by dressing in his clothing, Esau enters his father's tent and asks his father Isaac to bless him. At this moment, Isaac suddenly realizes that he has been deceived. Though Isaac quickly understands that Jacob did indeed deserve the blessing - for Esau admits that he had sold the birthright to Jacob previously - Esau is devastated with the recognition of what he has surrendered. Bless me too, he begs his father. But Isaac informs him that he has already given Jacob everything. Esau begins to weep, and in one of the most moving and heartrending episodes in all of Torah, he cries:

> *Ha'bracha achas* hi lecha avi, baracheini gam ani avi.
> Have you [but] **one blessing**, my father? Bless me too,
> my father!
> (Genesis 27:38)

The words "bracha achas" are simply translated as "one blessing," but they can also mean "the blessing of oneness." You have the blessing of oneness, Esau says to his father, cognizant in this moment of brokenhearted clarity that it is the recognition of God's absolute unity that has distinguished his grandfather Abraham and his family from all of the other people on earth. I, too, want this blessing, he admits as the tears begin to flow. He truly desired to experience the oneness that he sensed in his essence even if it seemed very far from him. Even the most egregious "sinner" has moments of clarity in which s/he glimpses her/his inner Godliness, though they may be infrequent and short-lived. We can - and must - feel for Esau here, like an addict who sobers up for a moment and perceives a glimmer of what his life could be if he were not controlled by his addiction. We can see his struggle and weep with him for his inability to be who he has the potential to become. All of us have these glimmers, these flashes of what we truly are and of how beautiful life could be if we could simply reveal the truth that is within us. Like all of us who are imperfect, Esau had to deal with the painful tension of his fiercely competing internal drives. In a moment of complete honesty, he begged his father for the blessing of oneness. I want to be one, but it is so hard for me to control myself. Please help me!

Sadly, this introspection would not last long for Esau. As soon as he left his father's tent, a murderous rage burned within him. Rather than taking responsibility for losing the birthright through his own wanton actions, he blamed his brother Jacob and plotted his death. Jacob fled to the land of Charan, and Esau continued his wicked ways. Yet at the very end of his life, Esau's tremendous holiness and potential were finally revealed. The Midrash relates that on the day of Jacob's death, his twelve sons carried his body to Hebron to bury it in the cave where his grandparents, Abraham and Sarah, his parents, Isaac and Rebecca, and his wife Leah had been buried before him. But when they arrived, Esau and his soldiers blocked their entry. The final burial plot in the cave belonged to him, Esau claimed, denying the truth that he had sold his share to his brother decades earlier. Jacob's grandson Chushim drew his sword and decapitated Esau, whose head then rolled into the cave. Twins, Jacob and Esau were thus born on the same day and died on the same day. The Midrash relates that when Esau's head rolled into the cave, it landed in his father Isaac's resting place, as Targum Yonasan states: "Esau's head lies in the bosom of Isaac."[112]

The chassidic masters teach that there is profound significance to the burial of Esau's head, and head only, in the cave of Machpelah with the three holy patriarchs and matriarchs. The head represents our highest root and potential. As mentioned above, Esau's soul-root was extremely lofty - even higher than the root of Jacob, which is why Isaac desired to give Esau the birthright blessing. But whereas Jacob was capable of bringing the highest levels down into the lowest,[113] there was too great a gulf between Esau's head and his body. Throughout his life, therefore, the two aspects of his being - his Godly soul and his animal soul - battled

---

[112] Targum Yonatan, Genesis 50:13

[113] This is indicated by his Hebrew name, "יעקב/Yaakov," which is a combination of the word "עקב/ekev/heel" - which represents the lowest level of the human - and the letter "י/yud" - which is the first letter of God's name "יְ-ה-וָ-ה" and represents "chochma/wisdom," the highest level of the head. Yaakov was thus one who was able to bring the loftiest level down to manifestation in the earthly plane.

incessantly. It was only at his death that his highest nature was freed from the anchor of his body. His head rolled into the cave and rested with his father who had always recognized his immense Godly potential and tried to bring it down to express itself in this world.

Like Abraham, Isaac, and Jacob, our job is to expose the face of God wherever it is hidden. All of those who act "ungodly" in this world are simply unable to access their Godly essence and potential. It is the lack of belief in, or awareness of, the "Pnei Hashem/face of God" within them that makes them act in ways that are contrary to their true and highest nature. To transform the world, and to hasten the arrival of the time of peace and perfect vision, we must work tirelessly to help those who are lost to find and reveal the Godliness within them.

As Water Mirrors The Face

What is the best and easiest way to help others to see the "Pnei Hashem/face of God" within them? It is to show them the "Pnei Hashem" that is within you. This will be effective for a number of reasons. First, it will provide an image of something beautiful and admirable that one will aspire to her/himself. The peace and presence that are exuded by one who has discovered her/his inherent Godliness is rare and alluring. It manifests in a confidence and a composure which suggest some understanding of life's mysteries and a mastery of one's faculties. We all desire to be more balanced and content. Encountering others who display this type of serenity motivates us to seek what s/he has found and to see if we too can learn to live this way.

On a somewhat deeper level, when we witness others acting in kind and altruistic ways, it inspires us to call forth the "better angels" of our own nature. Seeing someone acting contrary to her/his own self-interest complicates the notion, which is so prevalent in the modern conception of human nature, that we are merely animals evolved. As we have discussed earlier,[114] the Darwinian model of evolution allows us to rationalize and normalize our egoistic and animalistic impulses. This

---

[114] Chapter three, section "In Me?"

further shrouds our Godly nature. But on those wonderful occasions when someone transcends our expectations and provides evidence of something more generous and noble than what we would expect of an evolved ape, then our self-concept is freed from the restraints of our biology. We begin to believe, even if only for a moment, that we can be far more than we have been until now.

On a more subtle level still, because we all contain the face of God deep within us, when we see it revealed elsewhere, it reminds of us of something we have always known vaguely and indistinctly. It is like a memory that is deep and distant, but so potent that though it is just beyond our grasp, it is on the tip of our consciousness. It evokes more of a feeling than a clear remembrance - a sense of something so familiar, but so elusive. It is like recognizing someone you have never met, and knowing that you are related. You are relatives because you come from the same place, you are made of the same stuff, you are the same energy expressed through different packaging. Eventually, we recognize that there are no strangers, only new wrappers that we have not yet opened. As soon as we open them, and as soon as we open ourselves, we see that the contents are the same. In this sense, we can understand the following verse from Proverbs:

> As water mirrors a face to a face, so is the heart of man to man.
>
> (Proverbs 27:19)

On the simple level, what this proverb informs us is that just as the surface of water acts as a mirror, reflecting one's face back at her/him, so too does our heart mimic and match the emotions and energies that it perceives and receives. Our reactions are typically commensurate with the actions that come our way, and similarly, our words, deeds, and emotions will tend to elicit a reciprocal response from those with whom we interact. In other words, when one treats another with kindness, then that person is inclined to respond with positivity. And conversely, if one is rude, mean, or aggressive, then s/he is most likely going to receive negativity in kind. We experience this frequently in life in simple ways. Smiles and laughter are contagious, and likewise others' tears often make our own eyes well. Though we tend to downplay it in our modern and rational world, energy is infectious. We are influenced, either positively or negatively, by those around us. When we surround ourselves with cheerful and peaceful people, we experience greater joy and contentment. And when we mingle with those who are bitter and hostile, we take on their stress and agitation.

This truth is recognized in both neurological science and social science. Neuroscientists have identified "mirror neurons" in the brain which render a person likely to respond sympathetically to the stimuli that s/he encounters. This accounts for our capacity for compassion and empathy. It also explains why yawning is contagious. Social scientists have identified a similar dynamic which they refer to as emotional reciprocity. This is the unspoken social contract which generally assures us that people will treat us with respect and integrity if we grant them the same courtesy. Cultural anthropologists have suggested that this social-emotional reciprocity is one of the uniquely human traits which enabled humans to survive and thrive. While other species do not have the nature or tendency to repay kindness with kindness, this uniquely human trait enabled humankind to create groups of allies that worked together to protect one another and promote mutual success.

Yet with their proverb "as water mirrors a **face** to a **face**, so is the heart of man to man," the sages are teaching us something even more subtle and insightful here than what scientists have attributed to neurological processes and anthropological developments. Just as water mirrors a face, and just as one heart responds reciprocally to what it experiences from another, so too does one's innermost face, her/his hidden "pnimyus/core," respond to the "pnimyus" of another. In other words, when we experience the "Pnei Hashem/face of God" radiating from another, the "Pnei Hashem" within us will be activated. And when we allow the face of God to shine from within us, it will reciprocally elicit the face of God from within those around us.

The reason this works is because at the most fundamental level, there is no difference or distance between one and another. When the infinite radiates, the finite can no longer interpose or exist. When one allows her/his core to shine outward, the other's core responds, and the physical casing that usually suppresses one's essential being no longer has the power to keep it hidden. This being the case, imagine the radical change our world will experience as each of us allows our Godly essence to be manifest. As increasing numbers of people become aware of the Godliness within them, there are ever more mirrors for those who have not yet peered inward and seen their inner truth.

———

א-RAY VISION

Of course, in order to reveal our "Pnei Hashem/face of God" to others in order that they should use it as a mirror to see the "Pnei Hashem" within themselves, we must remain conscious of our own "pnimyus/inner core." This requires us to see what is hidden, which is no easy task. As we have discussed at length throughout this book, the "olam/world" is designed for "helam/concealment," and therefore our vision is weak and faulty. Though we will eventually be able to see clearly and perfectly (as we described in the previous sections of this chapter), this is not yet our reality. But we have now been granted a glimpse of the light, and though we cannot be expected to see lucidly, we cannot pretend that we are blind. Torah has provided us a map to our deepest dimension, and the Chassidic masters have provided a cipher to interpret and follow the map more clearly. Yet in order to maintain the proper path through the darkness, we must train our vision and hone our ability to see Godliness in everything.

How do we do so?

In chapter seven, we began to explore the intricate regimen that Torah provides us to help us liberate ourselves from the veils that shroud our Godly core. As we discussed, the lifecycle ceremonies (along with the daily rituals, and the weekly, monthly and yearly calendrical observances) are all facets of an integrated practice through which we train ourselves to penetrate the darkness. The detailed and disciplined answer then to the question of how we can habituate ourselves to seeing the Godliness that is hidden within everything, is to take advantage of the tactics and exercises that Torah offers us.

Yet there is a shorter answer, which does not in any way contradict the previous answer, but which provides us something more elementary and immediate. And that is, that in order to train our eyes to detect the ubiquity of Godliness beneath the veneer of everything we encounter, we must actively and earnestly look for it. This may sound overly simplistic, but the plain truth is that if we are not seeking Godliness, then it will certainly be more difficult to find it. If we don't believe that it is there to be found, then we will have little impetus to look, and little ability to perceive it when it makes itself evident. It is true that there are those who stumble upon God's face even if they are not seeking Him. And it is true that God will often appear in people's field of vision precisely when they have concluded that He does not exist. Yet it is also the case that He provides everyone occasional opportunities to see Him that are frequently ignored because we are not interested in changing our life, even if that life that we are reluctant to change is not particularly pleasant or fulfilling.

As we quoted at the beginning of our search,[115] "happy of heart is the one who seeks God."[116] We questioned why one would be happy if s/he is seeking something, as the act of seeking necessarily means that the object of the search has not yet been found. The answer is that the one who is seeking believes that s/he can, and eventually will, find what s/he is after. This hope and joy will bring success. Without it, life is dark and cold. Even when light presents itself, it is not perceived because the person's eyes are closed.

The essential thing, then, is to open the eyes and to gaze constantly into the darkness. We must be alert, and patient, and sensitive to even the smallest sparkle or the faintest glow. We must be conscious with everything we see that this, too, is Godliness, even if we cannot yet see beyond its concealing outer layers. Our task is to develop x-ray vision, to see through all surfaces and penetrate to the core where the Godly spark resides. When we can do so, we will already be living in the messianic future, even as we simultaneously find ourselves in the exiled present.

The Lubavitcher Rebbe points this out by comparing the words "גולה/golah/exile" and "גאולה/geulah/redemption." The Hebrew terms are nearly identical, except for the presence of the letter "א/aleph" in the word "גאולה/geulah/redemption." "א/aleph" is the first letter of the Hebrew alphabet, thus corresponding numerologically to the number one. What this informs us is that the only thing that distinguishes "גולה/go-

---

[115] Chapter two, section "The Joy of the Search"

[116] Psalms 105:3

lah/exile" from "גאולה/geulah/redemption" is oneness. When we can see the "aleph" within the exile - when we recognize that all is one even as it seems to be separate and many - we are already experiencing the time of ultimate peace and joy because we have transformed the "גולה/exile" to "גאולה/redemption." This is not just x-ray vision, it is "א-ray (aleph-ray) vision," the ability to see God's Oneness within every aspect of His creation.

It is important to note that this penetrative vision does not preclude us from seeing the surface as well. Perceiving the underlying Godliness in creation does not mean that we are to abandon all of our worldly pursuits - our social, familial, and community engagements - and to focus exclusively on spiritual rituals. It means, rather, that within our daily lives - our jobs and our interpersonal interactions - everything is undertaken with the consciousness of our infinite potential and our divine purpose. It is not a retreat from the world, but an engagement with the world in which we are constantly seeking and revealing its covert and inherent unity. "א-ray vision" does not merely take us to the innermost depths of life, but it reveals to us that the surface is no less Godly than that which is beneath it. Unlike other spiritual systems which relegate "holiness" to specific places, times, or behaviors, Torah reveals the "Pnei Hashem/face of God" in everyone and everything at every moment. There is only "א/aleph/one," and, therefore, there is nothing other.

Facefulness

What we are proposing with this idea of "א-ray (aleph-ray) vision" is a certain type of focus or mindfulness. Mindfulness is a term that has become popular in a modern and mechanized world that is increasingly mindless and soulless. Mindfulness can be defined as intentional consciousness, as opposed to being merely conscious, or sentient but unaware of one's true circumstances and condition. When we are not mindful, we go about our lives under the thrall of our routine. We sleepwalk, existing without questioning or examining our existence. We are under the spell of those who profit on our passivity and exploit the ease with which we are manipulated, indoctrinated, and compelled. We play the game and keep its rules without knowing why we play or how to win. We live without knowing and celebrating what it means to be alive.

Mindfulness sweeps away the haze that leaves us numb and re-flexive. It pulls us from our predictable and mechanical lethargy. It is the awakening and the search for some more essential truth and reality. It forces us to see ourself and our context and to try to make some sense of all this. Why do I do the things I do? Why am I here? Where is here, and what is my place or function in this strange and uncertain existence. Who has been pulling my strings until now?

Mindfulness is an important start, but what Torah affords, and what we have described throughout this book, is a consciousness that is beyond mindfulness which we can refer to as "facefulness." Facefulness is the cognizance of our "pnimyus/innermost core" and the "Pnei Hashem/face of God" that is found there. It is the awareness of what we truly are and the rejection of the illusion that we are small and temporal and individual. It is recognition of our inherent Godliness and our unity with everything.

In some systems, mindfulness will lead to the confession and acceptance of one's insignificance. Because being mindful opens us to the consciousness of everything around us and not just our parochial and particular concerns, we therefore begin to see the much larger scope in which we exist. In the vast scheme of the universe, we are liable to con-clude that we are minuscule, and that in the endless expanse of time, we are merely an inconsequential blip. There is wisdom and value in this type of humility and relinquishment of egocentricity. It is certainly true that we have inflicted significant damage on our world, our fellows, and ourselves because we deem ourselves overly important or focal. Yet it is precisely "facefulness," the consciousness of the "Pnei Hashem" in our "pnimyus," that will rescue us from our self-consumed and self-destruc-tive culture. We are egotistical and confrontational because we feel small and empty inside. We assert ourselves aggressively because we secretly suspect that we are nothing, and therefore we must prove otherwise. When we are aware of our divinity, we will not need to justify our worth or power. We will choose to behave with dignity and love. We will act Godly because we are Godly - not because of ego, or guilt, or desire for reward or fear of punishment, but simply because it is what and who we truly are.

The goal of this book, then, has been to enable us to recognize our ultimate divinity. There is an obvious risk involved in such an awareness - that we will misinterpret this as a justification for self-assertion and self-aggrandizement as opposed to self-transcendence and translucence. While it is true that our inherent Godliness renders each of us incredibly holy and significant, we must express our greatness not by self-promotion, but by removing our outer trappings, releasing our ego, and expressing our Godly essence.

"Facefulness," or recognizing the "Pnei Hashem/face of God" within us, does not make us God, but rather it makes us nothing but God. There is a subtle but tremendous difference between the assertion "I am God" and "I am nothing but God." In the former case, I deify myself and therefore value and impose *my* will. In the latter case, I identify completely with the One and Only God, and I strive solely to channel His will through the vessel that He has created me to be. The sages discuss this subtlety in regards to a renowned mishnah from the Talmud that discusses the purpose of humanity's creation.

> *Ani nivreisi l'shameis es koni*
> I was created to serve my Creator.
> (Kiddushin 82a)

This statement succinctly establishes my raison d'etre. I am here as a servant and vessel for the One who fashioned me and placed me here. Yet in such a dynamic, there are two separate beings: the Creator, and "I." I recognize my subservience to Him, but I still consider myself a distinct and independent entity. An alternate version of the mishnah changes the language slightly:

> *Ani **lo** nivreisi **ela** l'shameis es koni*
> I was **not** created **except** to serve my Creator.

On the surface, these changes do not seem to alter the meaning substantively. In both cases, I recognize that the purpose of my creation is to fulfill the assignments of the One who created me. Yet, on a deeper level, the difference is profound. In the first case, "I was created" - I see myself as a creation. In the latter case, "I was not created" - I recognize that I do not exist "ela/except" as an expression of His desire and an agent of His service. There is only God, and I am simply a way that He manifests in this realm of seeming multiplicity. In the first case, I may be a *faithful* servant. But we are created to be more than faithful - we are created to be "*faceful*," to peer deep inside of ourselves and see the "Pnei Hashem/face of God" staring back at us.

Blessing

We have come to the end of this book, but only the beginning of this journey. From here, we will continue on our respective paths to finding ourself ("lech lecha") and finding the "Pnei Hashem/face of God," both of which we know by now are awaiting us in our "pnimyus/inner core." It is said that "chassidim (those who study the inner depths of Torah) never say farewell, for they never depart from each other."[117] We cannot part from one another, because we know that we are wholly and completely one. Yet in this realm of seeming multiplicity, we can feel as though we are going our separate ways. Therefore, we offer one another blessings for the journey ahead, as the Friederker Rebbe guides us, "Before embarking on a journey ... receive a parting blessing from your good friends."[118]

So we will conclude with a blessing, and there is no more appropriate blessing for this circumstance than the "Priestly Blessing" which God instructed Aaron the high priest and his descendants to bestow on the people throughout the ages.

> *Yivarechecha A-donai v'yishmerecha. Yaer A-donai* **panav** *eilecha vichunecha. Yisa A-donai* **panav** *eilecha v'yaseim lecha shalom.*

---

[117] Hayom Yom, 10 Adar Sheini

[118] ibid. The Friederker Rebbe, Rabbi Yoseph Yitzchak Schneersohn, was the sixth rebbe of the Chabad Lubavitch dynasty. 1880-1950

> May God bless you and watch over you. May God cause
> His **face** to shine to you and favor you. May God raise
> His **face** toward you and grant you peace.
> (Numbers 6:24-26)

We will notice immediately the multiple references in this blessing to God's face. What does it mean that God should turn or raise His face to you, and why is this the ultimate blessing that He can bestow upon us? On the simple level, the Priestly blessing requests God's favor, protection, and peace for those who are being blessed. But if we analyze the verses more closely, we will discover their far deeper implications.

> *Yivarechecha A-donai v'yishmerecha.*
> May God bless you and watch over you.

The first word of this first verse, "Yivarechecha," means "may He bless you." The root of this word, "barech" is familiar to us by now. As we discussed in chapter three[119] and several times since, the word "bracha" means "blessing," but it also means "to draw down," as in the phrase "hama**vrich** es hagefen/to draw down a vine" as well as the word "breicha", which means a "pool" or a place where water has descended and gathered. Reading the words "yivarechecha A-donai" with this alternate connotation, they can be rendered "may God be drawn down to you," blessing one with the ability to have God revealed to her/him below, just as He is above. As we have discussed at length, our goal is that the Godliness which is at the root of all things should not only be acknowledged intellectually or spiritually, but that it should be clear and visible within this realm of physicality and darkness. The final word of the verse, "v'yishmerecha" is from the root "shamor," which means "to guard." Once the Godliness is brought down and revealed within you, it should be guarded and kept in you. Otherwise, it may once again become lost, forgotten, or stolen by the forces of darkness that constantly work to deprive us of our vision in this "olam/world" of "helam/concealment."

The second verse of the blessing refers explicitly to God's face:

---

[119] Section "Blessed Are You"

*Yaer A-donai **panav** eilecha vichunecha.*
May God cause His **face** to shine to you and favor you.

On the simple level, this phrase wishes one God's kindness and grace, which are represented by the imagery of His radiant countenance as opposed to a dark countenance, which would symbolize anger or displeasure. Yet on a deeper level, this appeal for the "shining" of God's "face" is a clear allusion to the "Pnei Hashem/face of God" that is buried within our deepest "pnimiyus/inner core." It is a request that the face should "yaer/shine" brightly so that one can see it and be aware of it. The blessing is not merely that God should be kind to you, but that He should lavish you with the greatest of all kindness, which is that He should be apparent to you and revealed within you.

The final word of the verse, "vichunecha" is from the root "chein," which means "favor" or "grace." The ultimate divine favor or grace that we request of God is this shining revelation of His face. But the Alter Rebbe[120] points out that the word "vichunecha" also shares a root with the word "chanah," which means "to encamp." As in the first verse, where God is not only momentarily revealed, but thereafter guarded so that His presence remains, so too here in this second verse we pray that the face not only shines brightly within us briefly or temporarily, but that it "encamps" within us permanently so that we are constantly aware of our true essence and reality.

The face is specifically mentioned in the third verse of the blessing as well:

*Yisa A-donai **panav** eilecha v'yaseim lecha shalom.*
May God raise His **face** toward you and grant you peace.

In this final verse of the blessing, God "raises" His face toward us, as opposed to "shining" His face to us as in the previous verse. What is the difference between these two bestowals of His face? The Alter Rebbe[121] explains that the raising of God's face represents the removal of

---

[120] Likkutei Torah, maamar Koh Tuvarchu Bnei Yisrael

[121] Likkutei Torah, maamar Bayom Hashemini Atzeres

His visible presence from this lowest world. As such, it is the opposite of the "bringing it down" that was referenced in the first verse of the blessing. How, then, is this removal and elevation of God's face a blessing?

Here, the Alter Rebbe expounds, we find the secret of exile and darkness. God hides from us precisely in order that we should seek Him, and it is this very search that will enable us to rise ever higher. For by seeking His face, we come to find our own face, and we realize that we are far higher and loftier than we had believed ourselves to be. Indeed, the verse says "may God raise His face *toward* you," not away from you or above you. If He is raising His face, we would assume that it is becoming more distant, as we are ostensibly grounded and stuck here below. But in fact, as God raises His face, it approaches us, because the most hidden and precious truth is that we are not below at all. We are rooted in the highest of all heights.

This three-part blessing, then, is a three-stage progression. First, "yivarechecha A-donai," we should be able to bring God down so that He is manifest within us. Then "yaer panav," His face should shine so that it radiates from within us to illuminate the darkness for us and for all of those around us. And finally, "yisa A-donai panav," the face should be lifted to reveal to us our ultimate source and root which is far beyond this coarse and limited realm. And this progression will bring us the ultimate reward of "shalom/peace," as the blessing concludes "v'yaseim lecha shalom/and He will grant you peace." "Shalom/peace" is the ability to see the light within the darkness, and to know that there is nothing to fear because there is only, and always, One.

May you be blessed with this peace as you journey onward. And may you be a source of this peace and blessing for all of those that you encounter on your way.

Postscript

For those who are interested in exploring these subjects more thoroughly, there is another version of this book which was written for a reader that is already familiar with some Torah basics. It includes the Hebrew text for all cited verses, some additional explanation of concepts that were introduced more summarily here, and roughly 200 additional pages which, among other things, explore Torah's "liberation practice" more deeply. In particular, it explains Torah's daily rituals (prayer, Torah study, and practical mitzvos) as well as its calendrical observances (or holidays and holy days), demonstrating how each of the many detailed rituals of Torah practice are intended to assist us on our journey toward our "pnimyus" and the "Pnei Hashem" that is lodged there. The book is titled *Pnei Hashem* and it can be ordered at www.PneiHashem.com